In Another Place

With and Without My Father, Norman Mailer

In Another Place

With and Without
My Father,
Norman Mailer

A Memoir
by Susan Mailer

Northampton House Press

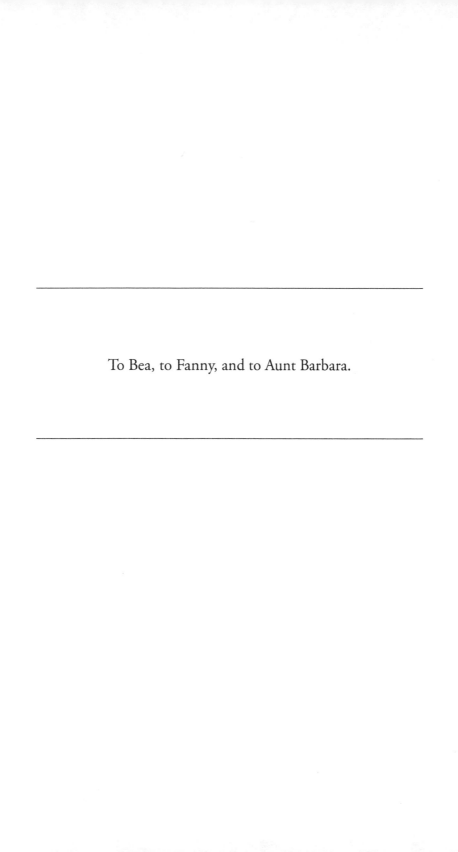

To Bea, to Fanny, and to Aunt Barbara.

Contents

Suppose a painter sees a path through a field sown with poppies and paints it: at one end of the chain of events is the field of poppies, at the other a canvas with pigment disposed on its surface. We can recognize that the latter represents the former, so I shall suppose that despite differences between a field of poppies and a piece of canvas, despite the transformation that the artist has effected...something has remained unaltered and on this something recognition depends.

—Wilfred Bion, *Transformations*

Part I

CHAPTER 1

The Butterfly Effect

MY EARLIEST MEMORY IS IN MY BELLY. While I was growing up, I loved to look at our family albums. Among the many photos was a small square, black and white image of me, at not quite two years old, with my mother. Every time I saw it, I got a fluttering, butterflies-in-my-belly sensation which made me turn the page as fast as I could. Sometimes, I'd even skip that page, anxiously trying to avoid the butterfly effect.

~

Mom left Dad when I was eighteen months old. That same day my mother met Salvador, a tall, handsome Mexican, and three weeks later they left New York City on a road trip to Mexico. Norman, my father, now free to pursue his bohemian writer's dream, rented a loft on the Lower East Side and moved in with his new lover Adele. And I was left with Dad's mother, Grandma Fanny, who took me with to live with her and Grandpa in Brooklyn Heights.

In the early summer we went to Long Branch and stayed with her sister, my great aunt Jenny, in her large white house with green shutters. The forsythia and azalea bushes colored the large garden while its big trees protected us from the sun. We often went to the beach, which was only a few blocks away. It was quiet and pleasant there. I can half remember settling into a comfortable routine with my grandparents.

I know Grandpa arrived every weekend after closing the office.

I suppose my father must have made an appearance once in a while.

Three months later, on a hot day in mid-July, Mom returned to fetch me. Grandma always said she'd hoped my mother would change her mind. Perhaps she wouldn't like Mexico, after all. Or maybe she would break up with Salvador. But none of that happened. My mother had not only fallen in love with the country, she was definitely in love with Salvador. She was moving to Mexico and taking me with her.

Grandma was very upset things turned out this way. She'd pleaded with Mom to stay in the city, even offered to take care of me while Bea went to graduate school. She had cajoled and pressured her son, my father, to prevent my departure. But nothing had worked. And now, my mother was about to arrive and pick me up.

Grandma sat me next to her on the sofa of her sister's living room and hugged me tightly. She told me, "Mommy is coming soon, and you will be leaving with her." Thinking back on that day, she remembered I didn't seem to react much. Only picked up my doll and wandered out of the room and into the garden.

Soon a car drove up and parked on the street. Mom stepped out and began making her way to the front door but stopped when she saw me pushing my doll carriage across the lawn. "Susie? Susie dear," she called to me.

I looked up, and said, "Mommy?"

She rushed to my side, picked me up, and hugged me.

Many years later, I asked my mother about that day. Mom, who was always so precise about most things in her life, was surprisingly vague about the details. She made an effort, though, shifted in her seat and closed her eyes to help bring that afternoon back.

"I was worried you wouldn't know who I was. I'd been away for three months, and you were only a year and a half old. But when you saw me you immediately said, 'Mommy?' And then, I remember, you kissed me once on the cheek."

Even after all those years it was painful to hear this. I wondered, why did I say *Mommy* with a question mark? Was it because I couldn't believe she had come back? Or perhaps I was asking her if *she* was the "Mommy" Grandma had said would take me away. Or did I in fact actually recognize my mother, as she had interpreted? But, if that had been the case, I figured I would have joyfully cried out "*Mommy*!"

I asked my mother about Grandma's reaction when she saw her. But Mom couldn't remember, nor could she recall how long we had stayed in Long Branch, or what I had done on the drive back to New York. She was pretty sure we'd left the same afternoon, and that a couple days later we boarded a flight to Mexico City.

There was no reference in her story to Norman. Had my father made an appearance before we left? Did he take us to the airport?

Nothing. No recollection.

Then I asked, "What about me?"

"You were just fine," she said. But after a few moments she added, "Maybe my going away did affect you. Because when I came back you sucked your thumb. And you hadn't, before I left."

There are photographs of that afternoon. In one, I'm smiling in Grandma's arms.

Smiling in Grandmas's arms. Long Branch 1951.

In the other Mom holds me in her arms, but our embrace looks awkward. I don't lean in to her; in fact, my upper body is turned away. I seem to be searching for someone, probably Grandma, while my mother's expression is tense. She appears unsure of herself. Her smile looks more like a grimace, and one of the hands that holds me is open in a gesture that seems to ask, *What's wrong?*

Awkward in Mom's arms. Long Branch 1951.

The photo I always wanted to avoid.

Years later, I found out from Mom that this picture had been taken the day I left Grandma to go to Mexico. And when I heard this, I felt the same uncomfortable sensation in my belly. Only now I wanted to cry for that little girl, twice ripped away from her surroundings.

My mother was so excited with the turn her life had taken, I don't think she dwelled much on my feelings.

"When Norman and I separated, it was final," she told me. "I never looked back, never missed your father, or my marriage to him. I was done with that period of my life."

The first few years in Mexico, my parents remained friendly. Dad lived in New York City, but spent a good amount of time, sometimes as much as three months, in Mexico City. There, he and Adele—his soon to be wife—and Salvador and my mother saw each other often. Sal and my father even became friends. But Mom never had much use for Adele.

∾

When I was old enough to formulate the question, I asked Dad why he'd let me be taken off to Mexico.

"I couldn't have done otherwise," he said, "because I had promised your mother that if she decided to move you could go with her. I felt bound by my word. And to be honest, I wasn't that committed to being a father. I wanted to have the freedom to live without a daughter or a wife."

Though eventually Dad came to regret it, at the time he was totally unaware of how this decision would shape our lives. Our relationship would always carry a burden of separation and longing. And each time he saw me Dad had to re-discover his daughter in the Spanish-speaking, "little Mexican" girl who greeted him.

CHAPTER 2

Norman and Bea

Norman and Bea in Provincetown. 1948.

Mᵧ FATHER AND MOTHER MET ON THE STEPS OF THE BOSTON Symphony Orchestra in late December 1941. Bea was studying music at Boston University, and Norman was at Harvard. They were both in their third year. Bea went to the symphony every week, and on that particular day Norman and his buddy Larry Weiss had arranged to meet her there. Bea was standing in line waiting to buy tickets when he arrived. She said something about that day's program, but soon found out he was more interested in meeting her than in classical music.

Norman was notorious for his tin ear. Bea's current boyfriend, on the contrary, loved music. He was also a great dancer, while Norman could hardly follow a rhythm. But that weekend Bea's boyfriend was sick and didn't make it to the symphony.

Norman's sexual experience was nothing to brag about. Almost nineteen, he was a skinny kid with big ears, and not much taller than 5'7". He had never had a real girlfriend, but he made up for it with his intellect and his sharp blue eyes. Always at ease with words, he let Bea know, in great detail, his plans to become a writer. His personality, a combination of sweetness and shyness, together with a know-it-all attitude and intense drive intrigued Bea, and in a few days her interest in him blossomed into a romance. Soon after their first meeting Bea told her boyfriend she'd met someone else and watched him walk out of her life.

Both my parents were very much loved by their mothers, which gave them a kind of inner strength, an aura that made people gravitate to them. They soon became a charismatic couple, the center of attraction in their circle of friends. I've often heard from Aunt Phyllis, my mother's younger sister, "When Norman and Bea walked into a room it lit up. They were our heroes." They were smart and outspoken and good-looking. They both found the old ways, the restricted diet, Hebrew school, and Friday at Temple to be stifling. And while Phyllis felt those traditions were a wall she had to bring down, her sister Bea acted as if the wall didn't even exist. She just glided past it.

Bea was an enthusiastic debater, a free spirit, and a champion of women's rights long before the Women's Liberation movement. She also believed in sexual freedom and practiced it.

Norman was basically shy, but he did have an opinion about everything, a trait that combined well with his striking blue eyes and intense stare. Exceptionally intelligent and well spoken, he was never at a loss for words.

Norman and Bea were undoubtedly equal forces.

At first Fanny, Norman's mother, wasn't happy with the match. Perhaps she thought her son was too young to get seriously involved with this obviously more experienced girl. More likely, she wasn't quite ready to see him in love, no matter who the woman was.

My maternal grandparents were also less than thrilled by their daughter's choice. For Grandma Jenny, Norman was "the little *pisherker* with big ideas." Grandpa Hyman thought he was simply rude; a smartass and provocateur who went out of his way to outrage their Jewish middle-class ethos, even though he came from the same stock. Only Grandpa Barney, my Dad's father, was happy with the match. He was taken with Bea's smarts and good looks, and their connection was mutual.

Norman's and Bea's parents and grandparents were Litvak Jews. Except for Grandpa Silverman's family, who was from the Ukraine, all my grandparents had come from small towns in what is now Lithuania. The Mailers left in 1900 and settled in Johannesburg, South Africa. The Schneiders, Grandma Fanny's family, had settled on the Jersey Shore, while the Silverman and the Toltz families went to Chelsea, Massachusetts. My first-generation American parents were totally and happily assimilated to the American culture.

Bea liked going to Harvard and hanging out with the boys at Dunster House. A fraternity for "meatballs" (meaning, Italians, Irish, Jewish and other non-Anglo-Saxon patricians) where Norman lived. Intellectual and well read, the couple went to concerts and plays, and discussed politics and literature. It was 1942, and my mother, always interested in world affairs, was obsessed with the fate of the Jews in Europe, and whether the United States would enter the war. She often said she'd worried about Hitler from the moment she became aware of him, in the mid-thirties, when she was barely thirteen.

Two years later they graduated from college. The next logical step was for them to get married.

"When Norman said, let's get married, I burst into tears," my mother told me. "Not because I was so happy. I didn't know if I wanted to get married at all, but it was expected of us. He would soon be drafted and would be going overseas to fight in the war, and I think we both needed to hold on to each other. So, I accepted, and Norman bought me a twenty-five-cent ring made in Mexico."

They married in Yonkers at the beginning of 1944. But when my grandmothers heard of the elopement, they joined forces and insisted on a proper wedding. That March, Grandma Jenny hosted a small ceremony with a rabbi and a *chuppah* in her apartment in Chelsea, for the immediate family. My father repudiated the ritual and wrote a scathing letter to his mother. My mother, on the other hand, regardless of how she felt about tradition at the time, had fond memories of that occasion, and was annoyed at Norman's bad manners and lack of appreciation.

There are no photos of the wedding.

A week later, on the 27th of March, Norman was ordered to report for induction. As a college graduate with an engineering degree, he could have been commissioned as an officer. But he wanted to write the great war novel and understood the only way he could get to know the army from the inside was as an enlisted man. At the same time Bea went to officer's training in the Navy and was commissioned ensign in the WAVES (Women accepted for Volunteer Emergency Service). Being a player in the war effort was very important to her. The idea of an office job, basically waiting out the war until Norman came back, was totally unappealing.

The army turned out to be a grueling experience for Norman. Once deployed, he felt certain he was the worst soldier in his platoon. The skinniest and weakest, with bad eyesight to boot. For the first time in his life he was in close contact with tough, uneducated young men. Big, strong guys who had grown up on farms, in mines or dusty towns in Texas; men who had not been coddled by their mothers, had barely finished high school, and were not Jewish. To call it a difficult experience would be an understatement. Norman often said, "The army was the worst experience of my life, and also the most important."

Writing the war novel kept him going. While Norman was stationed in the Philippines, and later in Japan, he wrote to Bea almost every day. Those 400-odd letters, which she safely put away, were the raw material from which he would eventually fashion *The Naked and the Dead*, his first novel.

∽

Norman was discharged in May of 1946, and my parents were happy to be reunited. "I was so relieved he was alive. Now that the war was over, I felt we were free to begin the rest of our lives. I was sure we would be happy. And I believed in Norman. I knew he would write a great book."

Together, they'd saved enough to carry them through a year. So, a month later they went to Provincetown, on the tip of Cape Cod, and rented a small beach cottage in North Truro, on Route 6A, for the summer. They also rented two bicycles to ride into town to buy groceries, and to have an occasional restaurant meal. Norman worked on his novel and Bea began a book about the WAVES. "We had twin typewriters," Mom reminisced. "I wrote in the kitchen and Norman in the bedroom. It was all very romantic; we were young and sure of the future. We would both be published and become known writers."

A year later Norman's novel was accepted for publication by Rinehart and Company, after first being turned down by Little, Brown. On the other hand, Bea's novel was rejected by several editors. Disappointed, she put the manuscript into a box, tucked it away in the closet, and said, "Writing is much too difficult."

The publisher was excited about *The Naked and the Dead*, but at the same time concerned about the obscene language in many of its passages. Even though Norman had substituted "fug" for "fuck" in the original manuscript, he bristled at the idea of deleting all the "assholes, shit, damn, bastard, pussy and sons-of-bitches," as suggested by his editors. He was not about to gentrify the real soldier's lingo. Eventually, he was forced to negotiate, and agreed to cut down on the swearing. A story went around after his novel reached the top of the best-seller charts, that when he met Tallulah Bankhead at a cocktail party in New

York, she held out her hand and said, "So you are the young man who can't spell fuck!"

Norman submitted the final draft of his novel in September of 1947. Then my parents left for Paris on board RMS *Queen Elizabeth* to escape the pre-publication jitters. Taking advantage of the G.I. Bill, they enrolled in the Sorbonne and traveled through Europe. They spent time in cafes and bars hoping to encounter Jean Paul Sartre and Simone de Beauvoir. That never happened, but they did make friends with other writers and artists, many of whom, like Norman's old roommate Mark Linenthal and his wife Alice Adams, were Americans enjoying the appreciative post-war welcome given to them in Europe. Norman and Bea loved French cuisine and wine, and on their $180 dollar-a-month budget considered themselves rich.

It was the longest vacation either of them had, or would ever have again. After ten months they both received diplomas in French civilization from the Sorbonne and returned to New York in July 1948. My mother could've happily stayed indefinitely; she adored Paris. But with the early success of the novel, my father was bursting to get back to the States.

The Naked and the Dead had hit the bookstores in May, almost two years to the day of Norman's discharge from the army, and it became an instant success. Suddenly, at the age of twenty-five, he was singled out as the best young novelist to come along in years. The book was reviewed in all the major newspapers and magazines, and considered one of the best novels to come out of World War II.

His sudden success wasn't easy for Bea. She'd wanted originally to become a concert pianist. But in her second year of college she realized that, although she loved music and was an excellent pianist, she didn't have enough talent to get to the top. She still considered herself Norman's intellectual equal, and certainly had ambitions. But now her husband, who had always known he would be a writer, was suddenly famous. While she had become "the writer's wife."

During the time he was writing the war novel, they'd been a team. Bea had been his partner and archivist, had kept his letters, had believed in and rooted for him. Adding to the sense of teamwork was the fact they were both writing war books. And though hers had gotten turned down, the real sting of this failure did not hit Bea until Norman became a "phenomenon."

Only then did she realize, with a shock, that she'd been under the illusion the book he was writing was *theirs*. Now she fully grasped that the novel was his creation. That all the recognition would go to Norman. He was the young star and she was only The Missus.

Bea knew she was supposed to be proud of her husband, and though she did put her best face forward, the seeds of resentment had been planted.

She searched for an occupation of her own. But for her, as for many ambitious women of her generation, married or single, few serious jobs were forthcoming. Back from Paris, though annoyed by the attention my father received, she went along with the business of being Norman Mailer's wife.

Then she got pregnant with me. Though not planned, I was welcome. Perhaps my mother thought a baby was the logical next step in their marriage, a new ingredient that might change their lives for the better.

If so, she was wrong. If anything, it made the situation worse.

In the summer of 1949, my parents moved to West Hollywood. Norman was intrigued by the idea of writing scripts and making good money. Faulkner, Fitzgerald, and many other writers had done it, so why not try it out?

My mother chose a beautiful home in Beverly Hills that had a baby grand piano in the living room. She could at the very least practice every day. They were soon doing the Hollywood circuit; going to parties and dinners, throwing some at their own home with the rich and famous: Charlie Chaplin, Burt Lancaster, and Montgomery Clift. Also, Shelley Winters and Marlon Brando, who were young and at the beginning of their acting careers. It sounds exciting, but my mother soon grew sick of the glittering scene, and openly resentful of my father's fame, as all eyes went to him.

I was born in the Cedars of Lebanon Hospital in August of that year. In a letter to his army friend Fig, my father complained about how my birth had him running back and forth to the hospital, "dicking around" and getting bawled out by Bea who "acts infinitely superior." It seems my birth had given her a sense of purpose and importance. Sadly, it didn't last very long. And now my father felt trapped in a marriage with a newborn baby, when what he really wanted to do was to go to bed with every beautiful woman who crossed his path. And there were so many. It was obvious the tapestry of their marriage was already unraveling.

Very soon after my birth, Norman was ready to head back East. He hadn't fared well working for Samuel Goldwyn. His intellectual, complicated scripts were not what the industry wanted. Ego slightly bruised, he figured it was time to leave, and was happy to get out of Los Angeles, a town he'd grown to dislike intensely.

My parents spent the summer of 1950 in Provincetown, staying in a clapboard house perched on a hill on Miller Hill Road. I took my first steps there. When that summer was over, they drove to Vermont and fell in love with Putney, a small artists' town. They decided to buy a beautiful nineteenth-century house and became landowners for the first time in their lives. Here my father could finish writing his second novel, *Barbary Shore.*

My parents moved into the new house in October. Norman did a lot of carpentry work on it, an activity he enjoyed and was good at. Bea played the piano and tried her hand at painting landscapes, winter scenes with bare trees stark against a blue and gray sky. She also cared for me with the help of a nanny, and took short trips to New York, where she and Norman had rented a studio apartment for visits.

Mom and me three months old, 1949.

By the end of 1950 my mother knew something was definitely wrong. Dad often went to the City alone. Sometimes she accompanied him, but visiting friends and going to concerts didn't help her shake the sensation that she was seeing everything from a distance, and through a thin pane of glass. Her usual zest for life was gone. She was bored of the country, of being a stay-at-home mom, and bored to the bone with being Norman Mailer's wife.

The day she found out about his affair with Adele Morales, they were both in New York, in the studio apartment. Dad was on the phone talking to Adele, and when Mother asked who it was, he admitted he was having an affair. She immediately packed a small suitcase and checked into a hotel. That night she'd arranged to meet Dan Wolf, a mutual friend, for dinner. When my mother arrived, Dan was already at the bar with Salvador Sanchez, a good-looking Mexican who spoke

English and had a great sense of humor.

Bea had been looking for a way out, and when she left Norman it was for good. My father, on the other hand, felt such a drastic move wasn't necessary. Despite their problems, he believed they could continue to live together and come to an arrangement. An open marriage, it would be called now. But Mom had made up her mind. When she left, she never looked back.

Her romance with Salvador, AKA Steve, AKA Chavo, was mercurial. In less than a week they were lovers. Three weeks later they drove to Mexico. Mom wanted to take me along, but was convinced otherwise by my father and Chavo. They said it wasn't the right time or place for me to tag along. However, they did take our dog, because no one was willing to care for him.

I, on the other hand, was left with Grandma Fanny, in Brooklyn. Dad saw me at Grandma's perhaps twice a week, but my life revolved around the stability she was to provide for me, then, and over the rest of her life.

In July, three months later, Mother came back to the States and went to Long Branch to fetch me. Together we flew to Mexico where I celebrated my second birthday. My parents' custody arrangement was that I would spend half of the year with my mother and the other half with my father. What actually happened, though, was that for the next several years, Dad and Adele stayed for three months in Mexico, usually from July to October, and then took me back to New York by car. We'd arrive in New York in November, where I remained until February; then my father would fly back to Mexico with me, delivering me back to Mom.

Bea lived in Mexico for the next eighteen years. She studied medicine and became a psychiatrist. She had a son, my younger brother Sal, with Salvador, whom she would later divorce. Dad would go on to marry five more times and father a total of eight children of his own. While I spent my childhood shuttled between two countries, immersed in two cultures, feeling always a bit of an outsider in both.

CHAPTER 3

Total Daddy Immersion

Dad and me in Grandma's house, 1953.

MY FATHER ENJOYED TELLING US, HIS CHILDREN, STORIES ABOUT when we were kids. One of my favorites was about those long drives from Mexico to New York in the early 1950s. It made for good after-dinner conversation and became part of our family lore, at least

Dad's and mine. Every time he told the story he changed some details. But it always reached a climax with his description of our conversation about God and the angels as we drove along the quiet roads of the Texas desert at 4 AM. He liked to say, "Susie helped me think about God in a different light, which years later developed into my own personal belief about Him, or Her." When I was growing up, every time he told the story I glowed with pride.

My recollections of those road trips are fuzzy. Did we take off in the morning or the afternoon? How did I say goodbye to my mother, and how did I react to leaving her and Chavo? Once on the road, what did the three of us do to pass the time as Dad drove? I can't imagine him and Adele singing kiddie songs. But I can recall him belting out "The Bodily Function Blues," a song he made up in college and continued to elaborate on, and entertain us with for many years.

> Ah can't piss, Ah can't urinate
> Ah can't shit, Ah can't defecate,
> Aou, Aww, Uhu…
> Ah can't fuck, Ah just can't copulate….
> Eeh, Aouuu!!
> Ah got those bodily function blues.

I probably didn't understand the lyrics, but I did enjoy his gusto. He also sang, "When the Deep Purple Falls" in his out-of-key, totally unmelodious voice.

I'd shout "*Dad-ee*, stop! You can't sing."

To which he'd say, with an amused twinkle in his eye, "What? I certainly can! Listen carefully!"

And, to my dismay, he would start all over again.

I also vaguely remember that he made up stories to pass the time. I must have also asked questions about where we were going, and about Grandma and his younger sister, Aunt Barbara. I'm sure there were quiet periods, too: me sucking my thumb and gazing out onto the winding road.

And what about Adele; how did she participate? It seems curious that such significant details about one of the cornerstones of our relationship, and one of Dad's most important acts of fatherly devotion, is almost totally hidden underneath layers of childhood amnesia. Only certain images, flashes of color, strokes of his story and mine, remain. I do see myself at four years old, in my child's seat between Daddy and Adele, stopping at motels with swimming pools. Waking up very early the next day, at 3:30 AM, and driving on the empty roads surrounded by darkness. Seeing only the headlights on the pavement, and the stars above.

Dad liked getting an early start, so I can picture him packing the Studebaker at dawn. He'd be irritable, swearing at all the usual small problems of travel, ready to pick a fight with Adele if she wasn't on the ball. Once everything was inside, he'd install me in a child seat with a straight back and two wide metal hooks curved like ears. These fit over the top of the car's front bench seat, so I wouldn't slide around. I was tied in with a thin safety strap.

This 1950s child's seat was an important item of equipment for our trips, because I could sit between my father and Adele, up high enough to be able to see out through the windshield.

Dad told me later, "I thought it was important for you to be able to get a clear view of the road, to see the same scenery we did. That way we could share the experience. And I also wanted you to be next to me, not sitting in the back and sucking your thumb, alone with your thoughts."

Two hours after leaving Mexico City, we'd see the dry-looking mountains of Queretaro. The music on the radio turned to static then, until we caught a local station. But the reception was always erratic. My father, exasperated by the intermittent blasts of music, would finally turn off the radio.

Dad and Adele chatted, their voices lulling me to sleep. I was in pause mode; disconnected, silent. Leaving my mother and stepfather and everything that was familiar, about to spend three months in New York City with Dad and Adele, and Grandma and Grandpa. I didn't cry or complain, just looked at the road with my thumb in my mouth. The soothing rhythm of the sucking coupled with a continuous caress on my ear lobe created an invisible circle of protection. I felt safe.

As I sucked and dozed, images of New York appeared: the smell of cold crisp air, the gray sky, the high buildings, the parks, the bland food. Grandma's apartment was clear in my mind, the soft armchair covered in light blue fabric, the red velvet couch with the gold-framed mirror above it. I saw her twinkling blue eyes and thought of how she bathed and towel-dried me, paying special attention to the crevices between my toes. She would cut my fingernails and toenails, put me into my pajamas, read me a story, and tuck me into bed.

In the morning she'd ask, "Susie, what do you want for breakfast?" Grandma Fanny made the best scrambled eggs, but my favorite was Cream of Wheat with salt and cold milk. I stayed with her and Grandpa Barney in their apartment on Willow Street in Brooklyn Heights and attended a nursery school close by. Dad would visit me often, just like in Mexico.

On the road, we'd stop in the mid-afternoon, to eat, sleep, and then get up again at 3:30 AM, in order to get a 4 AM start. Before dawn, sucking my thumb once again, I'd look out into a dark empty space, the sky studded with stars, while my father drove until the sun rose. At some point we'd pull off at a diner, usually at a truck stop, for a big breakfast with eggs and bacon and pancakes. Dad always had black coffee, no sugar. Back in the car we'd keep going until the desert sun, baking the roof of the car and the hot air coming in through the open windows, forced us to stop. Usually by 3 PM Dad called it a day and turned into the first motel with a swimming pool we spotted.

Now that was fun. I'd change into a bathing suit and jump in. Dad stood in the shallow end waiting to catch me, then he'd carry me back to the edge so I could repeat the same stunt over and over and over again, indefatigable. At last, exhausted, we would have dinner, and dragging my tired body to bed, I would be asleep before dark. Only to be awakened at 3:30 the next morning, to start all over again.

Each of those ten days seemed to repeat the same routine. A trick of memory, because as we got closer to New York the landscape changed and so did our rhythm. I'm sure we stopped in Arkansas to see Dad's Army buddy, Fig, and his wife Ecey. We no doubt passed through a few big cities. But what remains sharp and clear in memory are the dark desert roads, the stars, and those swimming pools.

And our conversation about God.

One morning just before dawn, when the morning light had not quite reached us, I was staring up into the sky. And I said to Dad, "*Los angelitos* are up there."

He glanced over. "The what?"

"*Los angelitos y los angeles*, too."

"Oh, the angels. So, you believe in *angelitos*?"

"Mmh, *si*."

"How do you know they are there?"

"I just do. *Tía* Lupita (Salvador's sister) told me the *angeles* live up in the sky and take care of us. We all have *un angel de la guarda*. They are special for kids, like me. And God is also looking out for us, but he has the angels to help Him."

Dad was a nonbeliever at the time and had no use for conventional religious beliefs. He wasn't about to let me get away with this kind of thinking. "Susie, see the stars?"

"Yes," I answered, nodding.

"I do too, so I know that stars exist." He pointed at the steering wheel. "You see this wheel?"

"Yes."

"So I know it's here and it's real. When things exist, you can see them. But I see no *angelitos*. And where is God, I don't see him. Do you?"

"No. But I know He's up there."

"How do you know if you can't see Him?" Dad insisted.

"*Por que si*. 'Cause I do."

After that I said nothing more for a while, just gazed out onto the road, quietly thinking. Suddenly I asked "Daddy?"

"Yes, honey."

"Daddy, do you think Grandma is in her apartment in New York?"

He looked a little surprised. "Yes."

"Why do you think that?"

"Well, because that's where she lives. You know she lives in Brooklyn, we're going there."

"But are you sure she's there?" I asked.

"Yes, I'm sure."

"How can you be sure if you can't see her?"

Dad burst out laughing.

Every time he repeated this story, Dad slapped his leg and chuckled, and I'd feel proud of that little girl. Sometimes I think I was never quite as smart again.

After a week and a half of total immersion, I felt comfortable with Dad. I got used to him and our routine. For all that time he was focused on me, on the road, and on Adele—we were a cozy threesome. But as the scenery changed into New England green, I felt a familiar weight settle on my chest. As we approached New York City, I'd stop chatting and fall silent. Put my thumb in my mouth again, and retreat into my private place, sensing we would be separating shortly.

As soon as we got to Brooklyn, Dad would drop me off at my grandparents' house, stick around a while, then head off for his cold-water flat with the hole in the ceiling. He always said goodbye with a guilty look, and a promise to come back soon. And I, once again the twice-a-week daughter, would watch him put on his coat and shut the door behind him.

CHAPTER 4

The Cold-Water Flat with a Hole in the Ceiling

DAD AND ADELE LIVED IN A COLD WATER FLAT IN THE LOWER EAST Side, on 1st Avenue. In one corner of my bedroom ceiling, right above the bed, I could see a black hole. About the size and shape of a tennis ball, it had clean edges and looked as if a fist had been punched through the plaster. The hole was a source of fascination and endless curiosity. Before I went to sleep, I would lie in bed and stare up at it, making it bigger or smaller depending on whether I opened my eyes wide or almost closed them. I'd do this over and over, feeling my body float up to the ceiling and lightly sink back to the bed, until I fell into a trance-like sleep. I was obsessed by that hole, which felt by turns like a playful *Alice in Wonderland* rabbit-hole, or the opening to an eerie dark place.

"*Dad*-ee, I don't like that hole. Why don't you fix it?"

"What bothers you about it?" he'd ask, but I couldn't really define my worries, and he never got around to fixing it.

Adele spent a lot of time in the flat, too. I thought she was beautiful, with short black, slightly wavy hair, and slanted dark eyes inherited from her Peruvian father. Her tea-and-milk complexion came from her light-skinned Cuban mother, Consuelo, and more ethnic-looking father, Al Morales. Though she was a first-generation American, and her parents generally spoke Spanish around the house, Adele must have made a serious effort to never learn the language. She didn't speak Spanish and only understood the basics. Adele was taller than my mother. Like Bea, she didn't wear make-up except

Adele, 1957.

for red lipstick, which she used only when she went out with Dad. Then she'd put on a tight-waisted black dress with a plunging neckline and full skirt. Run her hands through her hair to make it look casually stylish, stop by the mirror to put on the lipstick, and step into black stilettos. I watched her preparations closely, hoping I would look like her when I grew up.

Adele was a painter. In the loft there was a special place where she set up her easel. It was next to a window where she was sure to get the best light. When she worked, she wore beat-up jeans and one of Dad's old shirts stained with oil paints. She stood dabbing the palette with her brush, looking at the white canvas until she had an idea of what she wanted to do. I liked the pungent smell of turpentine mixed with the more subtle linseed odor of the oil paints. I was fascinated by how she mixed colors, and especially enjoyed the way she used a metal spatula to smear a thick coat of paint on the canvas. It seemed easy and fun. So, one day I asked if I could do it too.

The next time we were together she set up a small table for me with paper and a box of pastels. Not ordinary white paper; it was thicker and had more texture. Adele told me it was specially made for watercolors and pastels. Kneeling next to my table, she swept a stick across the block of paper, showing me how to use the pastels.

She said, "Take any color you like and draw something, anything, a circle or a line. You can smudge it with your finger to create a special effect. See how it looks? Now take out another stick and, with your finger merge the two colors."

When I complained it didn't look right, she said, "It takes time. You've got to be patient. Don't be afraid to make mistakes. Try drawing with different colors, put them together, get your fingers dirty. Soon you'll see which colors look good together."

I sat at my makeshift artist's table playing with colors, brushing my fingers across the grainy paper, while Adele used oil paints to transform her canvas into a multicolored and textured work of art.

I felt close to her then. We were fellow artists.

She let me look at her art books – reproductions of Matisse, Picasso and Klee—and told me I might get some ideas leafing through them. After several tries, I finally completed a work I liked. Adele approved and showed it to Dad.

"Susie, you've got something going there," he said.

It had a nice combination of shades of green, gold, yellow, brown and black; little squares close together in the middle of the paper with a few drifting, floating to the edges, Klee style. Dad said I had a flair for color and shape, and had the pastel framed for Grandma, who put it on her bedroom wall.

Dad and Adele went out a lot and also had parties at home. Loud gatherings with lots of drinking and marijuana. Many times, I'd wake up and tiptoe out, hoping to be included in the revelry. Once, Dad told me, he heard a ruckus coming from my bedroom and came in to see me jumping on my bed, totally excited, probably high on the weed fumes that had drifted in.

My father enjoyed carpentry, and with some help from his friends transformed the loft into something that looked like a real apartment. He and Adele had a bedroom and so did I; the one with the hole in the ceiling. We had a bathroom with a door, and also a kitchen. The rest was open space, with sofas and armchairs and Adele's easel in her special corner.

The flat with the hole in the ceiling remained stuck in my mind. For years I used to wonder why it had made such an indelible impression. At least until I met Adele many years later, after my father had died, at a memorial party.

In April 2008, Random House threw a cocktail party after my father's Memorial at Carnegie Hall. I saw Adele standing alone in a corner. I walked up, happy to see her after so many years. She was of course much older, but still Adele, a smaller, thinner version of herself. We embraced and, after catching up and asking the usual questions, took a stroll down memory lane.

At some point she asked, "Susie, do you remember the flat with the hole in the ceiling?"

"How could I forget it?"

"And do you remember that time when you were a kid, and couldn't wake up?"

I was surprised by the comment. "No, what do you mean?"

"You must have been five. We were going out for the evening and you wouldn't go to sleep. So Norman split a Seconal, a tiny piece, and gave it to you. You were out like a light. But the next morning, he couldn't wake you up. He shook you, talked to you. He was desperate, very upset. You were limp, like a rag doll. You finally opened your eyes in the early afternoon."

"What! He actually did that!" I was shocked my father would drug me and leave me alone in order to go out. I laughed to hide my surprise.

At the same time, I thought Adele must've still been pretty angry at Norman to say something like that to me right after his memorial. Obviously, she wasn't thinking of me and what that day meant to me, but rather of taking a final jab at her ex-husband.

Ever since I could remember, I'd had a recurring nightmare in which I was asleep, about to wake up. I'd try to open my eyes, but they were stuck together with a gooey substance. I'd try to open my mouth, but my teeth were glued as if with chewing gum. I could only grind them from side to side. I'd lie half awake and half asleep, trying to rouse myself. But I was pinned to the bed, in a state of unbearable anxiety, unable to communicate or move. Finally, bewildered and confused, with aching muscles, I'd manage to yank myself out of this trance state and sit up, relieved to be awake and finally free.

When Adele told me the "tiny piece of Seconal" anecdote, many formerly puzzling things came together. My obsession with the black hole in the ceiling was obviously tied to that experience. The feeling of floating up into the hole and then descending, of my body getting lighter and wider, and then heavier and compact, was clearly an out of body experience tied to a kind of anxiety that made me want to be in another place. Or at least in another state. It was my way of not being there. I don't remember feeling anxious or unhappy, though my reaction was typical of someone in distress. Much less do I remember my father actually giving me the pill. But I realized this knowledge had been in my body since childhood, and I'd been reliving it in that dream.

I didn't think to ask Adele if my father had only given me Seconal that one time. But I silently thanked her later on, because after talking to her that day, the old nightmare never came back.

CHAPTER 5

Princess of the Hill

T HERE I WAS, JUST FIVE YEARS OLD AND AT THE TOP OF THE SKI slope. I looked down the white expanse of snow, the small bumps, the poles with red flags on the sides. Waiting for Daddy's push that would send me cannonballing down the hill. I was eager to feel the cold, crisp air hitting my cheeks. It felt exhilarating to fly down the slope, shouting "Out of my way!" to all the slowpoke beginners snow-plowing down the hill. I was the Princess of the Hill. And for Dad, I was the best.

Every winter in the mid 1950s, Dad, Adele, and I would drive to Stowe, Vermont to ski for ten days. Packing the car was always tricky because my father had a short temper. If anything went wrong, like a missing rope to tie the skis to the roof of the car, he could start ranting, usually at Adele. "Christ! Can't you have these things handy beforehand?"

Eventually we'd get started and as soon as we got out of the city there was a shift in mood. Dad, now relaxed, would tell jokes and regale us with funny stories. And once his bad mood wasn't permeating the car, Adele and I could settle into our seats, shake off the tension, and enjoy the ride.

We stayed at a beautiful lodge, with a huge lobby and an immense fireplace, in adjoining rooms. Mine had a big tub in the bathroom, while theirs had a large double bed with a beautiful view of the mountains. After a good night sleep, we got up early, had a hearty breakfast of pancakes with lots of syrup and scrambled eggs, and set off to the slopes.

Adele always helped me get dressed: long johns underneath my ski pants, two pairs of socks, a long-sleeved t-shirt, a turtleneck, a sweater and a parka. I could hardly walk bundled up in all the clothes and was usually sweating as we walked out of the lodge to make the quick drive to the lifts. There, another ordeal lay ahead. Dad had to get the skis off the roof of the car and carry them to a room where everyone was getting their gear ready for the day. And then he had to put on my skis, and his.

We sat down on a bench, so he could lace up my boots. An activity that took a good deal of precision, because if they were too tight, they could cut off the circulation, and if they were too loose, you couldn't control your skis. As he was lacing them, he asked me, "Susie, does this feel right? Remember, not too tight, not too loose."

I nodded, and once I was ready, he did the same for himself.

Meanwhile Adele had gotten her boots on, and we were finally set to go.

At the time, there were no rope tows for little ones, so Dad took along a short rope that he tied to his belt. But first he put on my skis, then his. He tried to get me to walk over to the lift, teaching me how to take small side steps or else walk penguin-style with the skis. But I never lasted long; my legs were too short and not strong enough. After a few minutes I'd be exhausted and cranky, so he'd pick me up and carry me to the lift.

At the rope tow he would get in place and position me behind him, then say, "Susie, hold on to this rope tightly. When you go over the bumps, relax and you won't fall."

I stood, skis open in parallel position, bending my knees, holding tightly to his rope. His hands in thick leather mittens grabbed the rope tow and, with a jerk, we started up the hill. I bent my knees and crouched even more every time we went over a bump, as Dad had taught me earlier. But inevitably, once in a while, I lost my balance and tipped to one side. When I was lucky, I quickly regained my footing, but sometimes I fell, dragging him down with me. Each time we scrambled to get out of the way as quickly as possible, to make room for skiers coming up behind us. Dad would wait until there was a gap in the uphill flow, then we rushed into position and grabbed the towrope again.

As we approached the end of the tow, my heart always beat faster. This part of the operation, sliding off the rope tow, made me anxious with anticipation.

"Okay Susie, we're getting off now. Just relax and slide to the right with me. I'm going to let go of the rope now. Okay, very good, that's 'a girl! Good for you!"

On top of the hill, he instructed me to keep my weight forward, leaning into the slope, knees bent. Once the quick lesson was over, I was ready to go. I immediately forgot all the cumbersome paraphernalia, the drudgery of getting ready, going up the tow rope, falling down from the tow, the fear of getting off at the top.

All gone. I was ready to fly.

But sometimes my skis came off mid-way down and I'd take a tumble. Dad would immediately be by my side. First, he had to get the skis, then take off his mittens to fix the bindings and lace up my boots again. "Goddamn it, these fucking boots!" he'd swear with frustration as frostbite began to settle on his fingers and our feet. Once my skis were on again, I'd continue my run.

In later years, it became my responsibility to strap on my boots, carry the skis and, if they happened to come off, find them and put them on again. I much preferred Dad doing the work, but by the time I turned eight, I was on my own. If I asked for help, he was willing to give me instructions. But he always said, "Good skiers take care of their equipment. If you can't lace up your own boots, you'll never be an expert."

I never did become an expert. Not because of the boots or the skis, but because my father thought I was a natural and didn't need lessons. Whatever I needed to learn, he decided he could teach me. So, I remained at the advanced intermediate stage, just like him.

At mid-afternoon, as the sun was beginning to slide down the sky, we headed to the lodge. By then my hands and feet were aching, my cheeks red with the wind and cold winter air. Adele ran a hot bath for me, and as my hands and feet slid into the water they burned. A cross between pleasure and torture, until my body got used to the warmth and the cold left me.

Drinks were a ritual in the big hotel lobby with the huge fireplace. Dad had a whisky sour, Adele a martini, and I got a Shirley Temple. After dinner I was tucked into bed in my room, and they went back to the bar for more drinks.

Years later, I taught my own kids to ski. By then, there was no more rope tow, no lace-up boots, no long johns or heavy parkas. Instead, they wore clip-on boots, and quick-and-easy-step-in bindings for the skis. But it was still an ordeal. When their skis slipped off, I'd take off my gloves to assist, and my fingers froze. When they fell off the T-bar, I'd help them scurry out of the path of skiers going by. By the time we were up the beginners slope I'd be completely exhausted.

I realized then all the work that had gone into teaching me to ski. My father had laced my boots, devised a kiddie rope tow to help me up the slope, and taught me to lean back on the T bar while we went up the slope. He could've sent me off with an instructor. Instead he'd insisted I learn along with him; it was something we did together, and we treasured it.

My father valued and admired the act of mastering any physical activity. He'd been a frightened and timid child. I, quite the opposite, was fearless, eager to cannonball down the mountain. He relished this quality in me and enjoyed every advance I made on the slopes.

In the late 60s, for Adele's daughters, my sisters Danielle and Betsy, it wasn't the same. My father had changed. He no longer had any patience and was infinitely more irritable. His temper could flare at the drop of a coin, especially if his daughters didn't respond the way he expected. Yet he insisted on repeating the same ritual, taking them skiing every year.

When we were adults, Danielle told me that after a few lessons with him on the beginners' slope, lessons which included lots of scolding and cajoling, Dad usually decided it was time to move on to a more advanced trail, so that they could ski with him. The prospect was daunting, and they were terrified. But he was adamant, saying that once they went down the first time, the fear would disappear, and they would feel virtuous.

Danielle remembers staring down the long slope, putting her skis into plow position, hoping she could get to the end in one piece. At the bottom, she and Betsy would sigh with relief, grateful to have survived. But already anxious about doing it again the next day.

CHAPTER 6

Going to The Bullfight

AT HOME IN MEXICO, I ALWAYS ENJOYED WATCHING MY MOTHER get ready for a party on Saturday nights. She'd put on her silver hoop earrings, choose a low-cut dress, and then put on red lipstick. The preparation for the party itself took place earlier. Bags of ice, bottles of rum and tequila and beer appeared in the late afternoon, and once the sun had gone down, her friends would arrive. Sometimes a large crowd gathered. Salvador and Mom had a diverse group of friends that included ex-pats and Mexicans, musicians and lawyers, doctors and writers and taxi drivers. And also, one or two unemployed friends. When my father and Adele were in town, they also joined the party.

Whiffs of cigarette smoke drifted to my bedroom, along with laughter and the tinkle of ice in glasses. All these were a magnet for me. I'd immediately get out of bed and wander into the living room. Many times, my mother would be playing duets on the piano with her friend Luis. Her favorite was a popular 1950s bolero, *Usted es la Culpable*," which she sang with him while the guests gathered around to listen.

Once I woke to shouting, but I was too scared to leave my bedroom to find out what was going on. The next morning, I asked Mom what had happened.

She said, "Oh, your father got into a fight with someone and Salvador jumped in to help him." I saw some towels stained with blood lying on the floor. Following my gaze, Mom said Salvador had lost his two front teeth in the fight.

She didn't sound upset. Her attitude was "what the hell, it was a great party and a rowdy bunch." And this helped me turn the whole event into a funny story and forget I'd been scared the night before.

I was proud my father and stepfather were so friendly. It felt as if I had two mothers and two fathers, something that amused Norman, but didn't make Bea very happy. Sometimes, though, I wanted my two mothers and two fathers to switch places. Like most children of divorced parents, I secretly harbored the hope that one day Mom and Dad would be reunited. It seemed to me that Chavo and Adele looked good together, so it wouldn't be a problem if they became a couple. I must've picked up on some unspoken vibe, because years later I found out that while Chavo had been living in New York, he and Adele had briefly been lovers before they'd met my parents!

During my father's long visits to Mexico he fell in love with the bullfight. He was captivated by the delicate bodies of the toreros, clad in tight-fitting costumes of brilliant colors with shiny sparkles, black shoes that looked more like ballet slippers, and strange eighteenth-century Spanish hats. Yet these lean, feminine-looking men would go into battle with a huge, strong, spirited bull. The very symbol of virility. Dad was intrigued by the paradoxical nature of the scene: feminine masculinity versus the brutality of the duel. A ballet of death.

Ernest Hemingway had also been captivated by bullfights, in Spain. And for Norman, as for many of his generation, "Papa" Hemingway was a role model. Perhaps this was another ingredient in Dad's attraction to the blood sport. A way of getting closer to the alpha-maleness Hemingway exuded, which was becoming so important to Norman. He even took notes for a novel, perhaps his version of *Death in the Afternoon*. He also published an article about an eccentric bullfighter nicknamed "El Loco."

The first time I went to the *corrida* with Dad I was four, maybe five years old. Adele stayed home. She wasn't crazy about bullfights. This made the outing with my father even better. Just the two of us, alone together, going to a special place.

We left my mother's apartment in the early afternoon. As we arrived at the Plaza de Toros, the sun was high and bright, and I was very hot. Waves of people were standing in line to hand in their tickets and enter, but the line moved quickly, so pretty soon we were safely seated. Dad bought me a Coke and got a beer from the vendors who walked up and down the bleachers with trays hanging from their necks full of drinks, peanuts, potato chips, and *charritos,* or Mexican hot chips. Everyone was in a festive mood. My father had told me we were going to see a special show, and I couldn't wait for it to begin.

The Plaza was a circular, open arena with bleachers all around and wooden barriers at the bottom, along with two or three camouflaged openings. I wondered what they were for. Suddenly trumpets signaled the beginning of the Corrida, and the crowd fell stone silent.

I looked at Dad, trying to catch his smile, and grabbed his hand. He sat me on his lap, so I could have a good view of the action.

The *matadores* in full regalia, the *picadores* on horseback, the *cuadrilla*—that included the *banderilleros* and other bullfighters, all entered the arena to the rhythm of the *Pasodoble.* They all walked around the full circumference of the plaza, and then exited through one of the secret openings I'd noticed before.

The music stopped. The crowd waited so silently I heard papers rustle in the mild breeze.

Suddenly, from the opposite side of the arena, a black bull barged in, running, pausing, looking left and right, ready to attack whatever crossed his path. A beautiful, powerful animal. His hide shone with energy. He ran, then lifted his front legs as if to jump, ramming into the side barriers, then stopping to look around.

From another opening on the side of the arena the *torero* appeared, cape in hand. He slowly walked toward the bull and the two eyed each other, each weighing the strength of his opponent. As the *torero* got closer, he spread the cape to its full circumference and shook it, saying,

"*Aja toro.*" The bull followed the movement of the cape, lowered his head, and swept those sharp, dangerous-looking horns underneath it to the other side.

The crowd yelled, "*Ole!*"

The *torero* positioned himself, inching his way over to the bull in small side steps. Then he opened the cape once more. The bull again passed underneath it.

More shouts of "*Ole!*" The crowd sounded even more excited. I was following the torero and the bull closely, but also looking up at Dad. He shouted every time along with the crowd, so I knew he was enjoying the show.

However, I wasn't totally sure how *I* felt. I sensed something bad was going to happen to the bull, and didn't want the *torero* to make fun of him, or taunt him.

Dad told me not to worry, he was sure the bull was having a good time. Even so, I kept a vigilant eye, not quite sure about that. It felt like a balancing act between what I perceived, and what Daddy's reassuring words expressed.

Finally, my father, apparently sensing I was having second thoughts about the show, said, "Susie, just think of this as a contest. One of them will win. The loser will be sad because he lost, and the winner will be happy. That's what happens in contests."

"I want the bull to win," I stated with total assurance.

The was a pause in the action. The *torero* left the arena and the trumpet heralded the entrance of the *picador*, a man who rode a horse with blinders and a padded blanket. He carried a long stick with a sharp iron tip.

The bull studied the newcomer, not moving.

"What's happening, Daddy? *Quién es ese hombre* with the stick?" I asked in my sing-song Mexican accent. "And why is the bull not moving? *Tiene miedo?*"

Dad surely knew by now he had a problem; he must carry me emotionally unscathed through the *corrida*, since it was clear I had a strong bias in favor of the bull. But was it possible it truly had just occurred to him that the violent scene we were about to witness could upset a small child?

He appeared to weigh the situation, then said, "Susie, these guys are the bad guys. They're going to try to beat the bull, but they won't win."

As if on cue, right after Dad said this, the bull went straight for the horse at a full run and rammed his horns into the padding.

The *picador* stuck the pointed pole right into the bull's neck between head and shoulders. Blood started seeping out of the wound.

Furious, the bull pushed the horse with his horns, right up against the wood planks of the plaza's round walls. But the more he pushed, the more punishment he got from the *picador's* sharp pole.

"Daddy, I do not like this man." My heart was pounding. I was angry and scared. I wanted to leave, but also wanted to stay. I was worried about the horse and the bull, and hated the bad guy with the pole.

"The bad guy is trying to make the bull tired," my father informed me, "but he's also in danger because if the horse falls, the bull will be able to hit him with his horns."

"But Daddy, if the horse falls, the bull will hit the horse with his horns and hurt him. And the bad guy will run away, and nothing will happen to him."

"You're right, honey. But that's what makes it so interesting. You never know what's going to happen. I think the horse will be fine, and so will the bull, even if he does get a bit tired."

"Daddy, I want the bad guy to go away."

Just then the trumpet signaled for the *picador* to leave. He yanked the tip of the pole from the bull's neck, but the bull kept ramming into the horse's padding. He wouldn't let go. So, the *picador* waited while men with capes tried to draw the bull's attention away. Finally, man and horse trotted out of the arena through one of the special exits.

The bull stood still, breathing hard. I could tell he was tired and angry. I was anxiously waiting for the next move, and at the same time wanted the whole thing to be over with, right away.

The trumpet echoed through the arena once again. A *banderillero* walked out onto the sand. Instead of a cape he carried two multicolored sticks, one in each hand. The bull, still standing in the same spot, didn't seem to notice him. Not until the man arched his back, stood on his toes, and lifted the *banderillas* high overhead. Alerted by the motion, the bull charged, while the man waited to strike. Seizing the right moment, the man ran up to the bull and sank the *banderillas* into his neck, in exactly the same place the picador had hurt him before.

That *banderillero* ran out of the arena just as another one appeared with two more sticks. He and the bull went through the same ritual. Only this time one of the sticks didn't sink in, and it fell to the ground. Finally, a third man ran up to the bull, *banderillas* held high, and attempted to place them. But by now the bull was alert, and not about to let himself be hurt again. He lifted his head and tried to gore the *torero*. Unable to stick the *banderillas* in, he ran out of the plaza, to the loud booing of the crowd.

I was upset now. Clearly the bull was suffering, and he was bleeding. I wanted to cry. Instead, I said, "Daddy, I think the bull wants to go home. Why can't they stop now?"

"Darling, the bull's certainly tired, but he doesn't want to go home yet. He wants to finish this first. Sometimes when you're doing something, like playing a game and losing, you might want to leave. But it's important you stay till it's over, because you might get a second chance. I think the bull feels that way: he's thinking what his next move is going to be."

"But why do these men keep putting the sticks into his neck?"

"They want him to be tired. He's very strong, and the *torero* who's coming next has to pass the cape very close to the bull. If he's not tired enough, he could hurt the *torero*."

I was more worried about the blood gushing out of the bull's side than about him hurting the man with the cape. I knew the bull was badly hurt, so I again turned to my father. "Daddy, what about the blood? And those things they stuck into his neck, are they hurting him?"

With a perfectly serious expression my father said, "That's not blood, that's red paint."

"Why do they put red paint on the bull?" I exclaimed.

What Dad had said seemed unbelievable to me, even at age five. I could also sense he was thinking about something. Years later he would tell stories of how he took me to the bullfights, what a sport I was, a brave kid. It seemed so important to him that I be "tough." (Unlike the sensitive child he'd been in his early years.) But back then, at that bullfight, was there perhaps a pang of regret?

Not fully convinced, I asked, "Daddy, are you *sure* that is red paint?"

He nodded. "The paint and the sticks are there to make the show more colorful. But look! Now something really exciting is going to happen. And then the bull will be able to go home."

My father must have been right, for just then the *matador* entered the arena. Silence descended again on the waiting crowd.

I looked at the bull. He seemed so tired. His head hung low, and white foam was coming out of his mouth. He moved his hooves a little, kicking up some dirt, but didn't charge at the *torero*. He just stood there.

The matador said, "*Aja Toro!*" He opened his cape, shaking it, waiting, until the bull finally decided to run at it. Then the *torero* turned on his heels, cape twirling close to his body. Facing the bull once more, he opened the cape again. Gracefully, horns bowed, the bull ran through the rippling cloth again and once more, and then again.

The crowd shouted "*Ole!*" in unison each time man and bull moved to the rhythm of the cape.

I liked this part. They were dancing.

Then I heard drums beating. *Something is really going to happen now*, I thought.

From under his cape, the torero pulled out a long sword. He was about twenty feet from the bull, who was panting, about to charge again. The torero rose on his toes. Taking aim, he ran right up to the bull, sinking the sword gracefully into the animal's neck, between the head and shoulders.

Silence fell again in the Plaza.

The bull dropped to his knees. His head touched the ground. Then, very slowly, he keeled over.

The crowd cheered, and shouted, *"Oreja!"*

An ear, for the *torero's* great performance.

"Daddy, Daddy, what happened! Is he dead?"

"The bull is very tired, and he's going to sleep now," my father said, as two horsemen chained the animal's horns to a contraption and dragged him out of the arena.

Loud applause reverberated through the Plaza.

"Why are they taking him out like this?" I asked in a high-pitched, anxious tone.

"Because he can't move, he's so tired."

"But why is everyone clapping?"

"They're clapping for the bull, because he was brave and fought well. They want him to know that, even if he's so tired he can't walk out by himself."

"And even if he can't really hear them because he's asleep," I offered.

Little did I know that this was only the first bull. That there were five more to go. But I have no recollection of the other fights that day, because by the second bull I'd spaced out and fallen asleep, my head on Dad's lap.

Was I deliberately helping Dad with his story, or did I really believe him? I must've wanted to believe with all my heart. Because when he took me home that night, I told my mother how I had loved the bullfight, the music, and the costumes. I added that I was a little worried about the bull being hurt, but felt much better when Daddy told me he wasn't really hurt. That the red stuff was paint, not blood. And that they had only carried him away because he was so tired.

Mom listened quietly. Then, in her matter-of-fact way, she said, "Susie, I think Daddy made a mistake. The bull does die, and what you saw was blood."

But I didn't want to believe her.

Next Sunday I went off to the bullfight with Dad again.

～

Now, when I think of the *corrida*, the images of the bull brutally pierced by the picador and coming to his death by the sword of the matador, still make my heart race. At age five, my emotions were even more intense. I favored the bull and passionately hated the picadors. I probably knew that what I was watching wasn't really a show.

I wasn't the only child in the *Plaza de Toros*. Bullfights were a Sunday outing in Mexico, something fun to do with the family. There were many kids ambling about, which must have been a good excuse for my father to ignore my distress.

Afterward, I felt divided. I wanted to never go back, and at the same time I waited anxiously for him to pick me up on Sundays. I did enjoy the fanfare, the costumes, and the music. The excitement of the crowd was contagious, and I loved that part of the show. But I learned to close my eyes when the bull was hurt, and I fell asleep when it all got to be too much.

Looking back, what I really wanted was simply to be with my father. I knew he enjoyed thinking of me as a brave child. It was also an opportunity to do something with him that he loved, and which I half-enjoyed.

The *corrida* became a way to bond with Norman; one that was reignited in my adolescence.

In 1966, when I was sixteen, Dad asked me to help him translate Federico García Lorca's *Llanto por Ignacio Sanchez Mejías*. Four powerful poems written in honor of the matador Sanchez Mejías, who'd met his death in the arena. According to my father, Lorca's official translator hadn't captured the beauty and rhythm of those poems, nor the pathos of the bullfight and the exquisite quality of the battle. We embarked on a joint venture: I would make a literal translation of the four poems, then Dad would provide the poetic flavor.

While I was translating them, the sensual and brutal quality of the bullfight flooded my senses again. I remembered our trips to the *Plaza de Toros*, and the tumultuous emotions I'd experienced ten years before. But I was in no mood to pursue that line of thought. I was so proud we would be co-editors of Lorca´s translation that whatever uncomfortable feelings popped up about that little girl in the *corrida* soon faded.

Our work was published in 1972 in *Existential Errands*. The book was dedicated: To Barbara, to Susan, to Adeline and to Al. My copy had the following inscription: *Now that your name is in lights you may be ready for existentialism, dear M'gusu.* That last being short for Susu M'gusu, one of his favorite childhood names for me.

I wasn't really sure what he meant by being "ready for existentialism," but it felt damn good to have my name "in lights."

CHAPTER 7

———

La Cantina

DURING MY FATHER'S VISITS IN THE 1950S, I WENT TO THE BULL-
fight with him on Sundays. But every Saturday, Salvador took me
to his shop, el taller.

My stepfather was lots of fun. He was a handsome man, tall with
wavy hair and soulful eyes. He had an easy smile, a great sense of
humor, and a knack for storytelling. I loved him and felt his unwavering affection. Even after my brother Sal, his only son with my mother,
was born when I was almost six years old. And even after he and my
mother split up, when I was eleven.

Before my brother was born, on Saturdays Salvador would take me
to his shop in la Colonia Guerrero, a working-class neighborhood. The
taller was on the second floor of a run-down factory building. The area
was large and near a window was a small square area surrounded by
glass walls that served as his office and isolated him somewhat from the
din of the machines. The room had a desk with papers and contracts,
paper clips, a stapler, pens, and a phone.

We'd get there mid-morning. Salvador would hand me paper and
pencil and let me play secretary. He'd give me easy jobs, like cleaning
his desk and getting his stuff in order. On Saturdays there were fewer
workers in the *taller*, about five or six to the usual twelve on weekdays.

The guys ran large machines that cut out boxes for products like Colgate toothpaste or Fab laundry powder. The machines looked like giant, sharp steel cookie cutters. It was a noisy business. Each time the sharp blades came down on the colorful sheets of light cardboard they made a curious sound, like a giant pair of scissors slicing thick paper. The die-cut sheets were then assembled into boxes by another worker. It was like cutting out and assembling my paper dolls, only with a great deal of noise.

The guys were always friendly; they usually gave me a few boxes to put together myself. After a couple hours Salvador and I would leave on errands. Sometimes he'd take me to The Cantina, a neighborhood bar close to his shop. I was still blond back then, and so attracted attention in a country where almost everyone else had black hair and brown skin.

Salvador was fond of telling a story about one of those Saturday excursions.

"You couldn't have been more than four or five, because you still had blond hair. One day we walked into The Cantina, one of those dark, seedy neighborhood bars that smell of *pulque* and tequila, where I would go sometimes after work for a drink. I sat you on the bar, ordered a beer, and started chatting with a couple of the workers from the *taller*. Suddenly I had a feeling something was not quite right, because I hadn't heard a peep out of you for a while. I turned around to look, but you weren't there. Not sitting on any of the chairs or standing near any of the tables in the cantina. I asked the barman if he'd seen you, but he was busy and hadn't noticed whether you had gone out. I turned to the *borrachitos,* but they hadn't seen you either.

Ay jijos, donde se metió? Where did she go, I wondered. Then, one of the guys remembered that a local customer who'd gone up to the bar for a drink had offered to take you on a bike ride. '*A lo mejor se fue con el.* Maybe she went with him,' the barman said. So, I rushed out of the cantina into the sunlit street. At the end of the block I saw a man on an old rickety bike with a child who looked like you, sitting on the handlebars. As the figure pedaled closer, I saw your big smile."

For many years Chavo told this story, bragging about how independent Susie was. "You could walk out of a room with anyone, including an unknown drunken *borrachito*, a barfly from a neighborhood cantina. You had no fear of strangers, that's for sure," he'd add.

But once, when Mom heard me telling the story, she said. "No, it wasn't any old *borrachito*, it was Chucho, our friend. He'd come into the cantina, saw how bored you were, and thought a bike ride would put you in a good mood. Only problem was he just took you out without telling Chavo!"

It was one of my favorite Mexican stories about me. One that revealed the carefree manner in which we lived, as if nothing was really that serious or dangerous. In Mexico, anything that happened in your life was an excuse to tell a good story, as long as its most important ingredient was the humor and lightness with which it was told.

Thirty years later, my husband and I and our three children visited Mexico. One Sunday afternoon I was in Coyoacán alone with the three kids. Antonia, my youngest, was a very pretty four-year old with honey-colored ringlets. We stopped at El Parnaso, a well-known bookstore. I wandered through the aisles with her while my two older kids browsed in the children's book section. I was immersed in the new Latin American fiction display when Antonia said, "Mommy, I need to pipi."

"Just a minute, honey," I said, and kept looking at the books. No more than a couple of minutes passed, but when I looked down again, Antonia was gone. At first, I wasn't that worried, assuming she was with her siblings. But they hadn't seen her. The sales clerks were busy with other customers and hadn't noticed whether she had left the store.

I broke into a cold sweat. My hands started shaking, and my ears rang.

As on any Sunday afternoon in Coyoacán, the plaza was crowded with street vendors selling a myriad of wares, from balloons to food to arts and crafts. The walkways were packed with parents and children and strolling couples.

In a flash, I remembered cautionary tales I'd heard all my life about *robachicos.* Thieves, who stole kids to sell their organs. This could not be happening. She couldn't be lost! My heart was pounding as I ran out of the store, screaming, *"Mi hija! Donde esta mi hija?"*

An old vendor asked if I was looking for "a guerita," "a pretty, light-haired girl." When I nodded, he added, *"Pues se fue por ahi."* She went that way.

I looked where he pointed, and there was Antonia coming toward me, crying. I ran to her, hugged her with all my strength, and burst into tears.

The old cantina anecdote lost its charm that day. I realized then it had probably never really been funny. Not for Salvador.

CHAPTER 8

Susanita Sanchez

IN 1955 I STARTED FIRST GRADE IN MEXICO, AT THE AGE OF FIVE AND a half. We lived in a middle-class neighborhood, but the school I attended, ten blocks away, was in a poor section of town. My mother had tried to enroll me in some other, better schools. But since I wasn't yet six, she was told I'd have to wait another year.

So, I entered República de Cuba, the only elementary school that would take me, even though I was younger than the official age for enrollment.

Mom was happy to get me into any school. According to her, I was bored in my kindergarten class, around the corner from us. And since I could already read and do a little arithmetic, she felt I was ready for first grade. At the interview with the principal, Mom lied about my age and said my birth certificate hadn't yet arrived from the States. The woman either believed my mother, or was so impressed by her self-possessed American manner, she decided to accept me.

The school year ran from February to November. So, in the second month of 1955, I put on my favorite red-velvet dress, and Mom drove me to school.

Immediately, it became clear something was wrong. I had no uniform! All students had to wear the blue school uniform, but Mom either hadn't thought to ask, or hadn't been told.

I stood in line with forty other kids, waiting to be assigned a classroom, the only blond, blue-eyed girl in a sea of dark hair. Not only that, I was wearing red velvet, while the other girls had on blue jumpers and white blouses, and all the boys blue pants. Every child also had a gray sweater with the school's white, red, and green insignia patch sewn below the left shoulder.

The class was taught in a large room with windows overlooking a patio. A huge blackboard was faced by twenty sets of double school benches, where we sat in pairs. The teacher finally moved me to the front row because I kept getting up and wandering around, not yet understanding that, unlike in my former kindergarten, here I was supposed to sit still and raise my hand every time I wanted to say or do something, such as go to the restroom.

At roll call time the teacher looked at her roster and went down all the As: Aguirre, Alcantara, and so on. Then on to the Bs: Barbosa, Barrientos, Benavides. Finally she reached the Ms. "Susan?" she said, and then looked up at me. "You mean Susana?"

I shook my head. "No. Susan."

She looked down again, to check my last name. "Do you know how to spell it?"

"M.A.I.L.E.R," I answered, proud that I knew all the letters of my last name.

"Bueno, so it's Susana My-lehr. *Así se pronuncia.* That's how you should say it." Then she added, "That's a strange last name. Where do you come from?"

"De Estados Unidos."

"Oh. *Bueno. Entonces*, Susana Mylehr *de Estados Unidos*," she said firmly, then smiled.

My face grew hot. I felt she was making fun of me and was almost in tears. In addition to the red dress, the blond hair and blue eyes, now I stood out even more because of my name, and because I was a *gringa!*

At recess I watched the older kids play a game called "crack the whip". When one of the older boys invited me to join in, I eagerly accepted. Everyone held hands, making a long line. The head of this "whip" ran, picking up speed, and the others followed along, running around the school patio, hands locked. Other students kept out of the way.

Suddenly the leader came to a stop and swung his arm with a violent jerk, sending a whip-like ripple down the long line of kids. And I, who was the last one in line, sailed through the air. Terrified, I saw myself in slow motion, flying. From above I saw the ground approaching and knew the crash back to earth would happen any second. As I landed on all fours, my hands and knees scraped along the rough pavement. At last I lay still, curled in a ball, crying.

A couple teachers came running over to help me up. "Are you okay?" both asked anxiously as they rushed me to the principal's office on the second floor. One woman washed my hands and knees, and my face, which had also been scraped, daintily patting my wounds with mercurochrome. They wanted to inform my mother, but we didn't have a phone at home, so the principal's secretary fed me cookies and juice until it was time for Mom to pick me up.

Bea arrived two hours later. When she saw me, she flew at the principal in a fury. "How could something like this happen? Where were the teachers? What were they doing that they didn't see this coming?"

Though still angry, she drove me back to the same school a week later, this time dressed in a newly-purchased uniform.

After my painful initiation, and Mom's reaction, "the whip" was forbidden. The older kids were warned not to pick on the younger ones.

And I was getting smarter. The next time someone asked what my name was, without hesitation I said, "Susana Sanchez." I had decided to use Salvador's last name. I became Susanita Sanchez for the rest of the year. That is the name on my first- and second-grade report cards.

When I told my mother about the unofficial name change, she thought it was hilarious. Grandma Mailer, however, wasn't amused. I don't know if my father ever heard about my sudden change of identity.

During that first year Mom picked me up every afternoon at 5 PM. I wanted so badly to blend in, but that was pretty much impossible.

I felt uncomfortable about my mother's American accent, and about the fact she wore slacks when all the other mothers wore dresses. I was mortified by the way she was so obviously not Mexican. But most of all, I was troubled that she picked me up at school in a 1950 Ford. No one else in the whole class had a car. So then, besides being the blond, blue-eyed *gringuita*, it became clear to my classmates I was rich.

Soon after second grade started, I asked my mother to let me walk home alone. She wasn't convinced and refused.

But I kept insisting, "It's only ten blocks away."

"Okay, let's do this," she said at last. "I'll follow along behind to see how well you cross the street, and if I'm convinced you can do it safely on your own, I'll let you walk home alone."

I walked, and she followed slowly in the Ford, until she was convinced I could actually cross the street on my own.

Many of my classmates lived nearby. My friend Conchita's home was less than a block away, so often I'd go over there to play after school was out. She lived in a *vecindad*, a gated slum community. To get to her two-room dwelling we had to open the front gate and walk down a long, open-air corridor with dirty white stucco walls. Each apartment we passed had a window and a door that faced the corridor. There were many doors, all painted in once-bright colors now faded by the sun. Often music blasted from the open windows. People stood by their doors or sat on stoops, chatting with neighbors. Kids ran up and down the patio playing games.

Conchita's front door was in the middle of that passage. Her apartment had only two windows: one next to the front door and one in the back, which made the rooms pretty dark. Another door in the back room led to a tiny patio with a tin roof, where the kitchen and bathroom stood side by side, the smells of food and human waste mingling there.

Conchita's mother usually greeted us with a cup of Nescafe made with hot milk, and a slice of *pan dulce*, slightly sweet bread. We would eat our snack, then go out to the communal patio where all the *vecindad* kids got together to play in the afternoons.

Conchita's mother thought I was very well behaved. "You are so *sencilla*, so respectful, in spite of being a *niña rica*, a rich girl," she often said.

The kids in the vecindad were curious about *la guerita*, the light-skinned girl. I was a novelty, a real *gringa* who looked different yet didn't make a big deal of it. Soon I was accepted and became part of the gang. And I had such a good time playing out on the patio there, I barely noticed the decaying, stained walls, the dirt, the strong fumes from bags of rotting garbage where clouds of buzzing black flies hovered.

In fact, I wanted badly to live in a *vecindad*, and told my mother we should move to one. To simply step out of your home into a passage full of friends with lots of music and games, was my idea of heaven. Our house felt too quiet. When I got home after school my mother was either off at work or studying for her Med school classes. The maid would be in the kitchen, or upstairs ironing and listening to radio shows. Salvador did not arrive until late afternoon. Most afternoons it was just me and my little brother, who was barely a year old. I often felt lonely and bored.

One afternoon at Conchita's, she and I and Chabela and Trinidad, her friends from the *vecindad*, skipped rope, played hop-scotch, and tag. Then we went into Chabela's house to listen to the evening soap opera on the radio. Her mother invited us for a light supper of black beans, tortillas, and a cup of *café con leche*. I lost track of time listening to the *radionovela*. The dramatized story was about a woman who lived on a ranch in Jalisco and was married to a really bad guy. Suddenly she died. But she wasn't really dead! She had something called Catalepsy. But no one knew about her condition, so she was lying in a coffin, about to be buried.

We were breathless, glued to the radio.

Suddenly I realized it looked very dark outside. I should have already left for home.

I ran the whole ten blocks. It must have been close to 8 PM when I finally neared the house. I'd already figured I would be in some sort of trouble for being so late. But when I saw so many of our neighbors out in the street looking for me, I realized the trouble was going to be big.

Then I saw my mother. She was standing in the middle of the street, waving her hands, frantically looking both ways down the avenue. When she noticed me running toward the house, she cried in a loud, anxious voice, "Susie, Susie, where were you? I was so scared something terrible had happened to you. We were so worried!" She grabbed my arm, shook me by the shoulders very hard, then slapped my bottom.

Mom had never hit me before, so I knew I'd done something horrible. I was startled by the slap, but also relieved to get the punishment over and done with. Still, I started to cry, because it scared me to see her so unhinged. I said, "Mommy, I'm sorry, I didn't notice it was so late. I promise I will never do this again."

"You'd better not, or I'll have a heart attack. You must remember to tell me when you will be coming home late. If you can't reach me, then you have to come home on time. No excuses, no exceptions! You understand?"

I nodded. Because by then, I truly did.

The two Sals, 1958.

When I was in fourth grade, the public-school teachers went on a national strike that kept everyone out of the classroom for three months. I soon discovered a new group of kids who lived around the corner from my house, and spent many hours playing with them in the street. My brother Sal, now almost three, tagged along, riding his tricycle up and down the block.

One day a neighbor woman, Pepita, who also happened to be a teacher, bumped into my mother. "*Beatriz*," she said, "I see Susie running around here all day long. Maybe you don't know that I'm teaching fourth grade. I belong to a local syndicate that supports the strike but has decided to keep its schools open. We don't think it's fair to the kids to lose a whole year, or to go on to the next level without knowing anything. Why don't you send her to my class?"

A few days later I was enrolled in Escuela Primaria Ezequiel A. Chavez. I wasn't sad to leave my old school because, thanks to the long months playing outside during the teacher's strike, I'd made more friends, and many of them went to this school. In my new class most of my classmates came from middle-class homes, so although I was a *gringa*, and different from the people they knew, at least my mother's Ford didn't stick out.

I soon found out that all my girlfriends were going through an important rite of passage: The First Communion. I wanted to have one too, so I decided to ask my mother.

She was sitting at her desk studying a medical textbook when I posed the question. She looked up, surprised. "Why in the world would you want to have a First Communion?"

"Because everyone I know is doing one," I replied eagerly.

Mom must have sensed my determination, because she smiled and said, "If you find someone to sponsor you, it's okay with me." Then she went back to her textbook.

The most obvious candidate was Tía Lupita, Chavo's sister. Unlike Salvador, who was a declared atheist and Marxist, she was a devout Catholic. A few years earlier, without my mother's knowledge, she'd taken me and my brother Sal to be baptized. She was thrilled when I told her I wanted to have a First Communion, and immediately began the preparations.

I went to Sunday School every week for four months, until I was ready. Lupita had a dress made for me of off-white satin. She bought a small veil with tiny fake flowers on top, plus white gloves and white shoes.

I got dressed up in the outfit, but when I looked in the mirror, I wasn't crazy with what I saw. My friend Pilar's dress had been a long, flowing white affair, almost like a wedding gown. But mine was shorter and less formal. I didn't look as pretty as I'd imagined in my daydreams.

On a Friday morning I received the sacrament and carefully swallowed the wafer without chewing it. Lupita invited her family and mine for the traditional breakfast to celebrate my entry into the Catholic Church. There were only ten people in my breakfast party instead of the large crowds I'd seen at Pilar's event. So of course, I also didn't get as many presents as I'd been expecting.

Immediately I was a disappointed Catholic.

Salvador, Mom and me on the day of my First Communion, 1958.

At first, I attended Mass every Sunday. Sometimes with Lupita, but mostly I tagged along with a school friend. I knew this was my obligation as a good Catholic, but church was supposed to be a family affair. All my friends went with their parents and siblings, so even though I was invited to come along, I couldn't help feeling like an orphan. Also, in spite of the weeks of intensive Sunday School, all that kneeling, sitting, and standing was still a mystery. The ceremony was still performed in Latin then, so I had almost no idea of what all the mumbling and bowing at the altar was about, either. Mass soon began to feel like a chore.

I stayed true to the rite of confession, though, and went once a month. That wasn't easy either, because I didn't really feel that my sins were so bad. I'd usually tell the priest, "Forgive me, Father, for I have sinned. I lied to my mother the other day. I wasn't nice to one of my friends. And I was envious of my best friend."

One day, I got a very old priest who asked if I went to church every Sunday. When I admitted I didn't, he reprimanded me severely. "You know you have to go to Church every Sunday. As a good Catholic it's your responsibility and it's a sin not to do so! You will kneel and ask Christ's forgiveness by praying ten Hail Marys and five Our Fathers."

This really pissed me off. I'd been seeking some empathy. I wanted him to understand my plight. Instead he scolded me and sent me packing with nothing but a penance.

I decided there and then that I didn't want to be a Catholic, after all.

That fall I went for my usual visit to New York. In my grandmother's Brooklyn apartment, I told Dad about my found and lost religion.

He widened his eyes, whistled softly, and then asked, "What did your Mom have to say about this?"

"Oh, she just said that if I found someone to pay for the stuff, she was okay with it."

He shook his head disapprovingly. I suppose because, even though he wasn't a practicing Jew and had his own unique ideas about God, this business of my becoming a Catholic grated. He was clearly annoyed at my mother's casual attitude, but instead of bad-mouthing her, he asked me a number of questions about what it had been like to briefly become a Catholic. He was especially interested in finding out all about the Confession, and whether I had done it.

"Yes, of course. Everyone has to confess to receive the wafer."

He looked at me seriously. "What do you do when you confess?"

"I kneel in the confessional booth, and the priest opens a small window. I confess my sins to him. Then he tells me to pray, like, five Hail Marys or maybe ten Our Fathers, so I will be forgiven by God."

He frowned. "Susie, you know what upsets me? That you confess to another person, a human being like you. Why not just confess directly to God?"

"Well, because that's not the way things are done," I told him, with an eight-year-old's crystal-clear logic.

But Dad had a point.

Grandma, however, wasn't nearly as philosophical. "I can't believe your mother let you go through with this nonsense!" She added, "Susie, this is ridiculous. You're Jewish, and you are not to go to confession again, you hear me?"

Soon after the First Communion imbroglio, because of my frequent throat infections, Mom was advised by her medical colleagues to have my tonsils taken out.

When they divorced, my parents had signed a financial agreement. In the settlement, they divided their assets equally. She would not receive alimony, and they would split my expenses down the middle. This meant that my father would be financially responsible for my needs while I was visiting the States, including the plane fare. While my mother would pay for everything I needed while I was living with her in Mexico.

According to the settlement, my mother received $17,000. With that money she bought two cars and two taxi license plates. She then hired a couple of guys to drive them. A good decision, because the taxi income supported her through her medical studies. There was even some left over to help Salvador open his *taller*.

After the tonsillectomy was scheduled, Mom wrote to Dad and

asked him if he could contribute $300 toward the cost.

He replied that he was about to go to Europe with Adele and wasn't exactly swimming in money. He also reminded her that she'd agreed to pay for my living expenses in Mexico, adding, *I don't believe in tonsillectomies and don't approve of this procedure.*

My mother didn't respond, but I could tell she was furious.

After that, their communications dwindled. The tension between them grew. And when I read his letter, many years later, I definitely felt he'd crossed that line that separates resentment toward your ex-wife from doing harm to your young daughter.

Dad had been an asshole.

Those years in the 1950s, my mother was busy with medical school. She went to classes very early in the morning, had lunch at home with us, and studied in the afternoon. But no matter how busy her day, she always found time to play the piano.

The piano was central to Mom's life. When she moved to Mexico in the early 1950s she had it shipped there. The parlor grand followed us to every house we lived in. It was almost six feet long; the first, most imposing object you saw when you stepped into our living room. My mother practiced almost every day. I often sat on the floor beside the bench while she played. Sometimes I'd bring along books and do my homework. Often, though, I simply listened to the music in a dreamy mood. She played Bach fugues, and Beethoven and Mozart sonatas. She loved Chopin, and sometimes practiced Rachmaninoff's piano concertos, which I could tell were particularly challenging.

Whenever she played, my mother's face was a study in concentration. She'd purse her lips and stare intently at the score, oblivious to interruptions. When she made a mistake, she'd frown and repeat the fragment until it was perfect. Then her face relaxed. I could tell she was happy the piece was flowing and her fingers were obedient. Like all pianists, Mother moved to the rhythm of the music she produced.

Occasionally she would bend her head close to the keys, as if listening to an almost imperceptible conversation. And sometimes, especially during a powerful piece like a Chopin nocturne, she put so much pressure on the keys she elevated herself slightly from the bench. When practice was over, she'd ask if there was anything I wanted to hear.

I usually asked for Beethoven's "Moonlight Sonata" or Brahms' "Lullaby." Invariably, somewhere along the middle of the latter, I'd burst into tears.

Mom would stop and ask, "Dear, is everything all right? Why are you crying?"

"Because it's so sad." But I'd insist she go on.

Though I kept certain feelings tamped down, well-hidden from my daily life, when Mom played the "Lullaby" they welled to the surface. I probably ached for that lost period of my childhood when Mommy or Grandma had held me in their arms. And even though my chest hurt, and my throat swelled with tears, I somehow needed to feel those sensations. I never asked her to stop, and always wanted her to play it again.

Watching my mother at the piano was a bit like observing my father while he was writing. Except in this scenario I was not only invited to witness my mother's love of music, I could also take part. I saw her labor over the difficult phrases, and then be rewarded with a special piece I was invited to choose.

With Dad I usually felt walled off; left on the perimeter of his work. When he read a passage out loud I could sneak a look, or hear him repeat phrases, but he was mostly conversing with his private muse.

Sitting by my mother's side while she practiced, the woman who always seemed indestructible was now sensitive, even vulnerable. Her playing created an aura that was unusual for us, one of warmth and intimacy that overwhelmed me, and brought tears to my eyes.

CHAPTER 9

―――――――

Diamond Eyes

IN OCTOBER OF 1956, WHEN I WAS SEVEN, DAD BOUGHT A HOUSE IN Bridgewater, Connecticut. A typical New England colonial, white with green shutters, it included an old barn and several acres of pine forest. On the right side of the entrance hall a wood-banister staircase led up to the bedrooms. A large door to the left opened to the library, while down the hall was a living room with a brick fireplace. Two bow windows faced the lawn. The dining area sat at one end of the living room, where to the right a swinging door opened to an old-fashioned kitchen with lots of white wall cupboards and a big pine table in the middle.

My bedroom was on the second floor, next to my father's and Adele's, but after my sister Danielle was born in March 1957, I moved to the attic, to a small room with a slanting roof, nondescript but cozy. I didn't spend much time there; I was usually in the living room watching television or playing with my toys, or in the kitchen talking to Adele and helping her cook.

I arrived in New York, as usual, in the month of November. This time Dad didn't come to Mexico to fetch me. Instead, my mother took me to the airport, and left me under the care of the airline hostess, as they were called at the time, who looked after me during the flight. In New York Dad would be waiting at Idlewild Airport. As I walked out of customs holding the airline agent's hand, I saw him upstairs, behind a big glass window, craning his neck to find me in the midst of the crowd of arriving passengers. In February, when I was scheduled to return to Mexico, my father would hand me over to another airline representative, as the process was reversed. I enjoyed those eight-hour plane rides. I felt important to be traveling alone, cared for by a pretty lady, and then zipping through customs like a VIP.

Once I passed through the Arrival lounge sliding doors, Dad rushed up and hugged me tightly. Then we collected my suitcase and drove to Connecticut. On that first ride to Bridgewater, he described the house, and the two large black standard poodles he'd bought, Tibo and ZsaZsa. "You'll enjoy playing with them. They're very smart and lots of fun. We'll take them for walks in the woods."

The next morning when I went outside, I was impressed by the grounds. In front of the house was a large lawn, and to one side stood the red-painted barn. In the back were acres of forest. It was my first Fall in the country, and the leaves, which had turned many shades of red, orange, and yellow, shimmered and glowed in the morning light. The house itself was large and old, and I was immediately in love with it. Perhaps, in part because it was white with green shutters, like houses in my picture books. Also, it was the first time in my memory that Dad had actually owned a home of his own. It seemed different, and a hell of a lot nicer, than the loft on the Lower East Side. Immediately, I felt at home.

That year Dad decided I should learn to read and write in English, so he took me to be enrolled at the local public elementary school.

Unlike my school in Mexico, everything there looked clean and pretty. The classroom was large. On the walls hung colored pictures of each letter of the alphabet, paired with animals and objects. In the back stood a bookcase with books we could take home. I was welcomed by my second-grade teacher, who introduced me to the class and gave me a bag filled with brand new textbooks.

Still, I didn't know anyone, and could barely read or write English. But Dad had said, "You'll make lots of friends. Then you won't be so lonely."

I went along with his plan, although deep down I would have much preferred to stay home. The kids weren't unfriendly, but I made no close pals during that time. I did learn to read and write in English and was soon on the same reading level as my classmates. I also enjoyed the weekly spelling bee. As usual, I tried hard to fit in, but felt ill at ease most of the time.

Recess period and lunch were especially hard. I had to choose with whom to sit or play and felt insecure because I was never sure of being accepted. Most of the kids were polite, not bullies, but not truly welcoming, either. Though I did what I was supposed to do, I missed my life in Mexico, and secretly looked forward to returning to my own school.

One day, a week or so after my first day in class, I was apparently scratching my head furiously. Soon I was called into the nurse's office. She went through my hair with chopsticks and surgical gloves. Then, calmly peeling the gloves off, she asked me to step into the waiting room. I already knew what was going on, and while I waited, I wondered if she would call Dad, or tell the teacher. Would she let everyone know about the lice on my head?

When Dad arrived and was informed of the situation, he seemed wary, as if he didn't quite know how to bring up the subject without hurting my feelings. He asked if I knew why I'd been called into the nurse's office.

I could finally confess my secret.

It had been a tough year in Mexico as far as head lice were concerned. My mother hadn't been able get rid of them for long, though she'd tried all the usual concoctions, dousing my hair with a special product, then putting a nylon stocking cap on me for the night. The theory behind this was that the tight covering would concentrate the power of the solution and smother the lice. And to a degree, it worked. In the morning she'd wash my hair with vinegar as I watched the dead lice fall into the sink. Then with a very, very fine-toothed comb she'd tease out all the nits and squash them between her thumbnails.

And I would be free of the infestation until the next month, when the whole process would start anew. Having friends with lice was, of course, the root cause.

So, I'd arrived in the States, unbeknownst to Mom, the New York family, and me, with a head full of nits. And they'd hatched a week later.

Like any Jewish-American middle-class father, Dad was shocked. Kids in towns like Bridgewater didn't get lice, especially not in the mid-1950s! After a family conference call, Grandma included, Dad made a phone call to Mom in Mexico and got the prescription from her. He might have even passed it on to the school.

I was kept home for a few days until I no longer posed a danger of infection to anyone. When I went back to school the few kids I knew went into great detail about how they'd been taken to the nurse's office, where their hair was looked at under a magnifying glass as she poked around with something that looked like chopsticks. I listened and didn't say a word. I told them I'd stayed home the last few days because I was sick and had missed the ruckus.

Although I had been accepted there, I felt like an illegal immigrant who'd somehow managed to smuggle herself across the border into White Man's Land. None of my classmates knew I was responsible for introducing cooties to the upper-class, Protestant township of Bridgewater. Still, I felt tainted. My guilt was intensified by Dad's anger at my mother. Why had she let this happen, and why had I even been at that school in Mexico, he demanded. Was she taking good care of me? He and Grandma told me to not talk about the situation with anyone, because it would only make me feel bad when I was with my classmates. An unnecessary warning; I would rather have been tortured with the fires of Hell than tell anyone my shameful secret.

My hair had been a battleground for my estranged parents even before this. When I was six, at my request, Mother had taken me to the neighborhood beauty parlor for a perm. It was a disaster. My hair puffed out in a frizzy halo. When I got to New York shortly after, Dad took one look and said, "What the hell did your mother do to your hair!"

Later that week he took me to the fancy East Side salon that Judy Feiffer, Jules Feiffer's wife, had recommended. I came out with a cute, pixie style haircut.

Me with pixie haircut holding Danielle, 9 months old, in Bridgewater. 1957.

It was the start of my funny-looking period: no front teeth and very short hair. Dad loved my trendy look, though. "This cut brings out your eyes and the shape of your face. You look great!" That felt good.

But later, when I got off the plane back in Mexico, Mom, who'd recently begun working at the local psychiatric hospital, shook her head. "I could've taken you to the psychiatric unit, and you would've gotten that same cut for free."

I was hurt to the bone.

My hair became something to be criticized or commented on by both my parents. Another way they expressed their growing hostility towards each other, and a painful and sensitive issue for me.

~

Life in Bridgewater was slow. I watched lots of TV, mostly cartoons and the "Mickey Mouse Club." I loved Annette Funicello and wanted to be her friend. Or better yet, to be *her*. She seemed like the quintessential American. I so wanted to have that kind of life and live in Disneyland surrounded by cute, carefree friends.

Once in a while Dad took me ice skating on a nearby pond. I assumed skating would be a breeze. After all, we skied every year. But as soon as I was on the ice, I realized it was a completely different sport. My ankles wobbled, I kept falling, and ice is much harder than snow. When I took the skates off my ankles burned. I was tired and discouraged. Skating had looked like fun, but turned out to be mostly a lot of pain and effort.

A couple of times we went on excursions into the woods. There we played war. Adele was a prisoner in the big house, and we had to liberate her. We crept up slowly through the snow, Tibo and ZsaZsa leading the way. When we reached the house, my sergeant-father would order me to peer in the window and see if any enemy soldiers were in sight.

"None on the horizon," I'd whisper.

We'd tiptoe inside, silently, making sure the enemy didn't hear or see us as we searched for Adele. She was usually in the kitchen, seven months pregnant with Danielle, cooking our evening meal. Her specialty was spaghetti with meat sauce.

Dad wrote every day, and in the afternoon, he liked to work out in the barn. He had fixed it up as a gym. A heavy punching bag hung from a one roof beam, and there was a small boxing ring where he'd horse around with friends, daring them to a two-round match. Adele's father, Albert Morales, had actually been a boxer, and when her parents came to Connecticut, Al and Dad jumped into the ring to practice. Alberto was twenty years older, but still a good fighter, and during one of their matches he knocked Dad down. Norman always credited Al with teaching him how to counterpunch.

My father also worked out on a bongo board, which consisted of a solid slab of wood about a foot wide by 30 inches long and nearly an inch thick. This was balanced on a solid wooden cylinder, not unlike a big rolling pin. On each side of the slab were strips of grip tape. You put a foot on each side and started it rocking, like a seesaw. It was lots of fun and demanded a great deal of balancing skill, something I was good at. Dad enhanced the basic bongo board by adding a rotating disc on top. Then I had to stand on the disc and, with knees slightly bent, rotate my lower body right and left while the board kept moving sideways. All of this without falling off, which was almost impossible. Dad's reasoning behind pursuing this extreme exercise was, "It'll improve your skiing."

This period in Connecticut was a difficult time for him. After the release of *The Naked and the Dead*, he'd been lauded and pampered by the press, hailed as the next great American novelist. Hemingway's heir. Now, less than ten years later, many in the literary world had concluded Norman Mailer had had only one good book in him. Critics had panned his second novel, *Barbary Shore*, published in 1951. *Time Magazine* had called it "paceless, tasteless and graceless," a jab that never lost its sting. His third, *The Deer Park*, came out to mixed reviews. And though it was a bestseller, moving over 50,000 copies in hardback, the bad press still irked him.

By the fall of 1957, his ego was hurting. He was clearly angry. He drank. He smoked marijuana. He took Benzedrine and Seconal, uppers and downers. He was often moody, and many times got a strange look in his eye that disturbed me. I tried to ignore his moods and instead concentrated on the fun times, like Christmas celebrations with a tall, beautifully decorated tree and lots of incredible presents for me.

But two memories color this idyllic picture in an entirely different hue.

I was eight years old, and my sister Danielle, Dad's second daughter and Adele's first, was nine months. I was playing in the living room next to the chimney when Dad walked in and asked me to step into the library. "Hey, Diamond Eyes, come in here. Let's have a talk."

His serious tone made it sound important. I felt a sudden desire to run out into the snow-packed forest and play with the dogs instead. Anything, just to get away. But I went in obediently, thinking, *Daddy's in one of his moods.* I sat in an armchair directly in front of him. He gazed at me somberly, and said something like, "Hey, Diamond Eyes, you're looking good today."

He had a habit of commenting on my appearance. In my teens his judgments could make me feel as special as a wet dishrag, or suddenly elevate me to a Sophia Loren-like self-image. "Diamond Eyes" was one of his nicknames for me, because he said my eyes sparkled and were crystal clear.

"I wanted to talk to you about something. You know you're very important to me and I love you. I want you to know that. But it wasn't always so. There was a time when I didn't know if I loved you enough. I was afraid I wouldn't be able to give you what I'd received from my mother, your grandma. I didn't know if I could feel that kind of love when you were born, because I don't think I was ready to be a father. I wanted to be free, and your birth was a responsibility that felt like a chain around my neck. Your mother and I were already not happy by that time, but we didn't think of divorce. I was famous and she resented it. And for me, being a father was a burden. You were a great baby—don't get me wrong—but I wasn't ready. Then, when you went to Mexico with your mom, I didn't really consider what it meant. I think I might have even been a little relieved.

"I want you to know, honey, it's been hard not having you around most of the year. When you come to the States, it's always awkward, isn't it? And just when we start getting used to each other, really digging being together, you have to leave. It's hard on the soul. You know what I mean?"

I was sitting very still by then. I didn't feel much except a great desire to have this "talk" over soon and be free to leave. But I was stuck. No escape yet. "Yes, Daddy," I said.

"Every time you return to Mexico, I think it takes something out of us. Something we might never get back. I'm angry with your mother for going there, and angry with myself for having permitted it."

"Why did you let her go, Daddy?"

"Well, there wasn't much I could do. She was in love with Chavo, I was in love with Adele, and I didn't think it was fair to say, 'You can't take Susie with you.' You know, Grandma wanted you to live with her. She loves you very, very much. But I felt it just wasn't right."

I didn't want him to go on a rag about my mother, so I said, "It's okay. I like living in Mexico." and I meant it.

I was eight years old, and my father was telling me he hadn't really loved me when I was born. I wondered, What about Danielle? Did he love her now more than he had loved me, back then?

His piercing blue eyes were staring directly into mine, so it was hard to avert my eyes. This was a habit I later acquired from him: the intense, into-the-soul Mailer gaze. But just then, in that room, I was afraid of this Dad with the intense look, who was giving off a strange vibe. It certainly didn't feel good to hear I hadn't been loved when I was born, and of course I never forgot those words. But at the same time, it felt special he was being so honest with me. I realized he must think I was strong enough to hear these truths.

This attitude became my trademark. I would later employ it in my work as a psychotherapist, and listen to almost anything without blinking, without taking it to heart, without getting enraged or having my feelings hurt. At eight, Dad's speech fed into my tough-kid persona, but even so, underneath that affirming recognition, that armor, I felt hurt. Why was he telling me this? By then my father believed that total honesty, even if it was painful, was an important stepping stone in his relationship with his children. But I doubt he was thinking about *my* feelings. That speech was more about indulging in a personal theory of honesty; his senses were heightened with marijuana and booze, his judgment probably clouded.

And I was a good subject, because I loved him, and was pliable and even-tempered, though sometimes moody. But most of all, I desired his approval. I knew that appearing to understand and empathize was one sure way to get it.

A few days later something else happened. I'd gone to bed up in the attic room and was having trouble falling asleep. Dad's heavy footsteps came up the stairs. I saw him approaching through half-closed eyes. He sat on the edge of my bed and leaned over checking to see if I was asleep. I didn't move. First, he kissed me on the forehead. He hugged me tight, and then even tighter, with a kind of desperate urgency. I was surprised and curious, but I didn't say anything. Soon he was crying. Not sobbing, just quietly weeping.

My father always hated sentimentality and usually banished it from his emotional repertoire. He could be gloomy, morose, irritated, angry, or tender and funny. But he was not sentimental, and certainly not weepy. That's what made that night so acutely uncomfortable. I could tell he was in pain, and it obviously had to do with me.

Even though he'd resented infant Susan for curtailing his freedom, in later years he felt pain every time we had to separate, and our communication shrank to occasional letters, and even fewer phone calls. During the 50s my father and mother had corresponded quite often. Sometimes there was a hand-written page with a drawing for me included in Norman's letter to Bea. But most of the time he wrote to me directly and asked me to answer his letters. He said we had to build a bridge to keep in touch, and letters were the best medium to accomplish this. Sometimes he called, but our conversations were monosyllabic on my part. I felt uneasy when I heard his voice on the phone. So, he resorted to letters again.

Still, every time I saw an envelope with his return address on my bed, my stomach tightened. I wanted to brush away that by-now familiar sense of discomfort. When I was in Mexico, I stopped speaking English, and always answered my mother in Spanish. Though I understood it, the language was banned from my life down there. I put my father and the Mailer family in another compartment that didn't touch my life in Mexico. His letters were an impingement on the continuity of my everyday life. I'd put off replying for days, until my mother would finally sit me down with pencil and paper and force me to write back.

"But I don't know what to say, Mom. Do I have to write?"

"Yes, you do. Just tell him what you did today. That will be enough."

Then, not very happy, I would comply. All my letters had the same tone. They usually started like this:

> Dear Daddy,
> Today I went to school and had a good time.
> When I got home, I played with my friends
> and then went to bed.

These short missives generally ended with:

> Miss you Daddy. Give my love to Grandma
> and Grandpa and Adele.

During my visits to the States I stopped speaking Spanish. And found it just as hard to answer my mother's letters. Those months living with Dad were intense, but they never developed a natural rhythm. While we were together, the shadow of my departure was always just around the corner. And when I left there was an empty space between us. In 1954, in a letter to his close friend Robert Lindner, he wrote:

> Mexico was rough on me…one day I literally
> had to fight off weeping twice while I was
> with Susy because of the pain of leaving
> her. And the weight she carries in her heart
> and the wisdom. She fell asleep the night before
> I left, the last time I would see her, and I think
> she knew that it was far better to be unconscious
> when I left than to go through the pain of the
> scene. I really think she loves me, and I want no
> one to love me more than I want Susy to.

I can see myself falling asleep, not wanting Dad to be around when I wake up the next day. This turning away, looking in another direction to isolate myself and be cut off from that ache of separation, was to be my modus operandi for many years. The stamp of our relationship. Not until I was an adult and going through psychoanalysis was I able to sift slowly through all that pain. Until at last I could see little Susie not as the great, fearless kid my parents always told me I was, but as a child who did her best to withdraw from pain by creating a great division between her two lives.

This photo was taken by Dad.
On the back it says: Susie a few days after arriving in New York. 1957.

The night in question, did my father cry because he was in anguish over my departure? Or was he feeling guilt, now that he had another daughter, Danielle, an infant he could actually enjoy and live with? Was I jealous of Danielle, who had been born only a few months before? Was I more silent and detached than usual, now that I was leaving his home, the first beautiful place we had lived in since I could remember.

Was I resentful he would be staying there with Danielle and Adele?

I'm sure I never said a word of this. I doubt I was even conscious of these feelings. I probably just wanted to go back to Mexico and forget about this tight-knit-family from which I would soon be exiled.

There were other things going on, too.

During Norman and Adele's country idyll, his drinking and pot smoking, his intake of uppers and downers, all grew worse. He was irritable and took it out on Adele, who was anything but meek. Their arguments got out of hand. I wasn't aware of any of this. If they fought when I was around, I didn't hear them, or more probably I blocked out the loud angry voices. I don't remember ever seeing them drunk. My only recollection of bad times is occasionally having the thought, *Dad is in one of his moods.*

Added to all the drinking, during this period my father lost two good friends. Apparently, the novelist William Styron made a disparaging remark about Adele, and my father called him on it in an angry letter. The writer James Jones, whom Dad deeply loved, sided with Styron; they both felt Norman had changed for the worse. He was drinking too much and had become contentious, even violent. This break with two old friends, which lasted twenty years, weighed on my father's psyche. It clearly hurt. He sorely missed his buddies, especially Jim Jones.

In 1959, not long after I returned to Mexico, Dad and Adele decided to leave Bridgewater. My father had thought it would be good to be away from the frenzy of the city, and they'd tried to make a life in the country, but finally decided to move back to New York. They sold the beautiful big house and rented a dark apartment on Perry Street in the West Village. As with the house in Vermont young Norman and Bea had bought almost ten years before, this second experiment in country living did not work out, either. And now, serious trouble was brewing in his relationship with Adele.

CHAPTER 10

Silent Spaces

A FEW YEARS AGO, WHILE I WAS AT MY SISTER DANIELLE'S HOUSE IN Connecticut, our conversation turned to one of our favorite topics: the family.

She said, "Hey Sue, something funny happened the other day. My friend Alice was telling me some complicated thing about her family that I won't go into right now. But then all of a sudden, she says, 'Of course you wouldn't understand, you Mailers have a sense of entitlement. You have a pedigree.'"

Danielle and I burst out laughing.

"The Mailers have a pedigree?" I said. "Now that's something I haven't heard before."

In the late afternoon, I was on the train back to New York and our conversation came back to me. Did I feel like someone who had a pedigree? I'd always thought of others, such as the Kennedys, or other children of well-known politicians, or artists, or actors, as belonging to some aristocracy of arts and letters. But I'd never thought of us, Norman's children, as kids with an important lineage.

We were, of course, the offspring of a famous writer, but this particular author had a stain on his past that always tainted my perception, setting us apart from the families of other well-known authors and artists. And while I wasn't totally aware of this in my childhood and early adolescence, I'd certainly experienced its repercussions.

In September of 1959 my sister Elizabeth Ann, nicknamed Betsy, was born. My father and Adele were living with my two sisters, in the West Village apartment on Perry Street, when I visited them in the winter of that year. The recollection is not a pleasant one.

The apartment was gloomy, the furniture old and shabby. I remember playing with Danielle, who was then two years old and going to a progressive school, City and Country, nearby on 12th Street. The rest of my visit is cloaked in a gray mist that only lightened when I had dinner with my grandparents and slept over, or when I went to visit Aunt Barbara, who lived right around the corner on Bleecker Street.

I returned to Mexico in February of 1960. Later that same year, in September, Dad and Adele moved to a large apartment on the Upper East Side, on 94th Street. They had been fighting continuously. My father's intake of booze and drugs had accelerated, and Adele also drank her share.

To make things worse, my father had been brewing the idea of running for Mayor of New York, on the ticket of the 'Existential Party.' (A party that did not actually exist, then or later.) In November he threw a huge party at their apartment to announce his intention to run.

During this period, Adele was in a continuous state of anxiety. She actually believed Norman might win and didn't know if she could cope with being the Mayor's wife. He resented her lack of aplomb, as well as her doubts and insecurities. Norman became increasingly angry and aggressive, especially with those closest to him. He even hit his sister, my Aunt Barbara, during an argument, and broke her glasses.

Although many people came to the party, most of the celebrities and important politicians he'd invited didn't show. This perceived slight sent my father into a simmering rage. Adele was no help, either. She was drunk and goading Dad, even though it was clear he was like a bull in the ring, ready to gore anyone who came within range. He'd been in a disturbed mood for some time, but that night it reached a peak. He argued with some of his guests, then went outside and had a few skirmishes on the street. Finally, he tried hard to pick a fight with two friends: journalist George Plimpton and boxer Roger Donoghue. Both men refused to be goaded into a brawl, though.

At 4 AM, when Norman came back into the apartment totally wasted, Adele confronted him. In her memoir, *The Last Party*, she said, "…you little faggot. Where's your cojones, did your ugly whore of a mistress cut them off, you son of a bitch?" At that point my father threw most of the remaining guests out of the apartment. Then he took out a penknife, walked up to Adele, and stabbed her. First in the back, creating a superficial wound. The second thrust was to the upper abdomen, a more serious puncture that touched the pericardium of her heart.

Then he walked away and sat quietly in a corner.

One of the few guests still in the apartment noticed Adele was pale and in obvious pain. He took her to a friend's apartment in the same building, where they finally called both an ambulance and the extended Mailer family. Aunt Barbara and her husband Larry arrived first, followed by Grandma Fanny, who came to pick up baby Betsy and Nettie, the nanny. Danielle was already asleep at her apartment, looked after by Grandpa Barney.

Adele was admitted to the hospital. Dad arrived a bit later with Aunt Barbara and talked to the surgeon, who asked them to sit in an adjoining room while he treated the wounds. He didn't think it would take too long. So, Norman and Barbara sat next to each other in silence, for four grueling hours, until the doctor at last came out. Adele was stable, but it had been a close call.

The next afternoon Dad went to a scheduled interview with Mike Wallace to talk about his mayoral campaign. Later he went to the hospital to see Adele and was met by two cops who were waiting to arrest him. By then his mood had changed. He was no longer in a rage; he was quiet and subdued.

My father was committed to Bellevue Psychiatric ward, where he spent three weeks. During that time, he put all his energy into convincing the psychiatrist he wasn't crazy; that he was not a paranoid schizophrenic.

He insisted instead that he'd committed an 'act of passion.' Why couldn't a Jewish intellectual commit such an act? he argued.

In the end, the doctor took a chance on him, and signed release papers.

Adele came home after a couple of weeks at the hospital. She felt it might damage her daughters to put their father in prison. She also harbored the illusion she and my father might still repair their shattered marriage, so for that reason, as well, she didn't press charges.

But there were still criminal charges to reckon with. Dad was advised by his lawyer to plead guilty to second-degree felonious assault to avoid a trial and all the negative publicity that would come with it. At Norman's hearing, the judge released him on a suspended sentence, and ordered him to report to a probation officer once a week for three years.

Adele and Norman tried to make a go of it one last time. But he was still drinking and partying hard and she was understandably frightened of him. They separated for good in March of 1961.

These are the facts as I pieced them together from various sources, including what my family and my father later told me about that night. I've lived with this story most of my life. But only in the last few years have I begun to understand the long-lasting impact that stabbing had on me and on our whole family.

Until the late 1950s, my sisters and I were the daughters of a young, celebrated, successful writer. The morning he stabbed Adele was the beginning of "The Trouble," as his friends euphemistically called it. This act landed with the force of an earthquake, creating shock waves that rocked us to the core. Yet the family and many of his friends locked the whole event away in a sort of mental freezer. As a result, although we never forgot what had happened, and talked about the incident once in a while, all mention of "The Trouble" came devoid of emotion. The mere idea that something as terrible as that could happen was simply too much for all of us, especially his children, to comprehend. So, we tried as best we could to put it away in a box and go on with our lives.

A couple of years later, when I was thirteen, I finally did put the question directly to Dad, and asked him what really happened with Adele.

He told me, "It's very complicated Susie, and I think you're not ready yet. When you get older, we'll have a long conversation about it. I promise."

For many years, whenever someone asked if I was related to Norman Mailer, I knew the next comment was not going to be, "Oh, he's a great/lousy writer." Or maybe, "Hey, I liked that last book of his!" Instead it was always, "Umh, uh . . . didn't he stab his wife?" And then, "Was she your mother?"

In self-defense I created my own icy bubble around "The Trouble" to separate the event from my feelings for my father. But dissociation works only up to a certain point. At the very least, the family stain, and the shame that came with it, made the idea that we had any sort of 'pedigree' seem absurd.

In my teens and early adulthood, I rarely felt proud of Dad. When he drank, which was often, he usually put on a false Irish brogue, or walked in a certain deliberate, aggressive way, hunching his shoulders like a fighter about to pounce on an enemy. Scared of him, I tried my best to steer clear of him. I certainly never considered I had some fancy lineage; instead I felt something was wrong and didn't want people to know who my father was. I also wondered why so many of his friends seemed to be drunks and losers, or "bums" as my grandmother defined them. Even before the stabbing, I wondered why Norman Mailer wasn't respected like other writers.

For example, in January of 1959, over a year before the stabbing, my father was invited to appear on The David Susskind Show with Truman Capote and Dorothy Parker. That night I was sitting with my grandparents in their living room waiting for the show to come on, really excited about seeing Daddy on TV. But when he did appear onscreen, walking with that strange, tough-guy swagger that said *don't fuck around with me,* he looked like someone else. I wanted him to stop acting that way.

As the show progressed, it was troubling to see Capote, Parker, and

Susskind gang up on him. I turned to Grandma "Why don't they like Daddy?"

She answered with a Fanny Mailer firewall. "Oh, don't pay attention, they're just jealous of him."

But I knew better. I could tell he was acting strangely. Even though this was well before the stabbing, the signs were already there.

I was eleven the year "The Trouble" happened in November 1960. It was the month I usually flew north to visit the Mailer family in New York. But this year, for some reason unknown to me, when November came around, I was still in Mexico.

One Friday afternoon, after school, I went to Tía Lupita's store to spend the weekend with her. As usual she was standing behind the counter, taking customers' orders. The mingled smells of cold cuts, chorizo, and cheese immediately made me feel at home. But this time when I walked in Lupita greeted me with a worried look.

What's the matter? I wondered.

She said, "Susie, I'm so sorry, but you can't stay this weekend. Your mom will be picking you up very soon." Then she asked, abruptly and rather confusingly, "How do you feel about Adele?"

"I like her very much."

"Did you hear what happened?"

My stomach tightened. "No, why? What happened?"

She had heard on the radio about my father stabbing Adele. Only she used the word *acuchilló*, an apt way of putting it since it has the word knife in it. So, she actually said, "Did you hear your father knifed Adele?"

Just seconds before, I had been thinking about what I'd be doing with Lupita and her daughter Cristina over the weekend. Now came this bit of news I didn't really understand. The words *knifed, Adele, your father* lingered in the air, but I felt nothing. Or at least nothing I was supposed to feel. I knew I should cry, or feel sad, or worried. Instead I immediately flipped this new, unwelcome information out of my mind. I wanted to play, to move around, to do anything but think about it. And, I didn't want my mother to arrive. I wanted to stay at

Lupita's for the weekend. Dad and Adele, Chavo and Mom, *they* were my family. I needed everything about them to remain the same.

Asking about Adele's condition didn't occur to me. I simply did not want to know.

When my mother arrived, I could tell she was furious at Lupita. She'd wanted to break the news herself, but it was too late. I had already retreated to the flat "yes" and "no" mode children adopt when they really do not want to communicate. We drove home in silence, me sullen and angry because I still wanted to stick to the original plan and sleep over at Lupita's. I knew that once we got home, Mom would sit me down and ask me how I felt about the new information. But all I wanted was to forget the terrible news. To lock it away somewhere, far from my everyday life.

I could tell my mother was nervous and upset. On the ride home, she remained silent but kept looking over at me. She sighed several times, and once almost ran a red light. When we got home, still getting no response, she finally realized it was best to let me be.

Over the next few weeks Mom would occasionally make a comment like, "It could've been me. I did well to leave him when I did."

I was deaf to such remarks. Even though I didn't react, it hurt. What was especially hard was when she pointed her psychiatric artillery at the state of my father's mind. Her diagnosis was the same as that of the court-appointed doctor in New York: Norman was suffering from a paranoid schizophrenic disorder. So now, certain that Dad was unstable, possibly even dangerous, she wouldn't allow me to go to New York that November.

With this decision she incurred the full brunt of my father's wrath.

"How can you do this to me! Don't you understand Susie is terribly important to me? She is one of few persons I can trust. I need her," he insisted on the phone.

And for my mother, this rather grandiose statement only proved my father was totally unstable. She remained adamant. I stayed in Mexico that winter.

This argument was the end of their friendship. They still spoke once in a while, but only saw each other when absolutely necessary, such as at my college graduation. The amicable relationship they'd created after their divorce ended with that telephone call. To be replaced by barely disguised hostility and mutual resentment. Bea thought Norman was psychotic and delusional, while my father believed she had bad taste, an ugly voice, and had not lived up to her potential. Whenever he wanted to attack her, he'd say to me, "You look just like your mother." Or, "You dress just like your mother." Or even, "Your mother can't cook and all men like a good meal." And the real killer, "You have your mother's bad taste."

I immediately felt these jabs as a terrible judgment. Not until I was in my fifties did it occur to me to retort, "What's so terrible about looking like my mother!"

For me, the stabbing went to a silent and private place inside me; one that I didn't even know existed until much later in my life. At first, I don't think I gave it much thought. That year I was beginning junior high in a new school and had just discovered boys. I had new friends and lots of activities, although I still played in the street sometimes with my neighborhood friends and my brother Sal, who was six. Few knew about what had happened in faraway Manhattan, and Mother rarely brought it up.

Then, in early December of 1960, barely a month after "The Trouble" in New York, my mother kicked Salvador out of the house. Their relationship had started well. It had been passionate and fun. But after eight years the bare threads were becoming all too visible. Salvador loved women, any woman, and he wasn't hard to get for a night. My mother was too busy with medical school to notice his womanizing, but once she graduated, the flirting and late nights he spent out were staring her in the face. They fought, he denied, she insisted. Until finally she caught him in the act with Catalina, his business partner from the shop.

The night Bea kicked Salvador out, their fight woke us up. Little Sal and I tiptoed out of our bedroom, peeked into the living room, and saw our parents yelling at each other. Suddenly Mother picked up a lamp and threw it, grazing Salvador's forehead. As he took out his handkerchief to wipe away the blood, my mother yanked open the front door to show him the way out.

Sal and I cried, crouched in our corner. Mom came over to hug us. I said, "I don't want Chavo to leave! I don't want you to break up." She promised it would only be temporary. But, of course it wasn't.

After that night, every time my stepfather came around to fetch my brother I tried not to be there. If by chance I answered the door, I'd quickly make an excuse and leave them alone. It hurt to see him now and going out with him was close to unbearable. He always looked at me sadly, with those soulful eyes that said, *I totally understand.* When I was older, we became close again. But at the time, it was just too painful.

Both my families had shattered in less than a month.

Very soon Mom was living with Martin, her new partner, fourteen years her junior. My father had taken up with a British woman. Salvador had various lovers who changed every few years. And Adele retreated into the background. After "The Trouble" I didn't see her much.

I took refuge in my friends and was rarely home. I survived.

~

"Guess who just arrived in Mexico?" My mother asked one afternoon in July, about eight months after the stabbing.

"I don't know." But by her pursed lips and sarcastic tone, the one she used when speaking of my father, I knew Dad must be in town. I shrugged, as if I couldn't care less, but my shoulders tightened.

The next day Norman came to our apartment with his new girl-friend, Lady Jeanne Campbell. He was sweet and seemed a little shy with me. He did ask if I knew what had happened in New York.

I quickly replied, "Yes." I must have said it in a very curt way, because he never brought it up again during the whole time he was there. He was probably relieved.

On that visit we took a trip to San Miguel de Allende with Jeanne.

She was taller than Dad, with bright green eyes that squeezed shut in merriment when she laughed. Her light brown hair was wavy and unruly, and she was funny. Jeanne was the daughter of a duke. Her grandfather, Lord Beaverbrook, owned the London *Times.* She spoke in a delightful British accent and, like most members of the English nobility, loved horses and was a good rider.

In San Miguel they decided to take a ride. Dad rented three horses from a nearby stable, plus a guide to take us on the scenic route. Slowly we plodded up the steep mountain trail. At the top my steed broke into a feisty gallop across the plain. I was terrified and tried to slide off, but one foot was caught in the stirrup. I hung on sideways, gripping the edge of the saddle, scared to death, praying, "Oh God, please make this stop!" Finally, my trapped shoe slid free. I fell to the ground and hit my head.

Dad and Jeanne rushed me to a doctor in town who diagnosed a concussion. He told them I must rest in a dark, quiet room for a couple days, until my headache went away.

There I was, not quite twelve, and in San Miguel with my father and his new girlfriend, who was *so* not Adele. And what was my reaction? I was a good daughter; still a "great kid." I didn't ask embarrassing questions and tried to have a good time. My calm demeanor was a striking contrast to the mare's crazy gallop across the plain. As if she were acting out the suppressed anxiety of which I was only dimly aware.

Alone in that dark, quiet, small hotel room, I slept most of the time. My state mirrored the silent space deep inside me.

I must admit, though, that the three of us got along beautifully. I had just become interested in boys and confided in Jeanne and Dad. On the drive back from San Miguel to Mexico City we spent the time making up limericks. One of which was dedicated to "Susie's boyfriends," and recited by Jeanne in her beautiful accent. It was truly a memorable visit.

I might have been easily charmed by Jeanne, but my mother was not. She immediately had acid comments about the "eccentric" woman who'd now hooked up with Dad. In her opinion, they were both crazy.

Hearing this said so openly made me cringe; in fact, it made me dislike my mother. I *needed* things to be normal. So much so that I couldn't acknowledge what was right before me. My father, who had only months before been committed to a mental health facility for a violent assault, was already intensely involved with another woman.

Jeanne seemed to be equally enthralled by my father, a man who, she must have known, had just spent three weeks under observation in the violent ward of Bellevue for stabbing his wife. And when he introduced her as his girlfriend, I accepted the development without hesitation. Absorbing this new upheaval, as usual, with apparent ease.

~

Ripples from The Trouble appeared in other ways over the years. After the stabbing my parents' dislike for each other was relentless. I created a space as wide as the distance between Mexico and the United States to keep them apart. Mother never knew what was going on with Dad, and the same held true the other way around.

If Dad happened to ask, "How's your mother?" I'd answer "Okay, nothing new."

"How's her work going?"

"I don't know. I guess the same."

When Mother's sarcasm bit into Dad, I'd mask my hurt with indifference. *I don't care what you say about him. It's all the same to me,* was my attitude. I tried not to mention what we did on my visits to New York, because I could sense her jealousy. She didn't have to say anything; I could read it in her body language. I built a wall between my parents and patrolled the no-man's land in between.

~

About two years before my mother died, in the spring of 2014, I was sitting in her living room reading J. Michael Lennon's recently-published biography of my father, *A Double Life.* I made a point of only reading it while she took her naps.

But on one occasion she walked in unannounced, surprising me red-handed with my iPad, absorbed in the book. "What are you reading?"

"Dad's bio," I answered blandly.

"Oh." She paused, then said, "Is it interesting?"

"Yes."

"Do you think I would like it?"

Now *that* was a surprise. "Yes! It's very well written, and you'll like what Mike says about you."

"Hmm. Oh, well. Maybe I'll get it from the library."

I didn't push it; I just changed the subject. Even after so many years, I still couldn't be too enthusiastic about Dad in my mother's presence, or she got a look that showed her disapproval. I could tell she was jealous. I suppose she still asked herself questions, like, *Does Susan love him more? Why does she get along so well with her siblings? Well, he must've done something right.*

~

At first, living far from my father kept my love for him protected, insulating me from what he'd done to Adele. And yet, as much as I tried to shield myself from that frightening figure, the man who had stabbed his wife, the same aggressiveness seeped into our relationship.

He liked to stage staring contests with friends, and sometimes with me. It always began with, "Hey Susie, want to play a game." A rhetorical question, really. "I'm going to stare at you, and you stare at me. Let's see who can keep it up the longest."

"Can I blink?" I would ask.

"Yeah, you can. But you can't look away."

We'd sit face-to-face staring into each other's eyes for what seemed a long time. *How long do I have to do this?* I'd wonder. And without planning to, I'd look away.

"You can do better than that! Let's try it again."

"Daddy, I'm tired, I don't think I want to do it right now."

"No. Let's do it!"

Again, we'd stare into each other's eyes. Soon my body itched. I longed to scratch myself. One eye, disobeying my order, would start to flutter.

Daddy is so serious about this game. I wish he'd stop. I'd think. And then look away, losing once more.

"Susie, this game will hone your will and your instincts. You can tell a lot about a person by staring into his eyes, and if you stare some-one down, he'll be afraid of you. Remember that: he will respect you."

Whenever he drank, I could tell immediately when he was looking for a fight. Or a heart-to-heart talk, which could be even worse. On those occasions he'd bare his feelings, or have a deep conversation about God, or about cancer and plastic, or whatever his interest was at the moment. He would lecture, and I'd listen intently, understanding only half of what he said. Partly because I was so anxious, and also because the topics and language were way over my head. I could sense, though, that there was danger ahead: a flare-up of his temper, or a putdown. I knew enough not to provoke him, so it never occurred to me to say, "Not now, Dad." Or, "Gotta go," the way my own children would answer me, in their teens, when they were simply not interested.

Not me. I was a captive listener, and there was no place to run.

CHAPTER 11

Return to Albert Einstein

Chelo and me dressed for a play. 1962.

I FIRST MET CHELO IN EARLY FEBRUARY OF 1961, THE WINTER OF "The Trouble." The winter I didn't go to New York. She was quite petite, about two inches shorter than my 5'2", with striking looks: hair the color of new corn, large eyes, even bluer than mine, set in a pretty freckled face.

That day there was a large crowd of kids and parents in the school patio of Secundaria Albert Einstein. We had all been anxiously waiting since 8 AM to find out the results of our admission tests for middle school. After what seemed forever, two women came out and began posting the lists, and as soon as they were done, a mad dash to the bulletin boards ensued. Immediately, a stern voice through a loudspeaker ordered us to stand in line and wait until it was our turn to look.

When I finally reached the front and stood before the lists, I searched out the M's, and saw my name. I was so thrilled, I started jumping and hugged the nearest person, who happened to be Chelo. We started talking and walked away from the noisy crowd. Then I invited her to my house, which was only four blocks away.

The first day of school, at the end of February, I met Carina, who became my other close buddy. She was not in our class, but as soon as she saw us in the schoolyard she walked over and struck up a conversation. Carina was even more petite than Chelo, with dark curly hair, beautiful green eyes, and a big smile that revealed lovely white teeth. The three of us stood out at school because of our light eyes and complexions. Perhaps because of this we felt special, like the cool kids, and became an inseparable threesome.

I was eleven years old when I entered Albert Einstein middle school. Suddenly I was a teenager, with the freedom to get around on my own. I didn't study much; I got away with cramming just before an exam and usually still got A's. Weekends, on the spur of the moment, we organized parties. These usually took place in the late afternoon, mostly at my apartment, which was large and comfortable. Of course, boys were central to our lives by then, and being a good dancer was the key to success. So Chelo, Carina, and I faithfully practiced our rock n'roll, mambo, cha-cha-cha and salsa steps. If my brother Sal was around, he was included. He was always a happy trouper.

Often, I'd take the bus to Chelo's or to Carina's house, feeling excited to discover new neighborhoods on my own. This new freedom was exhilarating, and I took full advantage. My mother left me alone as long as I told her where I was going.

Sleepovers weren't customary in Mexico in those years, so having Chelo or Carina stay overnight was a big deal. Mother would drive out to Chelo's house and sit with Julia, Chelo's mom, in the small room that served as dining and living room in the daytime, and as bedroom at night. Julia took out fancy plates and offered Bea coffee and *pan dulce*. Mom always accepted, even if she wasn't hungry. In Mexico, a guest never refuses food. It's considered an insult.

After an hour of chatting my mother would ask, "Julia, I think I'll go home now, and I'd like to take Chelo and Susie back with me. Is that okay with you?"

Julia always hesitated. "*Ay*, Beatriz, Chelo has to wash her clothes and do the dishes." But she couldn't flat-out refuse my mother's invitation after Mom had taken the trouble to drive all the way to their house.

But whenever I went there alone, Julia wouldn't budge. Now Chelo definitely had to wash her clothes and do the dishes. "You haven't cleaned the bathroom and the patio," her mother would add. *Mami* Juli, as we called her, derived pleasure from tantalizing us. After all the chores were done, she still withheld permission and invited me to stay the night. Chelo and I would run to the corner store and wait in line for a half hour to use the pay phone that served the entire neighborhood, to ring up my mother and let her know I wouldn't be coming home.

When it was time to go to sleep, Chelo, one of her sisters, and I, plus *Mami* Juli, all four of us got into a double bed, two sleeping vertically with heads at the front of the mattress, and two with heads at the bottom. Her other two sisters and two cousins slept in the second bedroom, while her father and brother bunked in the main dining and living room. Finally, I was living in a *vecindad*; a house full of people with a lively street scene outside.

Chelo, Carina, and I shared everything, including boyfriends. Our lives felt so exciting that even going to a café in another part of town was an adventure we relished. First we would shed our school socks and borrow nylons from Chelo's older sisters. Then tease our hair, make up our eyes with blue powder and thick mascara. We probably looked ridiculous, but we felt sure we were fit to compete in a beauty pageant.

Life was perfect. I had no desire to leave Mexico ever again. All I wanted was for things to stay the same.

∿

In 1994 I visited Mexico City for a class reunion. At first it wasn't certain I'd be able to make the trip, because I had a fever, a runny nose, and aching muscles. In fact, I felt awful, but couldn't bear to miss the occasion. So, I stocked up on Tylenol and decongestants and boarded the plane. My old middle school, Secundaria Albert Einstein, was celebrating its fiftieth anniversary. Many close friends I hadn't seen in more than twenty-five years were going to be there. Chelo and Carina had been busy for a couple of months organizing the "junta."

It was 9 AM when we finally entered the school courtyard, which had been set up as a huge dining area, with long tables draped in white cloths. At the front stood a podium. We sat together eating breakfast and not really listening to the boring speeches. When the ceremony was over, we walked around the school remembering past escapades.

We'd planned to spend the rest of the day together, too. When it was time to leave, we walked over to the apartment building where I had lived for seven years with Mom, her partner Martin, and my brother, until I went off to college. Back then it had been an attractive red brick eight story building, with open spaces between each apartment. Now it looked run down. The large black iron entrance gate, where I used to stand for hours talking to my boyfriends, was in dire need of repair; the hinges creaked and the paint was peeling off. Lots of bricks were missing from the façade. Apartments had faded curtains hanging from the large windows whose cracked panes looked out over a park. The soda fountain on the street had closed, the lock and chain wrapped around the door handles signaling its demise. Looking at this grungy, dirty building made us all sharply feel the passage of time.

We immediately decided to go to Chelo's house, three in each car, and drove south on the *Periférico*. Traffic was slow, as usual, so we had lots of time to catch up. After we arrived, we saw that Luis, Chelo's husband, had bought *carnitas,* fried pork, *tortillas, chicharrones, chorizo,* and chicken to throw on the barbecue. But Chelo decided we needed even more food and went to the *tianguis,* the street market across from her house to get *botanas,* typical Mexican appetizers. She came back with a full array of Mexican finger food: *sopes, chalupas, quesadillas* and *flautas* with red and green salsas, plus guacamole with lots of cilantro.

I was still feeling unwell and wasn't sure how long I'd last. But the fresh smell of cilantro and avocado, the crisp pork rinds, the black beans and corn tortillas all made me forget the headache, the aching body, the runny nose.

We sat on the patio that sunny afternoon drinking Corona Extra with lemon. With the *botanas* we had a couple shots of tequila with lemon and salt, a good remedy for colds. Then more beer with the main course. By 8 PM we were ready for the next meal and another round of drinks. This time, rum and Coke, with lemon. At 11 PM a couple of friends finally called it a day and left, zigzagging out to their car. No one thought of calling a taxi, and there was no designated non-drinking driver. At two AM, the last of our friends had left. By that time my cold had also disappeared, to be replaced the next day by a ferocious hangover.

Our group had been very close, as tight as teenagers can get. That afternoon I realized my house had been a haven for all of them, a more relaxed and easy-going place they could escape to from their more restrictive and traditional homes. My mother was welcoming, but she could also be brusque, and sometimes too candid. More than a few times, one of my friends would ring the doorbell right before lunch. In Mexico it was common to invite anyone who arrived at that hour to sit down and eat, too. But if a friend says, "No thank you. I've already eaten," you're supposed to insist until they sit down with you at the table.

But whenever this happened, instead my mother would reply, "Okay, then sit on the sofa until we're done." The whole cultural dance about refusal and insistence never made sense to her. "If they're hungry, they'll eat. If not, they'll say no thank you."

This embarrassed me. But my friends didn't mind. They were intrigued and seduced by Mom. She was an oddity: a female doctor, twice divorced, with a *gringa* accent, and good-looking to boot. Most important of all, she let us throw parties almost every weekend.

My memories of those high school years had always been clear. The images had occupied a space in my mind that replayed a time when I'd been happy. But that day, while reminiscing with my old friends, something uncanny happened. I suddenly stepped into the past and *became* that teenager again. I wasn't merely remembering a scene from my past, I was actually inside and living it. I became once again that thirteen-year old with great lightness of being, happy and bouncing with enthusiasm.

CHAPTER 12

_____

Educating Susan

BY THE END OF MY FIRST YEAR AT SECUNDARIA ALBERT EINSTEIN, my mother felt it was safe for me to go to New York again. In November of 1961 I stayed with Aunt Barbara, who was still on Bleecker Street in the West Village. Dad would swing by in the afternoon to see me. He'd walk in with the customary swagger, trench coat haphazardly buttoned, its belt carelessly tied, curly hair unruly.

He wasn't the same Dad who'd come to Mexico with Jeanne only four months before. Gone was the carefree happiness. His mood was always dark now, and it made me ill at ease. He tried talking about Adele and what had happened, but I didn't want to hear it. For some reason he wanted me to know about his stay in Bellevue. He described how hard he'd worked to convince the shrinks he wasn't nuts.

"They were out to diagnose me with some form of schizophrenia or paranoia. They insisted on giving me antipsychotics, but I knew they would dull my brain, so I refused. There were some interesting guys there, though, maybe I'll write about them one day," he added.

Once we drove past Bellevue and Dad pointed out the window where he had often stood staring down onto the street. As he talked, I remembered the psychotic patients I'd seen the few times my mother had taken me to the psychiatric hospital where she worked. Men and women mumbling to themselves, shuffling down the halls with no aim or purpose. Imagining my father in the same surroundings was something I made an effort to avoid.

Dad also told me about his parole officer and how he still had to sign in at the precinct every week. Whenever he wanted to leave the country, like the time he'd gone to Mexico with Jeanne, he had to ask for permission. He often talked about how we would soon have a nice place where we would live with Jeanne. I didn't care. I was happy to stay with Aunt Barbara, whom I adored. It was perfectly okay with me if he only visited in the afternoons, and also okay if he didn't come by every day. Being alone with my father made me nervous. I had a better time when we were with other members of the family.

I don't remember much about that winter. I can't recall seeing my sisters, though I'm sure I did, nor do I remember being with Jeanne. My life revolved around Aunt Barbara; a candy, comic, book, and toy store on the corner of 11th Street and Bleecker, and dinners with my grandparents. Living with Barbara was always a bright spot for me. She had an easy smile and a willing ear for her disgruntled niece. Every night she'd read to her son Peter, who was five years my junior, while I sat on his bed and listened. Every story she read to us, even *Babar*, which by then I considered kid stuff, gave me a warm and fuzzy sensation. It felt like home.

Aunt Barbara also played the piano, although not as well as my mother. Many afternoons as I sat next to her on the bench, she'd open her music book and ask, "Susie, what should I play today?" A rhetorical question, since she already knew the answer. My absolute favorite was a Scottish ballad, "Loch Lomond," which I sang with real gusto. I still remember the lyrics:

> O ye'll take the high road, and I'll take the low road,
> And I'll be in Scotland afore ye.
> But me and my true love will never meet again,
> on the bonnie, bonnie banks of Loch Lomond.

At the time I was also addicted to comic books. I preferred *Classics Illustrated*, but also enjoyed reading *Superman, Little Lulu*, and to a much lesser degree *Batman and Robin*.

One day, Dad went into my room and saw the pile of comics lying in a corner. He picked up a few and seemed intrigued by the *Classics Illustrated*. "Why do you read these?" he asked.

"Because the stories are great."

"Oh, so you like good stories? Come with me. I'll get you some great ones."

We went to a nearby bookstore, a place that exuded the fresh odor of new books, a smell that would soon become a magnet for me. Dad and I walked out with two bags: Tolstoy, Dostoyevsky, and Dickens in one hand; Twain, Louisa May Alcott, and Jane Austen in the other. Dad said these authors had written good stories I would enjoy, adding, "You should start with *The Adventures of Tom Sawyer*."

It was such a relief to finally discover something we could do together, a thing that was actually fun. I became a voracious reader, closing the door to my small room to lie in bed for hours with a book. After *Tom Sawyer* I went on to *Pride and Prejudice*. By age thirteen I was reading *Anna Karenina*. I was so young that most, if not all of the nuances and complexities of that novel were lost on me. But I never forgot the elegant balls, the Russian country scenes, the characters, and Anna's tragic end. I still enjoyed listening to Aunt Barbara reading aloud, though, and remained loyal to our nightly ritual.

Years before, in Mexico, I'd used to take the loose change in my mother's purse and save up enough to buy a notebook. With time I grew bolder. No longer content with change, I had graduated to stealing small bills from her wallet. With this I'd bought more notebooks, pencils, and sometimes board games to play with friends. Comic books, as well. But I was particularly attached to those notebooks. I loved the crisp sound of new paper, its fresh-pulp smell, the neat parallel lines that invited me to write. I acquired various pencils, some colored, others just black graphite. Sitting at the desk in my bedroom, notebooks on one side and pencils on the other, I would pick up a notebook, open and bring it close to my nose. Then take a deep breath and begin practicing cursive or drawing with the colored pencils. I'd be the teacher to imaginary friends, using the notebooks to grade my students' handwriting and spelling.

Though I played teacher, not writer, I think I was really conjuring my father by going through the same rituals I had seen him perform while he worked. And it's not lost on me now that these notebooks were bought with money stolen from my mother's purse. Perhaps the only way I could be close to Dad was by secretly taking something away from Mom.

Once Dad began my literary education, I went on to read other classics, and not in illustrated form. Works by Balzac, Stendhal, Zola, Thomas Hardy, D.H. Lawrence, James T. Farrell, and Hemingway. Also, García Lorca's plays and his poems, some of which I later translated with my father. By the time I was fifteen I felt ready to read Norman Mailer.

I began with *The Naked and the Dead,* reading it at first with some trepidation. I wasn't sure what to expect, though I'd always heard it was a great book. I read it non-stop. After turning the last page, I immediately wrote Dad a letter to let him know how much I'd enjoyed it. That must've felt good to receive. After all, it was the first time a child of his had been old enough to read his work.

Not long afterward, he sent me a copy of *An American Dream*, which I'd watched him write in monthly installments for *Esquire Magazine* in 1964. I was eager to read it, too. But the sexual scenes and the main character's violence disturbed me. I was repelled and at the same time fascinated.

In the first chapter, protagonist Stephen Rojack has a violent argument with his wife Deborah and strangles her to death. Afterward, he enters the German maid's bedroom and proceeds to have anal sex with her. Near the end of the novel, he opens a window, steps out onto a terrace, and dares himself to walk the parapet of the penthouse atop the Waldorf Astoria Hotel.

Back then everyone, myself included, assumed the character of

Deborah had been based on Lady Jeanne. Although there were certainly more than a few shared characteristics to strengthen this assumption, I'm pretty sure my father was also describing his state of mind when he stabbed Adele. Or at the very least he'd poured into this novel the charged mood of potential violence he inhabited while drinking heavily. Rojack's emotions in the novel were probably not that different from those the author had experienced, himself, five years earlier, on that fateful night.

As I grew older, I became one of Norman's readers. If I was in New York he'd talk to me about what he was writing, just enough to whet my appetite. As soon as a book was published, he'd send me an inscribed copy, and he always expected comments in return. But it wasn't always easy sailing.

In 1969 *The Armies of the Night* won the National Book Award and a Pulitzer Prize. The nonfiction book tells of the March on the Pentagon in October of 1967, a protest against the war in Vietnam. My father had been invited as a speaker, but he got drunk, crossed a police line, and was arrested. He ended up spending most of the demonstration in jail. When he was asked to report on the event he decided to do it from the third person point of view—the story of Norman at the March told by a retrospective Mailer. One marched, and the other wrote.

It was a brilliant piece of journalism and an innovative experiment. By putting himself inside the narrative he questioned the principle of objective reporting, and in effect helped change the genre. Yet, even with that third person perspective, I was unable to create enough distance between what I was reading and my real-life father. His voice, his manner, the drinking, and his put-on accents were on full display. It was so close to reality, I could not enjoy the book.

On the other hand, *The Executioner's Song*, which also won a Pulitzer Prize in 1979, blew me away. It told the story of Gary Gilmore, a man who spent most of his life in prison, and his brief encounter with freedom and Nicole, his soul mate. Dad's portrait of Utah, of Salt Lake City and the Mormon community, was written in the simple straightforward language of the people of the West. As the book progressed and the tale became more complex, the prose grew in depth and lyricism. Norman evoked the passion and desperation in Gary's and Nicole's love affair with such intimacy it seemed as if he'd inhabited both of them. As with *The Naked and the Dead*, I forgot my father had written the book and got lost in the characters and story. Of all his works, it is probably my favorite.

CHAPTER 13

In Brooklyn Heights

MY SISTER KATE WAS BORN IN AUGUST OF 1962. A FEW MONTHS before the end of that year, Dad and Jeanne had broken up. In a letter written to me earlier, in the summer, Dad had promised a family life, a home we would all share. He told me he'd bought a brownstone in Brooklyn Heights, remodeled it, and turned into a one-family home. Jeanne lived on the first floor, Dad on the fourth. I was promised a special bedroom on the third floor, a small independent studio apartment with a tiny kitchen and bathroom. According to Dad, Jeanne had decorated it especially for me. The walls were padded and covered with a floral cloth design in green, orange, and yellow.

But by the time I arrived in

Jeanne and Kate, 1962.

November, Jeanne had left Dad, taking the china and cutlery with her. Another of Dad's favorite stories was how one evening he came home to find me upstairs on the fourth floor, alone as usual, sitting on the kitchen barstool, staring into space and sucking my thumb. Something I still did when I was feeling painfully unhappy.

He'd say, "I walk in and the first thing I see is Susie sucking her thumb. She barely looks up when I greet her. So, I get angry and say, 'Susie! Take your goddam thumb out of yer mouth.' She looks me in the eye and says, 'Poor man, his woman left and took the dishes.' "

Every time he told the story he'd chuckle and add, "She's a tough one, don't mess with her." Enjoying the quick jab.

I spent a lot of time alone in that apartment. My grandmother lived around the corner, so after school I'd drop in to visit and have dinner. Then I'd go home to an empty brownstone and wait for Dad. Sometimes he walked in before I went to bed and we tried to chat, but it was usually a stilted dialogue. We made a miserable pair. It clearly pained him to see me in such a sad state, but he was depressed himself and didn't know how to deal with a gloomy thirteen-year-old.

Finally, getting annoyed, he'd say, "Susie, stop smelling your armpit! There's nothing worse than self-pity."

But most of the time he hung around the apartment for a while and then split as soon as he knew I was in bed.

I was so lonely it hurt.

Very soon after my arrival in mid-November, I entered eighth grade. Elizabeth Irwin High was what was then known as a progressive school. The white brick, five-story building on Charlton Street in Greenwich Village had classes for grades 7 to 12. Many intellectual and famous parents sent their kids to E.I.. Arlo Guthrie, Doon Arbus, and Bobby and Jane Miller went there. They were juniors and seniors, though, so as a lowly eighth grader I only caught an occasional glimpse of them. They were stars in the firmament, to be admired from afar. My

classmates' parents were mostly highly-educated, sophisticated professionals, so my father was probably the most famous parent in my class. But that didn't make me feel any better.

It was very different from Albert Einstein Middle School. At E.I. we addressed our teachers by their first names, classes were small, and we were expected to think. For me, math was easy, but English was tough because I didn't know the basics of writing. Not even how to write in paragraphs, let alone proper grammar.

All this was difficult, but what most concerned me was how to belong to the in crowd. A near impossible task to achieve for a late-comer to E.I., because most of my classmates had been there since kindergarten, and the cliques seemed to be set in steel. It wasn't that they were nasty; they just ignored me. To make things worse, I'd arrived in the middle of the year.

I did make one friend, Eliana, a lonely girl like me. Her parents were originally from Spain, and she spoke Spanish, which brought us together. I liked her, and we spent lots of time together, but I had the nagging feeling we were the odd couple. I still wanted entrance to the cool kids' circle.

One afternoon, near the end of 1962, I was once again sitting alone on the bar stool in the kitchen when Dad walked in earlier than usual, accompanied by a young, good-looking woman. He introduced us and then informed me, "She'll be living here for a while."

This second Jeannie was twenty-one and had just been discharged from Bellevue after a serious suicide attempt. She still had the bandages on her wrists. She and Dad had been friends for some time, perhaps casual lovers. Knowing first-hand what it meant to be in Bellevue under observation, he'd gone to see her. She was desperate to leave the hospital and asked him to be her guardian. He had agreed on two conditions. The first being that she was to not make another attempt on her life, at least not while she was in his house and taking care of me, which was the second condition. He was aware it was a gamble but told me it seemed worth a try.

I liked Jeannie immediately. She was fun, kooky, and full of energy.

I looked up to her like an admired older sister. Going home after school was no longer gloomy; now I had Jeannie. If I needed clothes, she'd ask Dad for money and we'd go shopping. She helped with my homework unless Dad was around and willing to listen. We talked about boys, and about my lack of friends, and soon came up with the idea of having a party.

By then, Dad had rented the first three floors of the brownstone, except for my studio apartment, which had a separate entrance. The fourth floor became our shared living space, and it was a teenager's dream. The hardwood living room ceiling sloped down in a gradual curve, like the sides of a boat. The area that lead to two bedrooms had a triple height "A" frame skylight with ledges, rope ladders, and long ropes hanging from the ceiling. A hammock was hung halfway between the floor and the tall A-frame ceiling. To get in it, one had to stand on a ledge about twenty feet from the floor, grab one of the ropes, pull the hammock close to the ledge, and jump in.

I invited my whole class of twenty-five thirteen-year-olds to the party. Jeannie was the chaperone, and Dad arrived a little later to help supervise. My classmates climbed up and down the ropes, onto the ledges and stepped out on the roof to see the New York skyline. Some jumped into the hammock, and fortunately no one fell. There must've been a guardian angel watching over us. After that success I was no longer the lonely ugly duckling. I became a member of the cool kids' clique, finally invited to parties, get-togethers, and sleepovers after school.

However, my friendship with Eliana did not survive. I don't know if I abandoned her or if she took a step back. Perhaps it was a little bit of both.

∼

In December Mom moved to Iowa with my brother for a two-year residency in psychiatry. Martin, her partner, stayed in the apartment in Mexico, though he visited her in the Midwest a few times a year.

She asked if I wanted to join her, but I chose to stay in New York. As unhappy as I'd been in the city, the idea of moving to the hinterlands of Cherokee, Iowa held zero interest.

Those first few months in New York, prior to the party, I had gained ten pounds. A lot of weight, considering my petite frame. I was chubby for the first time. My breasts ballooned, my hips widened, and all I wanted was to be back in Mexico. I wrote many letters to Chelo, pouring out my heart. Her oldest sister, who knew some English, sent a letter to Dad offering to take care of me in Mexico until I finished middle school there.

After reading it, Dad asked me how I felt about staying. But before I could answer, he said, "Susie, I think you have to give New York a fair try. You'll feel bad about yourself if you give up too soon. Tell you what, let's make a deal. If at the end of the school year, you still want to go back to Mexico, I'll agree to it."

He was betting on a better future for us. Convinced, I agreed. He wrote a lovely letter to Chelo's family thanking them and inviting her to visit us some time in New York.

~

My party at the brownstone marked a distinct Before and After. Though I still needed to lose weight, now I wanted to live in New York. I was busy, finally doing well in school, and had lots of new friends and activities. Also, there was Jeannie, my super-hip companion. Bringing her into the house had been an audacious move on Dad's part, but this time he aced it. I had a welcoming home, I was happy, and I felt protected.

I lived in Brooklyn Heights the entire time my mother was in Iowa. Before Jeannie arrived, besides Grandma and Aunt Barbara, Annie Barry, Dad's secretary had been my other companion. Just out of Radcliffe, she was a petite, cute 21-year old who was in awe of my father. A great secretary, she was also interesting and smart. One day she took me to her apartment in Little Italy. It was so tiny, the bathtub was in the kitchen. When it was time for dinner, Annie lifted a large slab of wood, sort of like an old door, that had been propped up by the entrance. She set it on the bathtub and turned it into a table. If she hadn't been so busy keeping up with all of Dad's stuff, I'm sure she would've been recruited as my part-time companion.

~

Very early one morning before I left for school, Dad walked in with a stranger. He had an Irish accent, and was accompanied by his girlfriend and another woman, a beautiful blonde. They were all in such high spirits Dad decided I should stay home from school. The funny-looking man turned out to be the poet Brendan Behan, and his companion was Valerie Danby-Smith. The blonde was Beverly Bentley, who was soon to become my fourth stepmother.

I was immediately in awe of Beverly. Her teeth were very white, her smile engaging, her green feline eyes sparkling.

Jeannie was uncharacteristically quiet that day. Perhaps she intuited her place would soon be taken. In any case, she was already going out with Paul Krasner, editor of *The Realist*, an upbeat, pioneering magazine popular at the time. She would soon get pregnant with their daughter Holly and move in with him.

But for me that morning was magical. Dad and his friends had been out all night and were still riding high. He was falling in love with the blonde, who was witty and totally charming. Brendan Behan was being himself, eccentric and outrageous.

Dad noticed I was enjoying myself and said, "You know Susie, Brendan is a very good poet. You might want to read his work one day when you're older."

To which Brendan retorted, "Actually, I'm a drinker with a writing problem."

I thought it was so funny, I couldn't stop laughing. It was thrilling to stay home and be included in my father's fascinating life. I even got a Virgin Mary with their next round of drinks.

Beverly had plenty of stories, too. She had been Miles Davis's lover for years; had been part of Papa Hemingway's entourage in Spain during "the dangerous summer" of 1959. And she was an actress. Her latest movie, she told me, was the first smell-a-vision film, *The Scent of Mystery*, produced by Mike Todd.

As if that were not enough, Dad said "Beverly has a special car. You'll love it." It turned out to be a bright-purple Citroen with hydro-pneumatic suspension, and it looked like a space ship. Mysteriously, at least to me, the car rose a few inches higher when it was turned on. I'd never seen a vehicle like that!

Soon Beverly moved into the apartment, and Jeannie moved out to go live with Paul Krasner. By then, this was a Mailer routine. One in, the other out.

I missed Jeannie and felt jealous of Paul and the baby that was soon to arrive. But I moved on, as I always had to do. Once in a while I'd drop by Jeannie's apartment in Chelsea after school, and we'd go out for ice cream. There was a new, unbelievably delicious brand you could only get near her place. Called Häagen-Dasz, it came in four flavors: vanilla, strawberry, chocolate, and rum raisin. So, even though I was always on a diet, I'd order a double cone. Then we'd stroll back to her apartment, Jeannie's big belly in the lead and looking ready to pop.

Beverly, who was in her early thirties when she met Dad, rapidly took over managing the household. She did her best to be a good stepmother, provide meals, and manage chores. Things were complicated, though, because there was one bathroom on the fourth floor for the three of us, and on weekends Danielle, now six, and Elizabeth, a sweet, shy four-year old, also arrived. As a result, Beverly spent a lot of time teaching us basic cleaning skills and how to keep a living space neat.

"When you brush your teeth, clean the wash basin afterward. Don't leave the toothpaste cap off, and make sure none of it sticks to the sink. Don't forget the stray hairs. And never leave the bathroom without flushing the toilet." All sound advice which I follow to this day. But Beverly had a compulsive streak. As soon as I left the bathroom, she would go in to make sure I'd followed her instructions perfectly. That always put me on edge, because if she wasn't satisfied, I had to do it again. Both she and Dad were big fans of "doing a good job and finishing it well."

I lived with Dad and Beverly in the Brooklyn Heights apartment for the next year and a half, until the middle of 1964. They were obviously in love, and our daily life had an easy rhythm. Before Michael was born, Beverly was fun to be with; she had a good sense of humor and lots of energy. She organized the household so Dad could work without concerning himself with bills, repairs, grocery shopping, and bookkeeping. All of which he considered interruptions to his main purpose—writing. During that period, he turned out a blizzard of essays, reviews, interviews, and the complete serial version of *An American Dream*, for *Esquire*.

Me on Terrace of Brooklyn Heights apartment, 1963.

~

That November John F. Kennedy was assassinated. I was in a conference with my homeroom teacher when someone rushed in to tell us the President had been shot, and probably wouldn't survive the wounds to his head.

We were let out early, and Beverly picked me up. People on the streets appeared dazed. Traffic was moving erratically, since everyone was listening so intently to the radio. We finally got home and sat in front of the TV, which was showing Kennedy arriving in Dallas, then riding in the open convertible, and the impact of the shots as he slid to Jackie's side of the seat. And then the First Lady in a panic as she tried to climb out of the open convertible over the rear trunk.

We sat there staring at these terrible images, stunned, unable to believe our handsome young President-Prince was dead. A lump in my throat made it hard to swallow. One glimpse of my father's furrowed brow and anguished face, and I knew our world had shifted. Kennedy was irreplaceable to my father. He said that during JFK's administration, for a short time he'd felt hope for America. The Kennedys promised something new and exciting after the boring, stultified years of Eisenhower's presidency. And now we'd lost that dream. Dad was profoundly shaken.

Vice President Lyndon Baines Johnson was quickly sworn in as the new president. As we watched Kennedy's funeral, the most unforgettable image was of John-John saluting his father's coffin, not yet grasping what it all meant. Jacqueline, her slight figure clad in black, a long veil covering her face, looked both dignified and grand. Beverly and I remained glued to the TV for three days, except for short visits to the kitchen. Dad paced the floor, sat down only to jump up again and pace some more.

Suddenly Beverly gasped and shouted, "Norman, come quickly. You've got to see this!"

Jack Ruby had just shot accused assassin Lee Harvey Oswald in front of scores of reporters and TV cameras. How could such a thing happen in the presence of the Secret Service, FBI agents, and police?

Dad said we would probably never know the truth about what really happened. He wanted to believe the FBI had a hand in that shooting, but later, in a letter to his friend Mickey Knox, he wrote: *I suspect the real story is that two lonely guys, all by themselves, put more grit in the gears than anyone ever succeeded in doing before, and it's just a mess, a dull and miserable mess.*

In the same letter he adds that *An American Dream,* his most recent work, . . *of course falls by the side in all of this . . . With Kennedy alive it was a good book, but with him dead, it's just a curiosity, and somehow irritating in tone. I don't even mind the loss, in a funny way.*

At this moment at least, Kennedy's death and the end of all that his Presidency had meant to America, was much more important to my father than his own work. I think he mourned that loss off and on for the rest of his life.

Beverly got pregnant in the late spring of 1963, a few months after she moved into the apartment. This was to become the set script with my father and his wives, except for my mother and Adele. The rest usually gave birth to a baby sometime between the first and second year of the marriage. Age was an important factor, I'm sure. Both Jeanne and Beverly were in their thirties when they hooked up with Dad, so the idea of childbearing was probably already in the front row. Carol, who would be his fifth wife, was older. But she'd been Dad's lover for several years, many of them while he was married to Beverly.

I suspect his being a confirmed alpha male made my father seem like a good choice for a woman ready to conceive a child. His fame was no doubt an added attraction. But Dad also had very specific ideas about birth control. He hated plastic, so diaphragms and condoms were out of the question. He thought birth control pills were bad for the soul. He firmly believed all souls wanted to be born and this, together with a good fuck, could make an exceptional baby. Or, as he tersely put it in his 1971 book, *The Prisoner of Sex,* "Good fucks make good babies." Birth control only muddled the universe's plan, as far as he was concerned.

When Beverly got pregnant, everyone was sure it would be a boy this time. Except for Dad, who said he was resigned to having another girl. But he was wrong. Michael Mailer was born on March 17, 1964, Norman's first son after four daughters.

Michael was a cute baby with very blond hair and huge blue eyes that seemed to take up half his face. He also cried a lot. Beverly said he was very sensitive and that made him fussy. Today, I would probably say he might've been this cranky because Beverly was extremely anxious. Or, perhaps because he was a fussy baby, she then became overly anxious. Whichever was the case, life at home changed. The fun times dwindled into tense quiet ones; a "Shhh, the baby is sleeping and I'm exhausted" type of quiet. There were also frantic, busy moments getting things just so for Norman or the baby. That resulted in little time left over for stepdaughters. Fortunately for me, by then I was often out with friends, and could briefly escape the bad moods and pervasive tension.

Once he knew another baby was on the way, in the fall of 1963, Dad realized he needed more space for his growing family. The year before, he'd rented out the rest of the brownstone, and my bedroom on the third floor was now used as an office for his secretary. We now all lived together on the fourth floor.

To create a bit more room, he had a small bedroom built for me up on the roof, overlooking the harbor. Then, atop my bedroom another even smaller space was added, to serve as my father's study. We called it The Crow's Nest because it was perched on the highest part of the roof. Both additions were cozy, connected to the apartment by two small doors cut into the A frame. However, they had very little insulation, so in summer I baked and in winter I froze. Still, I cherished my little private room.

To get to the Crow's Nest Dad had to walk across a plank situated thirty feet above the roof, with only three handrails to hold onto. He was afraid of heights, so every day he had to dare himself to cross that plank. He said this daily exercise mastered his anxiety and got him in a sharp mood before writing.

~

I wrote my first serious essay in ninth grade. Having recently discovered Franz Kafka's *The Metamorphosis* and *The Castle*, I decided to do some research and wrote a fourteen-page essay. The title was "Franz Kafka's Relationship to his Father." The night I finished the paper I left it on the kitchen counter for my dad to read, and then in fear and trembling went up to my room.

Next morning a note on a separate piece of paper lay on top of the essay: "Congratulations Susie, I couldn't have written a better essay myself! Hand it in and we'll go through it later for style and grammar."

I got a double grade on the essay from Eleanor, my English teacher: A+ for content and C- for grammar. After she returned it, Dad and I went through the paper sentence by sentence. He explained some of the mysteries of style and advised me to always read out loud whatever I wrote. He said sentences had a natural rhythm that I could only hear if I heard them spoken. There were certain words I should stay away from as much as possible, such as *really, that, which, like,* and *very.* He told me to be selective with adjectives, to vary long sentences with short ones, and to choose simple, strong words, not convoluted, pretentious ones.

Around this time my father was writing the monthly installments of *An American Dream* for *Esquire*. To get the work done he kept a strict daily routine. In the morning, he would get up, go down four flights of stairs to retrieve *The New York Times,* then climb back up. He'd sit at the kitchen counter and eat a whole grapefruit, leaving nothing but the bare rind. Then he'd have two scrambled eggs, two pieces of rye toast with butter, and black coffee. No one spoke to him during this time. We knew he was getting ready for a day of work and needed to collect his thoughts. He got in the mood by doing the New York *Times* crossword puzzle, or playing a hand of solitaire. If we had any questions they just had to wait until he came back down from his writing studio. Once in a while I would say, "Good morning, Daddy." Usually he was too deep in thought, or in the fog of a hangover, to answer. If we did happen to ask something and he heard us, the usual reply was simply, "Not now, I'm thinking."

Dad disliked talking on the phone. Anyone who wanted to get in touch with him had to go through his secretary. In the afternoons, after work, he'd spend more than an hour answering the day's calls. But mornings were off limits for everyone. He was totally concentrated and oblivious to everything except his preparation for the day's coming work.

In the living room of the apartment, a desk stood in front of the window that faced the East River and the skyline of Manhattan. He sometimes worked there in the afternoons, revising pages his secretary had typed. We could hear his pencil scratching the surface of the page, stopping once in a while to be replaced by a murmur. He read sentences aloud again and again until he found the right rhythm, the way the words sounded best together. Many times, he'd tap on the desk, rhythmically, slightly bowing, as if he were davening the way Orthodox Jews do while deep in prayer.

One afternoon, a couple of months after Michael was born, Dad told me he wanted me to do something important for him.

"Susie, I have a job for you. I invested in some stocks and I want you to help me follow the flow of the market. I don't have time to spend looking at the Wall Street Journal, so how about if I teach you how to follow the stock market." As usual, a statement, not a request.

He gave me a special notebook in which I was supposed to annotate the daily rises and falls of his assets. I got a quick lesson on graphs and how to draw the fluctuations each day—one graph line for each stock every week, his idea being that at a glance he could tell if his stocks were going up or down. All this, of course, saved him precious time, and was also supposed to give me an education in economics. It didn't seem too complicated and the pay was great: ten dollars a week.

My father always insisted that any time one started a job, it must always be finished properly. But very soon I grew bored with drawing graphs and started skipping a day or two. I didn't think this was much of a problem, but when Dad found out he was furious.

He sat me down in the living room and turned on The Mailer Stare. "Hey Susie, you haven't been doing this job every day."

I looked down, avoiding his stare. "Hmm, yeah, well, I had a lot of homework."

"Look at me. Now, there's something you have to get straight. When you start a job you finish it, and finish it well, or it won't be worth the effort you've put into it. So, if you're going to do what we agreed on, do it. Don't piss around. Got it?"

"Yeah. Sorry. I didn't think a day would make such a difference."

"What do you mean, a day won't make a difference? The whole idea here is for me not to have to worry about the market going down. If you miss a day, I might lose a lot of money. If it goes up and I don't sell, I also lose money! You have an important job to do. If you don't think you're up to it, say so."

I obediently replied, "Yes Dad, I get it. I'll do it every day." Even though what I really wanted to tell him was, "Get lost. I don't want to do this anymore."

That spring, my mother's psychiatric residency came to an end. She was getting ready to leave Iowa and return to Mexico. On one of her visits to New York I made the mistake of telling her about my stock market discussion with Dad.

She was furious. "Norman's insane to expect you to handle his stocks at the age of fourteen! How can he even *think* of giving you this kind of responsibility?"

It also gave her a good excuse to put her foot down and insist I go back with her to Mexico. But I didn't want to leave, now that I'd found my place in New York. I was finally an insider, with friends. I had gotten excellent grades and been accepted as a staff member on the school newspaper. I didn't want to go back and live in Mexico now.

But for Mom there simply was no discussion.

Dad wanted me to fight back. "If you want to stay in New York, stand up to your mother. Your mother is a bully and like most bullies, she will step down if you're strong. I'm right behind you on this, but you have to decide first what you want to do."

Yeah, right. My mother is a bully. So where does that leave you? I thought.

Around this time, I woke up very early one morning for an exam. I was walking across the ledge as I always did to get downstairs to the bathroom. Suddenly I fell, landing on the floor with a thud that woke up everyone in the apartment. I was unconscious for perhaps a minute. When I opened my eyes, I saw hovering over me the concerned faces of my father, Beverly, and Aunt Barbara, who had been staying in the apartment with us for a few months. I had no idea about what had happened. I had blacked out and now felt groggy and confused.

I lay quietly on the floor for a while. Finally, Beverly insisted Dad take me to the emergency room.

"Oh, I don't think that's necessary. Look at Susie, she's fine. She's a tough one, a little fall won't break her."

But Beverly and Aunt Barbara wouldn't budge. They knew it had been a serious fall. After all, that ledge was about twenty feet above the floor.

Dad had no option left but to take me to the nearest hospital. We must have sat in the emergency room for more than two hours. My father kept asking the nurse at the admissions desk when the doctor would see us, only to be told there were many patients ahead of us, so we simply had to wait.

He looked at me and said, "You know something Sue, this could give me cancer. You're fine. You don't have a headache and you're not acting dopey. So, let's leave before we actually do get sick." Patience had never been one of his virtues, and by then I was more than happy to leave that crowded emergency room.

Still, the unanswered question remained: Why had I fainted?

Everyone, including myself, was mystified that I'd suddenly taken a fall after crossing the same ledge hundreds of times. One moment I had been awake and walking on it as confidently as ever. The next I was on the floor, with no recollection of what had happened in between.

Perhaps the whole thing had been my way of saying, "I don't want to make this decision. It's too hard. Mom will hate me. Dad will be disappointed. I just want to disappear. I want to black out."

～

I went to Mexico for the summer and tried to convince my mother to let me stay in New York, but to no avail. Even though Dad kept insisting I should stand up to her, I wasn't up for that battle. I was afraid to defy my mother, and certainly didn't want my parents to get into another war. That was too scary to contemplate. So, a few weeks after I arrived in Mexico, I wrote to Dad, telling him I'd decided to stay there.

I claimed I was happy with my decision, and that wasn't a total lie since life in Mexico was never bad. I still had my friends from junior high, and now the freedom to move around the city easily on my own. Also, I thought, *I'll be going off to college in three years, so if this will stop an open confrontation between my parents, I'm willing to wait and make the sacrifice.*

It turned out to be only a temporary peace.

CHAPTER 14

Underground Wars

I STAYED IN MEXICO, BUT AT A COST. I MISSED MY HIGH SCHOOL FRIENDS at E.I. It hurt every time I thought of the high school newspaper where I had been accepted, but wouldn't be able to work in. And in spite of the bumps and tension, I was sad to lose the daily routine with my father and Beverly, baby Michael, my sisters, and the rest of the family in New York.

My winter visits there resumed, however. When I got off the plane that November, Dad asked, "Do you have a nice dress? I want to take you to a dinner party where there'll be some interesting people."

That gathering was at Lionel and Diana Trilling's home. A few days later he took me to another at the home of Steven Marcus, who had just interviewed him for the *Paris Review*. During the rest of my stay in New York we went out to many cocktail parties and dinners. I knew a fair amount about classical music, thanks to Mom, and had read the literary classics, thanks to Dad. I was a precocious, interesting fifteen-year old and a novelty at those gatherings, so I enjoyed them.

I also met José Torres, soon to be the world light-heavyweight boxing champion, and his wife Ramona. Immediately, the three of us connected. He took me to his barrio and introduced me to his friends. With them I was a fish in water—I could finally display my Latin persona in New York, a rare occasion. My father did not appreciate Mexico, or the fact I spoke Spanish as well as a native. Sometimes he'd ask me how to say a phrase in Spanish and then repeat it back to me in a mocking accent that oozed disdain. Anything Mexican must have reminded him he had let me go many years before. I suppose this weighed on him, but I didn't understand it until many years later. So, his ridiculing tone hurt, and made me feel second rate.

Dad respected José, though, and enjoyed boxing with him. But he was an outsider and neophyte when it came to Puerto Rican culture. I observed him watching closely as José and I carried on in Spanish. I saw then his pride in me and, for the first time, felt he appreciated instead of resenting my Latino side.

But Dad was still the quintessential New Yorker. He thought that if a person couldn't make it in New York, they would never amount to much. He never tired of repeating this mantra, making me feel that whatever success I might have elsewhere in the world would never be worth mentioning. But with José and his family, my father was at a loss; his knowledge of their culture was so scant he needed me to help him understand it. When José won the championship in March of 1965, Dad was the first to jump into the ring and embrace him. Afterward, he threw a big party at the Brooklyn apartment.

Jose Torres, 1965.

Soon I was spending a great deal of time with the Torres family. In typical Latino tradition their home was always full of people, a throwback to my days in the *vecindad* and at Chelo's house. Gatherings there quickly evolved into parties with lots of drinking and dancing, and especially lots of singing. José's best friend Naro, short for Genaro, strummed boleros on his guitar. He stared into my eyes as he sang those romantic ballads. I was thrilled to have this good-looking older guy after me. But our flirting went nowhere because José was keeping an eye on me, making sure we didn't get into trouble. Genaro was not only considerably older than I, he was married and had a son, Narito. We remained simply good friends.

A year later they both came to Mexico City and I introduced them to Chelo, who also immediately fell for Genaro. Again, nothing came of the infatuation, because she was too young, and he was, of course, still married.

In choosing to stay in Mexico, I'd hoped to prevent a war between my parents. But soon after my return it was I who got into a battle with my mother.

A boy named Sergio lived on our street. He was seventeen, two years my senior, and soon we were going out. We talked about our favorite authors and composers. We went to concerts and to see European movies and soon fell in love.

At the time, I was in the school drama club and had been chosen to play the lead role in Friedrich Schiller's *Mary Stuart,* the verse play about the life of Mary, Queen of Scots. The role became a constant source of tension between Sergio and me, because going to rehearsals meant I had less time to spend with him. Sergio was insanely possessive and had serious doubts about what went on during those rehearsals. As a result, he interrogated me constantly. "Who is playing Lord Darnley? Why are you coming home so late? Where do you go after rehearsals?" The inquisition was endless.

I could have opted out of the drama to keep him happy, but I enjoyed acting too much to give it up.

Unbeknownst to me, my boyfriend came to the first performance. Once the play was over, he headed backstage, passed right by me, and went straight for the leading man. He grabbed him by the shirt, and said, "*Oye, imbecil.* Listen, asshole. If you ever kiss Susan again, I will beat the shit out of you."

We stood there, mouths agape. The lighting crew, my drama teacher, the actors, all of us too stunned to react. Except for Mom. She was furious at him, and shouted, "*No!* You listen, Sergio. How dare you make such a scene. You should leave now!"

He had no choice but to walk out. But before he left, Sergio gave me a look that clearly said, *We'll deal with this later.*

I was scared, and also embarrassed to my core; I couldn't even look at my friends. On the drive home, Mom told me "You are not to see that crazy lunatic again. I forbid it!"

She was right, of course, but at sixteen I wasn't about to listen to a sensible adult. Sergio was my first important relationship, my first love, my first sexual experience. For two more years I was stuck between him and my mother. Once again, mired in the middle.

Mom tried different tactics to keep us apart, but none worked. A couple of times she locked me in, but I simply climbed out the window of our first-floor apartment. Other times, Sergio climbed into my bedroom through the window in the middle of the night. Romeo and Juliet, revisited.

Mother caught us in the act one night. I thought she'd go ballistic. Instead she told him to get out, and then walked out of my bedroom. Perplexed, he and I sat on the bed, discussing the best way for him to exit. I thought he should just walk out the front door. But he was afraid my mother was in the living room and didn't want her to confront him. Timid Romeo finally climbed out the window.

The next morning, a Saturday, I got up at seven, made my bed, washed the dishes, cleaned the living room, and went to buy freshly-baked bread. By the time Mom, Martin, and my brother woke up, the table was set and breakfast was ready.

My mother turned to me. "Did your Romeo leave by the window?" Then she noticed the already-set table, the fresh bread. "I see you're trying to make some points today."

And we all sat down to breakfast.

We didn't speak of Sergio, or about what had happened the night before. It was so typical of Mom: to make an acid remark, and then go silent.

Our home remained off limits for Sergio after that, but the Romeo and Juliet routine continued. Whenever he was desperate to see me, he'd climb through the window at night.

Mom was obviously in denial about the consequences of unprotected adolescent sex. Instead of taking me to a doctor to get some kind of birth control she merely forbade me to see him and looked the other way. So, it should have come as no surprise that I eventually got pregnant. I had just turned seventeen.

When I realized I must be pregnant, I panicked. It was May and I was getting ready to leave Mexico to go to Barnard College in September. My trip to New York was only a month away, so I thought I'd wait until I arrived and tell Aunt Barbara, instead. I had been bleeding every two weeks or so, as well, so I couldn't tell if I was actually pregnant as the test showed, or if I was having a miscarriage. Sometimes I even convinced myself I wasn't pregnant after all. I would wake up in the night hoping it was all a mistake, merely my body playing tricks on me. Pleading *God, please make it go away!* When sleep eluded me, I'd sit up in bed and read Arthur Conan Doyle, until my mind was elsewhere and my eyelids were heavy again. I must've gone through all of the Sherlock Holmes series that way.

When I got to New York and confided in Aunt Barbara, she took me to her own gynecologist. Her face fell when he told her I was indeed four months pregnant, and then added, "The bleeding is due to a condition called placenta previa. Susan might bleed during the whole pregnancy. She should refrain from strenuous exercise. This is a delicate condition."

When we walked out, Aunt Barbara said. "Try not to worry. We'll figure out what to do."

I wanted to have the baby, marry Sergio, and go to the University of Mexico. But a voice inside me still whispered, with deep regret, *I was supposed to go to Barnard. Why does becoming a New Yorker always seem to elude me?*

I'll never forget Grandma Fanny's expression when we told her the news. She took a deep breath, and then let out a long, long sigh. I thought I saw tears in her eyes.

She just couldn't believe I had gotten myself into such a mess. "Oh, Sue, what are you going to do now? Will you still go to college?" And then immediately she recovered and said, "You can always count on me. And you'll have to tell your father when he gets here."

Dad sat and listened to me quietly. He seemed more concerned than angry. After I told him the details, he hugged me. "I'll support you in whatever decision you make. Sue, you don't have to marry Sergio, you can stay in New York and go to college, and we will figure out a way of taking care of the baby."

I, of course, was romantically inclined. I didn't care if Sergio and I lived in a mud hut; I just wanted to be with him. But he was in his second year of law school, still immature in spite of all the macho bluster, and too scared to tell his parents. Romeo turned out not to be brave at all.

I decided to stay with my father in New York and not go back to Mexico. I was seventeen and didn't fully understand I was about to become a mother, and how this would change my life forever.

～

When my father phoned my mother to tell her the news, I was standing next to him, terrified that she would hit the roof. Instead there was a brief silence on the other end. Then she said, "Norman, this kid Sue's in love with is not good for her. I think she should stay with you in New York."

Mom felt she couldn't deal with this problem anymore. One she'd been unable to solve. It was time for the Mailers to step up.

Over the years Mother has expressed more than once her regret about that period of our lives. She's apologized for not coming to New York immediately to see me, and for letting her anger cloud her better judgment. For me, that was the year winter descended between us. I felt cold and indifferent. I hardly ever thought of Mom and had no desire to be near her.

I've always felt, and have told her more than once, that the pregnancy might have been prevented if she had only accepted that she could no longer control me, or my body. I was not going to leave Sergio until I was ready. She should have understood that, and I'm still surprised by how she reacted. Mom had been a rebel in her own time, going against most of her own folks' expectations for her: virginity until the wedding, a traditional Jewish marriage, becoming a homemaker. In fact, my mother, as she loved to remind me, had been a feminist well before the 1970s movement. She acted and felt like an American Simone de Beauvoir; a free spirit, and very independent. But later, as a mother, she had grown used to being in control. I don't think she understood I was no longer a child and had become a rebellious adolescent, acting out my anger at her in a self-destructive manner.

After I told the Mailers about my pregnancy, Dad, Beverly, my four siblings, and I went north to Provincetown. One evening my father asked us to come into the kitchen to meet our sister Kate. After four years he and Jeanne had finally agreed on visiting privileges.

Standing in the middle of the kitchen was a cute five-year-old with a red bandana on her head: pretty, green-eyed Kate. We took her upstairs and showed her our communal bedroom, which we would all now share, and helped her unpack. How strange it must've been for her to go from zero siblings to five overnight. She'd been an only child until recently, but Jeanne had just given birth to another girl. A big change on top of meeting all of us as well.

Kate quickly fell in with the daily routine, helping with chores, sharing a room with her sisters, playing with us out on the deck or on the beach. Getting used to her new extended family.

A few days after Kate arrived, I woke up late one night, sticky and wet with blood. Alarmed, but also frightened about how Beverly would react to a stained mattress, I got up and groping in the dark found some clean sheets. I tried to go back to sleep, but I could feel more blood seeping out of me, which made me worry I was still leaving a mess.

In the morning, as soon as Beverly was up, I told her what had happened.

She reached out and hugged me. "Don't worry about the sheets. It's nothing, we'll wash them or get some new ones. I'm more worried about the bleeding. It's probably due to the placenta previa. So, we'll go to the doctor tomorrow."

But that night I came down with a mysterious fever. First, I was freezing, my teeth chattering uncontrollably. The fever only broke after it had spiked up to 103. The bleeding was all but gone by then, so both Dad and Beverly thought it had been a passing problem and that the fever had probably been due to a flu virus going around.

But when this happened again the following night, I woke them up. They drove me very early in the morning to the hospital in Orleans, twenty miles away. I was checked in, and that night got the shivers again, along with a similar high fever. The medical staff was confused. They couldn't figure out what in the world was the matter and decided to keep me under observation. Even the doctor had no clue.

Early the next morning, he came into my room to do some blood work. I recalled how worried he'd looked the night before. Now he was cheerful and chatty. He announced, "I think I've solved the mystery. Last night, after I left the hospital, I started feeling rotten. Figured I was probably coming down with some kind of flu and said to my wife, I feel like I have malaria. And then, all of a sudden, I knew. Malaria! That's what Susan has."

It was the *nostrum vivax* strain, which strikes every twenty-four hours with a high fever. I'd probably contracted it on a trip to the Mexican coast a few weeks before I arrived in the U.S. The combination of the placenta previa, which had made me bleed off and one since the beginning of the pregnancy, and malaria, sent me into labor that same day. By nightfall I gave birth to a boy. The baby, only 20 weeks old, was stillborn.

I wanted to see my baby, but the doctor didn't let me. When I asked about the sex, one of the nurses said, "I shouldn't be telling you this, but it was a boy."

That was the protocol for stillborn babies back then. It was believed to be better for the mother to not see or hold her baby, nor find out the sex of the child she'd lost. That way, I suppose the thinking went, the grieving period would be easier and faster.

I was so exhausted by then, all I wanted was to go to sleep. Right then I wasn't feeling much of anything.

After I got home, I stayed in my room for hours at a time, staring at the ceiling. I was in an emotional haze. I could hear my siblings playing on the deck or splashing in the water, all the noises of a house full of children. Alone in my room, I lay on the bed, aware of the changes in my body: my aching belly and swollen breasts. Tears welling up. All I could do was lie there in a fetal position with the covers drawn up to my chin.

After a few days I finally emerged. Yes, I was sad. I grieved for the lost baby, and for my failed relationship with Sergio. But at the same time, next to the sadness I felt a weight disappearing. I'd been given a second chance and would go to Barnard after all.

During this time, Beverly was kind to me in spite of her heavy drinking and hangovers, her black moods and frequent fights with Dad. My father was thoughtful and discreet. Later on, he took me to the cemetery to see the baby's grave and stood by quietly while I cried. As we walked back to the car, he hugged me tightly. "Sue, I love you, and I feel profound respect for the strength and dignity you have shown during this period."

I hugged him back with tears in my eyes.

~

There were no more surprises that summer. I got friendly with Jeff Michelson and his British wife Lottie, a couple who had been hired by Beverly and Dad to help around the house. They lived in the converted garage-bedroom of our waterside home on Commercial Street, and were supposed to clean, bartend, cook occasionally, and babysit when necessary. Jeff and Lottie were in their early twenties, and thought it was a gas to work for Norman Mailer. Soon they became part of the family. When they were through with work for the day I'd go to their room, where we'd smoke a joint and belt out songs from *The Sergeant Pepper's Lonely Hearts Club Band* album.

That summer Dad was making final edits on his fifth novel, *Why Are We in Vietnam?* His studio was a converted attic on the third floor with a panoramic view of Provincetown Harbor. He also wrote in a tiny rented cottage situated farther east on Commercial Street. He worked all day, as usual, and was off limits for conversation until the cocktail hour before dinner. Several days a week, though, he would take off a few hours. Then we would all pile into his old Range Rover and careen through the dunes of the National Park Seashore. Sometimes we walked across them. After a grueling hour of trudging through sand and sun, we'd jump into the ice-cold ocean. Dad taught my siblings to snorkel in the bay. We also walked on the low, tidal flats that seemed to go on forever, all the way to the other end of the bay. On those occasions we'd set out with pails and choose the best hermit crabs and shells, but horseshoe-crab carcasses were the best. They looked like science fiction monsters and were my younger siblings' favorite treasure.

Dad stretched a rope tightly across the deck, about three feet off the ground. He'd coax us to walk it with a pole, like circus performers, with his usual mantra, "It will strengthen your character and help you dominate your fears."

He also was determined to teach Betsy, then seven years old, to swim, even though she was petrified of the water. One scene sticks out in my mind.

I'm on the deck reading while my younger siblings play near-by. Dad appears outside in swimming shorts. I immediately sense trouble brewing.

"Hey Honey, I've been looking for you. Let's take a swim."

My sister clamps her lips tight and wrings her hands. "I don't want to, Daddy."

"Aw, c'mon. Listen, I'll do it with you. Let's get in the water. I'll keep you floating and won't let go until you tell me to."

Whimpering, she murmurs, "No, Daddy. I don't want to go in the water. I don't like the water."

"Tell you what, let's go in together. You hold my hand and we'll walk in. If you don't want to put your head in the water, fine."

By then she's crying. "No! I don't like the water, Daddy. I don't want to!"

At this point Dad's face changes. He is no longer smiling. His lips are tight, his shoulders tense. He quickly walks to where my sister is standing. I can tell he's lost all patience.

"Betsy, enough! You're coming in the water."

He scoops her up and marches into the cold water. Betsy doesn't move, she's frozen with terror. Knee-deep in water he drops her in, and her head goes under. I know Betsy won't drown. He won't let her. But I can't believe he's doing this! Still, I say nothing. Not a peep comes from any of us. His gestures are too menacing. Dad was not a tall man, but he always appeared like a giant to us when he was angry.

Of course, my sister did not suddenly get over her fear of the water thanks to this appalling exercise, though she did learn to swim years later. After that forced lesson she ran for cover whenever our father appeared on the deck wearing swimming trunks.

Kitchen duty became an ordeal that summer. In the early days Beverly had often asked us to help out with drying dishes, clearing the table, or putting away cutlery. But that summer in Provincetown she seemed to have suddenly turned into Cinderella's stepmother; especially when she drank and was hung over, which was often. At those times we did our best to steer clear.

By then Michael was four and Stephen was two. If the boys happened to wake Beverly before she had slept off a hangover, we were on her shit list for the rest of the morning. Her wrath terrified all of us, but for some reason it was Danielle, then ten, who got the brunt of it. Beverly assigned her to take care of the boys and to wash the breakfast dishes. When she woke, she'd conduct an inspection. If everything passed, only then could Danielle go out to play. Much like working for an evil fairytale stepmother!

At night cleanup was more a group activity. Beverly usually cooked. After dinner, with Jeff and Lotte, we'd wash, dry, and put away dishes, sweep and mop the floor, then show Beverly the result. This drill probably wasn't the case every night, but it happened often enough for my sisters and me to remember it as a chore we always did.

By turns, our stepmother could be irritable, fun, relaxed, compulsive, affectionate, or very scary. But to be fair, managing the extensive Mailer family, while trying to keep an acting career alive, was surely not easy. During her marriage to my father, Beverly not only ran the household, she acted in the three movies he produced and directed. She also played Lulu in his theater version of *The Deer Park,* which ran off-Broadway for several months in 1967. And she was definitely his equal when it came to drinking and partying.

At the time we were too young to understand her anger at Norman's womanizing, or the stress involved in managing a big house with six kids, four of whom were not hers. We just felt the brunt of her highs and lows and were petrified of provoking her verbal outbursts. When she was drunk, she could just as easily tell us a fascinating story about the old spirits that populated Provincetown as chew us out severely about some small task we hadn't done perfectly. It didn't matter which she started off with, either, because even when Beverly was in a good mood, she could still morph into that evil stepmother again at any moment. We tiptoed around her.

Beverly's emotional roller coaster made our father's emotional absence all the more evident. These were very busy years in his life, and the domestic expenses were huge. He often complained about how he was forced to constantly accept new projects just to pay them. Over the next few years he wrote *An American Dream, Cannibals and Christians, The Bullfight, Why Are We in Vietnam? Armies of the Night, Miami and the Siege of Chicago,* and *Of a Fire on the Moon.* The last four were finalists for the National Book Award, and *Armies* won it in 1968. He also produced and acted in three low budget *cinema verité* films. And, as if that were not enough, he ran for Mayor of New York City again, in 1969.

I silently questioned his behavior. Did talent and an enormous capacity for work give him some special dispensation to turn a blind eye to what was going on in his home, with his children? Why didn't Grandma or Aunt Barbara stand up for us? I was almost eighteen, but I was simply too frightened of my stepmother to say anything.

A fragile balance existed in Beverly and Norman's marriage. The threat of potential violence always seemed to hang in the air. Too close, too menacing. No one wanted to rock the boat.

When my father and Beverly broke up in the late summer of 1969, after seven turbulent years of marriage, Dad's longtime lover, the jazz singer Carol Stevens, moved to Provincetown almost immediately, while Beverly went off to Mexico with her new man for a short time. The typical *one goes out, another one comes in* Mailer routine.

Part II

CHAPTER 15

If You Want a Revolution

WHEN I WAS YOUNG, GOING AWAY TO COLLEGE HAD ALWAYS sounded like the most exciting experience in the world. The Promised Land. I'd imagine myself grown up and independent, sitting in classrooms with riveting professors and good-looking students. Walking down tree-lined paths with centuries-old buildings rising on either side, and me in deep conversation with classmates. I had inherited these images from stories Aunt Barbara, Aunt Phyllis, Mom, and Dad had all told about their college years. I could imagine walking around a Harvard Square bustling with students, living in a co-op house, going to concerts and movies with friends. Most of all I looked forward to sitting in smoke-filled cafes or dorm rooms, talking about philosophy and literature and love.

Following family tradition, I applied to Radcliffe. Both Aunt Barbara and Aunt Phyllis, Mom's sister, had graduated from there in the mid-1940s. I also applied to Barnard, because it was in New York. That winter, the night before my interview at Radcliffe, I went out to dinner with Dad, Beverly, and my mother's youngest sister Lorraine. Afterward, we stopped at a bar for drinks. By 2 AM the three of them were in high spirits. I was underage and hadn't had any liquor, but I was certainly caught up in the revelry.

Suddenly Dad looked at the clock above the bar and whistled. "Lorraine! It's late, we might not make it to the bus!"

We piled into his Corvette and raced through the empty streets of New York to the Port Authority Bus Terminal. My interview would be at 2 PM in Cambridge. We reached Framingham, where Aunt Lorraine lived, with just enough time left to wash up, yank on suitable clothes, and dash off to Harvard.

I felt hung over from lack of sleep and couldn't feel any connection to the woman who was interviewing me. After the exciting evening I'd had with my Dad, she seemed incredibly stuffy in her two-piece suit, straight hair pulled back tightly in a ponytail. Her questions seemed dull and uninspiring, too: "Why do you want to go to Radcliffe? What do you think you'll get out of your education here?"

I had been eager to talk about my dual identity, and the cultural differences I had experienced growing up in Mexico. But she showed no interest in anything that was not American. In the end, my performance seemed decidedly uninspired, even to me. By the time I walked out of that room, I was sure I wouldn't get in, and I was right.

I was accepted at Barnard, however, and even though I was disappointed about the Radcliffe rejection, I felt happy to be staying in New York. Dad had wanted me to go to Harvard, though, and always felt guilty about that night out on the town, figuring he was responsible for the disappointing outcome. But I think, he might've also wanted me to stay in New York too, and that was why he'd acted so flippant about getting me to my big interview.

I entered Barnard in the Fall of '67. Before the first day of classes, Dad took me aside. "Now that you'll be in college, I want you to keep something in mind. I don't want you smoking pot until you're twenty-one."

I didn't understand why I had to wait so long.

"You have a fine mind that's still developing, and smoking pot before you're ready will only fuck it up. Take it from me, wait a few more years. You will have powerful experiences with marijuana. It can make your mind stronger or stunt your growth if you smoke it before your brain is ready."

I didn't mention I had already been smoking it that summer. "Sure, Dad," I said. Meaning, *Yeah, whatever.*

Like most of my friends, I smoked all through my freshman year. But I didn't like the lassitude that overtook me when I was stoned, so pot soon lost its allure. Eventually I would stop, smoking it only on rare occasions.

My first year at Barnard didn't work out quite as well I had imagined. Instead of living in a dorm, I had decided to room with two sophomore friends in a sixth-floor walkup on Amsterdam and 125th, bordering Harlem.

Bad choice. Not only was the New York of that era gray, dark, cold, dangerous, and unfriendly; I wasn't prepared for the shock of living on my own. I had never had to cook all my own meals, nor dealt with a roach-infested kitchen. Hauling bags of dirty laundry down the stairs and to the nearest Laundromat was also a new experience. At home, in Mexico, clean clothes were set on the bed for me to put away in my closet; I came to the table to eat meals that had already been cooked, and only washed dishes when asked. Managing the basics had never been my responsibility before.

Beside these domestic duties, I needed to study. My roommates spent a lot of time with their boyfriends, smoking pot and listening to music. I had been through a rough time that summer and still felt the loss of the baby. I was lonely. Again, just as I had when I was unhappy and thirteen, I gained ten pounds. And I dreamed of being home in Mexico. Sunny, cheerful, colorful, friendly Mexico. But this time my solution would turn out to be less successful than the party I'd thrown at my father's apartment in my teens.

This time I tried to fit in by doing what everyone else did. I smoked pot and cigarettes, and talked endlessly about how miserable I felt. I often went to the West End Bar, crammed with students, its atmosphere thick with smoke and heady conversations, just to nurse a two-hour cup of coffee. Instead of joining in, I merely sat back and observed. I also spent hours in the Lion's Den, Columbia's main cafeteria, waiting for someone, anyone I knew to appear. I went to the main library to study but couldn't concentrate. I began to feel that all the wonderful professors there were wasted on me.

Except for one: My freshman English teacher

Kate Millett was writing *Sexual Politics* at the time, a book that was to be fundamental in the Women's Liberation Movement. It was also an excoriation of my father's ideas on sexuality and gender. The first assignment Professor Millett gave us was an in-class analysis of a poem by Dylan Thomas. After reading it two or three times I gave up. I couldn't understand it, let alone write about it in a half hour. With the clock ticking away, I finally wrote a note:

> Dear Ms. Millett,
> I'm sorry. I don't understand the poem and have no idea what Dylan Thomas is trying to say. Perhaps you can help me.
> Susan Mailer

When she returned the essays, she asked me to stay for a few minutes after class.

"Susan, I think you were probably the only honest student in the class. It's a hard poem to understand and most didn't get it. Tell me more about yourself."

After that she took me under her wing. Over the course of that semester, we met several times to discuss my assignments. I grew fond of Kate and felt a bond had developed between us. She never mentioned my father, or the book she was writing.

Still, the turmoil of the previous three years had definitely left its mark. It was hard to get up in time for nine o'clock classes. When I did make it, I was either bored or immured in self-obsessed reveries. Why was I overweight again? Why wasn't I back in Mexico? Why were people so unfriendly in New York? Why didn't I have a boyfriend? But in Kate's class I tuned in again. She provided what I so badly needed back then: one-on-one attention. With considerable sweat, I finally earned a B minus in her course. Yet I was put on academic probation for the remainder of the year, having failed Introduction to Anthropology, which didn't catch my interest in the least. I also got a C minus in Biology, and something close to that in Russian language.

The following semester the student revolution exploded at Columbia. But in spite of it, or perhaps because of it, my grades went up.

~

It happened on a bright spring day in April 1968, when the trees were blooming, and the air fresh. I was walking across the campus to class when I noticed a large crowd of students sitting on the steps of Low Library, in the center of the main quadrangle. I forgot about class and went over to sit cross-legged on the grass with the rest.

Perched on the highest spot, next to the Alma Mater sculpture, Mark Rudd was speaking fervently into a mic. He wore khaki slacks and a short-sleeved shirt; a thick sweep of dark blond hair almost covered his eyebrows. He was laying out the six points which became the mantra of the Columbia uprising.

NO to the divided entrance of the Morningside Gym project.

NO to racism. NO to the war in Vietnam, and NO to ROTC recruitment on campus. NO to Lyndon Johnson's presidency. NO to the deals between the IDA (Institute for Defense Analyses) and Columbia University.

I listened intently to Mark's speech. Everyone around me was responding in some way: nodding, smiling, or yelling out "Yeah, right on!" It was contagious. I felt excited about something for the first time since I'd come to Barnard. Without much reflection, I was swept into the revolution.

I'd already been moderately interested in another Columbia student named John Jacobs, known as J.J., who also rose to fame during the protests. He wore a green army jacket and looked like a Jewish version of a Cuban guerrilla fighter, his blond beard and intense eyes framing a sculpted face. Before the protests began, we had met a few times; he talked and I listened. His shtick was the revolution, capitalism, imperialism, and communism. For me, pretty ho-hum. The same-o stuff I'd heard from Salvador all during my childhood. I soon grew bored. But when I saw him that day, standing next to Mark Rudd, my moderate interest transformed into a crush.

Beginning three days later, on April 26th, students occupied a total of five buildings. Including Mathematics Hall, to which the most radical protesters, Mark Rudd and J.J. among them, led the way. I, high on pheromones and idealism, followed them inside. In "The Math Commune," as it was christened, we organized into groups: kitchen duty, cleanup crew, communications committee, and those who gave lessons on Marx and Lenin. Meanwhile the leaders went in and out of various political meetings, deciding the future of the movement.

Once inside, I realized I better get some stuff for what might prove to be a long sojourn. I went back to my apartment and collected a sleeping bag, toothbrush, and a basic change of clothes. When I returned, I chose my section of the floor. To my surprise, when J.J. saw me there in the hall, he laid out a sleeping bag right next to mine. I was in heaven. Although he was swamped with important meetings, he was still making time to be with me.

On the third night of the occupation we heard rumors that city police would storm the campus and take us out by force. On the 30th of April, after all negotiations with the University authorities had ended in a stalemate, the President of Columbia University, Grayson Kirk, agreed to let the New York Police Department enter the campus. At 2 AM, the Tactical Police Force (TPF) entered the University grounds and proceeded to empty the five occupied buildings by force.

The protest had initially been sparked in part by the building of a new university gym. This part of Columbia's Morningside Heights expansion had pushed a number of Harlem residents out of their homes, so the new gym was soon dubbed "Gym Crow." When the cops came, black students who had taken Hamilton Hall feared police violence, and the university administration feared a riot might ensue, due to the high tension the building had provoked in the African American community. The students in Hamilton Hall finally consented to a peaceful exit and filed out, escorted by the cops.

In the math building the situation for white protestors was different. Our duty was to resist. First, we poured liquid soap on the entrance floor and the staircase that went up to the classrooms. Then we turned off the building's main power switch, so we were in complete darkness.

In the end, I don't think any of this made much of a difference. The TPF were undeterred.

I was on the third floor in a teacher's office with four comrades. We blocked the door with the desk and all the chairs we could find. We stood glued to the window as we followed the TPF's entrance into the building. Wood cracked and splintered as, below our floor, doors were axed open. Furniture thudded as it was thrown around.

And then the shouts: "Hell no, we won't go!" and "Pigs! Pigs!"

The police methodically proceeded up each floor, opening every room, until they finally reached ours. We sat on the floor, dead silent. I wondered what was going to happen to me. My heart was beating frantically.

With a loud bang, the door was kicked in. As it flew open I closed my eyes, crouching in a corner of the dark room, waiting for the blows to fall.

Police officers in full riot gear stormed in with flashlights. They grabbed us and pushed us out into the hall, then down the stairway which was lined with more cops, and out the building's main door. The guys in our group were roughed up somewhat, enough to scare us; the women were shoved and pushed. But that was all that happened, at least to us.

It was dawn, and outside the air was cold. We were roughly thrown into police vans where we sat and waited, listening to the commotion still raging around us. People screaming, the hard thump and fast rhythm of boots stomping the ground. As more students poured into the vans they told us the TPF were striking bystanders who had been watching the police operation. I later found out that these spectators were clubbed and kicked. By far the most violent display I heard about that night.

We were taken to the Tombs on Center Street. The officers on duty wrote down our names, fingerprinted everyone, and then led us to an already-crowded, dimly lit cell with a toilet in one corner. Several black sisters were already in the cell, but they didn't pay much attention when we walked in. There wasn't enough floor space, so we had to take turns sitting on the floor, while the rest stood. It felt as if there was an invisible line on the cell's floor, separating the African-American and the white protestors.

I crossed the invisible line. I wanted to know what had happened in Hamilton Hall. But the young woman I spoke to hardly looked at me, and she didn't answer my question. I was pissed at the time. To my mind, we'd all been in this together, but I didn't yet know there had been a split between the Afro-American Society students (SAS) and SDS, the other organization.

After that failed attempt at conversation, I turned to one of my white cellmates. I hadn't slept all night, but it didn't matter. I still needed to talk. "What do you think will happen to us?" I asked.

Apparently more experienced, she shrugged. "I don't think they'll do anything to us. They'll let us go, but we'll have a police record after this."

I was ignorant enough regarding such matters to blow off the whole idea of a record, not knowing or worrying about how it could affect my future.

~

At 11AM, after six hours in that crowded cell, we were taken to a large courtroom that looked a lot like the ones I had seen on TV. The black-robed judge told us in a formal tone, "Ladies, the University has dropped all charges against you. You must not get into trouble again. I can assure you, you will not be so lucky next time."

In spite of all the bluster, I felt relieved. I walked outside to Center Street, stood on the steps of the court house, breathed in the morning air and felt warm sun on my face.

Immediately, I called Dad. I was sure he'd be interested in my adventure. My version of his experience the year before on the steps of the Pentagon.

"Where've you been all week?" he asked.

"I was in the Columbia protests, in the math building, and just got out of jail."

"Susie! I'm proud of you. You'll have to tell me all about it."

Shortly after that, my father hosted a large gathering at his apartment. A sort of cocktail party for Mark Rudd and other celebrities from our revolution, to talk about the Cause. It seemed to go well, though I was quiet for the most part, feeling I had nothing much to contribute. I was trapped in a sensation that was to repeat itself many times in my life; the "flower on the wallpaper" syndrome. It was tough to realize that these guys, my fellow students and the leaders of the Columbia uprising, only knew me as Norman Mailer's daughter. And that he was the actual center of attention, the reason they'd come.

After they left Dad said, "I'm disappointed Sue. I thought these guys would be interesting, but they're a pain in the ass. Their rhetoric is unbearable, and their arrogance borders on stupidity!"

By that time, I had no adrenaline left. I was faced with the sad truth that I wasn't that interested in "The Revolution." I didn't see myself as a political activist and found the Marxist jargon repetitive and full of clichés. But I wasn't ready to let my father know that. Not quite yet. After all, this had been *my* revolution, my adventure. I wasn't willing to let him see I was disappointed, too.

No matter how disillusioned I felt afterward, at that moment the most important result of the Columbia uprising, for me, was that it made me feel I had finally arrived. I truly felt like a college student, at last.

A few years ago, a young man came to my home to interview me about the Columbia sit-ins in 1968. He was writing and collecting filmed documents of the protests for his doctoral thesis. He set up his camera in my living room. His first question was, "Why did you join the protests?"

Up until then I'd always thought I participated in the demonstrations because I believed in the political issues behind them. But I realized at that moment it wasn't quite so simple.

My participation in the movement had not been solely political. Yes, I was against the Vietnam War, and I loathed L.B.J. 1968 had already been convulsed by the assassinations of both Martin Luther King and Robert Kennedy. In Mexico, everyone I knew celebrated the Cuban Revolution. Che Guevara and Fidel Castro were my heroes. So, when I walked into Mathematics Hall, I felt I too was making history.

All of those ingredients, along with J.J., of course, got me involved in the protests and into that building. But what had *kept* me inside was the sense of belonging to a community. The shared experience of doing things together for a common purpose; cooking and cleaning and talking with comrades, in a year in which I had felt out of place and lonely. I also suspect those adventures were my way of getting a taste of my father's life; an existence that seemed exciting, with the movie-magic quality I'd imagined for myself when I was younger.

I started by telling the interviewer, "I was going out with this guy, John Jacobs, called J.J., and--"

He stopped me. "You went out with J.J.?"

"Yeah, why?"

"He was the most radical of the group. Did you know he was one of the founders of the Underground Weathermen?"

It was news to me. "Wow, I had no idea. We lost track of each other once we left the math building. I might've seen him again once or twice."

"He was on the FBI most wanted list and emigrated to Canada. You know, he died a few years ago," he told me.

I'd hardly thought of J.J. for almost thirty years, yet I felt sad. He had remained frozen in time for me. Still the young, handsome radical of the Columbia Revolution.

≈

In June of '68, I went back to Mexico for the summer and shed the extra ten pounds and more. I was happy and in one piece. Being with my mother and my brother Sal again soothed me. After a year on my own, I appreciated being home. All the tense exchanges between my mother and me during the previous three years had nearly convinced me she had stopped loving me, and that the feeling was mutual. But once I got home, I knew our rift was healing. We'd both changed. We could talk now without the ice crackling. The air between us was clear. It was marvelous to be home again.

CHAPTER 16

In the Editing Room

THAT SAME SUMMER, WHILE I WAS IN MEXICO, MY FATHER WAS BUSY with his third and most elaborate film experiment, *Maidstone*. He gathered a diverse group at a large estate in the Hamptons: actors, close friends, extended family, and five of his children. Plus Beverly and his ex-wives Adele and Jeanne. Also, his special friend, Carol Stevens.

Norman hired several film crews led by Richard Leacock, Nick Proferes, Jan Welt, and D. A. Pennebaker. The movie had no script, but the actors, numbering over fifty, were given a rough story line: A famous and disreputable film director, Norman T. Kingsley, played by Norman Mailer, is running for president. Simultaneously Kingsley is filming a new movie about a male whorehouse called The Cash Box. His half-brother Raoul, acted by Rip Torn, is envious and wants to take his place, but is also assigned to guard Kingsley.

Along with these bare-bones directions the cast was instructed to follow their instincts while the four camera teams chased them around the estate. Mailer told the players they would be "a bunch of forced existentialists."

Most of the action revolved around Kingsley and Raoul, who managed The Cash Box. There was a tense undercurrent between the brothers, and according to the skeletal script, a strong possibility one or the other would be killed at the culminating event, The Assassination Ball. But once filming reached the scene at the Ball, neither one made a move on the other. Thus, to everyone's disappointment, the projected assassination never occurred.

The next day, Beverly, who played Kingsley's wife, Norman, and my five siblings were all filmed walking down a hill, a bucolic setting with tree branches swaying in a mild breeze. Norman was in the lead, walking ahead of the rest. Suddenly, the camera caught Rip Torn running up behind Norman with a deranged look and a hammer in one hand. He sneaked up on Dad, jumped on his back, and hit his head with the hammer several times.

Blood spurted from of my father's scalp as he wrestled Rip-Raoul to the ground, biting his ear ferociously. As they rolled in the grass swearing at each other, Rip shouted several times, "You know I had to do it, you know it didn't make sense if I didn't. I had to kill Kingsley. Not Mailer. Kingsley had to die!"

My father yelled back, "Are you crazy! You hit my head! *My head!*"

Beverly rushed up and pounded Rip's back with her fists, screaming at the top of her lungs, "Get off him, you crazy cocksucker!"

The camera followed all this action, while my siblings could be heard off camera, crying, "Daddy! Daddy!" and "Oh God, he's hurt, is he going to die?"

My brothers and sisters remember it as one of the most terrifying experiences of their childhood.

When I got back to New York in early September, Dad took me to Leacock and Pennebaker's studio, and we went into the editing room. I sat down in the room, which was dark except for the small screen in front of us. Dad sat in the middle, me on one side and the editor on the other. They were editing a scene in which Kingsley tongue-kissed and fondled the breasts of a young blond actress.

I stared uneasily at the flickering screen, thinking, *Eew! I don't know if I want to watch this!* But I didn't say anything, just stayed put.

Dad was focused on the editorial work, telling his editor, "Let's see that again. I think we should take this frame out. Play it again. No. Not quite right. Again. Okay, that seems to be the right sequence."

It felt like the scene had been replayed endless times before they finally decided to move on. So I saw my father kissing the blonde over and over. I understood, because Dad had already explained it to me, that in this part the character Norman T. Kingsley was in the midst of casting female actors who would appear in the kinky sex scenes that took place in the whorehouse full of male prostitutes. But only if they passed the tongue test.

The problem was that the character Norman T. Kingsley obviously *was* my father. I thought of leaving, but at the same time I wanted to look hip and act cool. That made it hard to just say, "Enough Dad! Too much information, I'm leaving." Because then I knew he would say, "Sue, stop smelling your armpit, get over yourself. It's a character in a movie, not me."

Dad said this would be a learning experience for me. "Who knows, you might become a film director, or an editor." He was proud of his experiment in *cinema verité*. But watching those disturbing scenes made me feel sixteen again, and reminded me of the slow-motion shock I'd experienced when I read *An American Dream*. As with that novel, again I felt like an unwilling witness to my father's sexual fantasies. I was seeing something I shouldn't, like peeping through the keyhole of his bedroom door while he was having sex. There was a tightness in my shoulders. My chest felt constricted. By the time we left all I wanted was to get the hell out of that dark suffocating closet. So, I declined Norman's invitation for dinner and drinks afterward.

A week later Dad called again.

"Hey, Sue, we're editing an interesting scene tomorrow, and I'd like you to come. I think you'll enjoy this one better."

He noticed my uneasiness! I thought. I hesitated, then decided to go.

This time they were editing the hammer scene. He'd finally agreed it was needed as the climax, as Torn had insisted. After the experience of the previous week, I'd taken some time to prepare myself. When I went into the editing room I was actually feeling cool and collected; distanced from what I saw on the screen. Merely watching a movie. So, even though Rip Torn looked crazed and his face was twisted into a truly evil grin, I wasn't horrified. It didn't even occur to me how bizarre it was that my younger siblings had actually witnessed this bloody scene. I thought it was effective and discussed it calmly with my father. This time, I didn't let it touch me.

After that second visit, though, I didn't return. Dad couldn't understand why I wasn't more interested in his film work. He seemed disappointed. I don't think he had a clue about how I'd felt. Or if he had intuited anything about that, he didn't pay any attention. Common-sense boundaries were never my father's strength.

Many years later, I saw the complete film of *Maidstone* with my siblings, in Provincetown. Once again, I was fascinated and repelled, but for the first time I had enough emotional distance to see some value in Dad's experiment. People who for the most part were not actors, and did not even know each other well, had gathered at an estate in the country for a single weekend to act in a movie with no script and little direction. Nobody had known what would happen, or where the plot was heading. It could have ended in chaos. It could've turned out to be anything from a masterpiece to a joke. The project had stayed true to my father's conception of existential experiences: situations where the outcome is unknown.

Certainly, the bloody hammer scene was not something Dad, or anyone else, could have foreseen. That violent act had emerged from the interactions of the two main characters. A reenactment of the biblical myth, the Cain and Abel rivalry. When Rip Torn shouted, "Norman, you know I had to do this, it was the only solution, the movie didn't make sense without it," I agreed with him. But it had been a dangerous move, nonetheless. The movie could well have ended as a real-life Greek tragedy.

CHAPTER 17

Fair Weather Father

I RETURNED TO BARNARD IN THE FALL OF 1968 AND SIGNED UP FOR Plimpton Hall, a new dorm on Amsterdam and 118th Street. Each suite had five bedrooms, a full kitchen, and a small dining area. And best of all, no roaches. There I made friends I would keep for the rest of my time in Columbia, one of whom I still meet up with every time I'm in New York. In my sophomore year, I finally felt good about myself. I went on blind dates with guys from Princeton and Yale and had a great time. That year I met Eric, who would be my boyfriend during the remainder of my undergraduate years. I also figured out how to study; what to ignore in the mountains of required reading; how to concentrate on the essentials. I chose my courses well. Now I *was* sitting in smoke-filled bars discussing Marx, Freud and Wilhelm Reich with friends. And going to the Thalia Theater on Broadway to see Fellini, Antonioni, and Bergman films, or listening to Claudio Arrau at Lincoln Center.

In early May 1969, I woke in the middle of the night doubled over in pain. In the morning I called my grandmother, who took me to a specialist on the Upper West Side.

After he examined me, he said, "I'm sure you have gallstones, but we still have to take an X-ray. Before we do this, go downstairs to the cafeteria and ask for Joyce. Tell her the doctor has prescribed a gall-bladder breakfast."

I hadn't been eating at all. Even a sip of water brought on spasms. This cafeteria breakfast turned out to consist of eggs and bacon with toast and lots of butter, the worst ingredients for triggering a gall blad-der attack. Almost as soon as I began eating a grenade exploded in my stomach. In less than five minutes my gall bladder went into a severe spasm and I doubled up in pain. Grandma Fanny got me back upstairs to the doctor's office. He was now convinced of his diagnosis, so we took a cab to New York Hospital. I was to be operated on immediately.

Earlier that same year, my mother had moved back to the States. During her residency in Iowa five years before, she'd realized her time in Mexico was coming to a close. She'd reached a professional plateau. Besides earning considerably more in the States, she felt the work would be more satisfying. She also wanted to be in Massachusetts, near her family. In particular her parents, who were by then in their seventies. Only her relationship with Martin had been keeping her in Mexico. When he promised to follow her to the States, she took the leap.

Martin never made it, though. As it turned out he really wasn't happy about the move but had said nothing to that effect. Instead he stayed on in Mexico, eventually married, and had two kids of his own.

By the beginning of 1969, Mom was living with Sal in Worces-ter, Massachusetts and working at the State Psychiatric Hospital. She rushed down to New York as soon as she heard about my illness and was furious when she learned about the so-called gall-bladder breakfast. Being a doctor herself, she knew it was a sadistic, unnecessary attack on my body. She was with me during surgical prep, holding my hand while nurse inserted a naso-gastric tube. That procedure was almost worse than the spasms. I couldn't talk, could hardly swallow, and the plastic tube kept scratching my throat. It was a hostile alien invading my stomach through my nose.

Things did not feel much better when I woke from anesthesia. Added to the naso-gastric discomfort, my abdomen was swollen, I felt nauseated, and my whole body ached.

To make matters worse, my father and mother were both in the room. I don't remember if they were talking or silent, but even in a post-operative haze I could feel the unspoken hostility floating in the air like poison gas. A nurse came in to give me a shot of Demerol, an elixir that soothed my emotional distress as much as my physical pain. After that, every time my parents were together in the room, I'd ask for a shot to blur and soften their presence.

Grandma, Aunt Barbara, and Mom took turns visiting. Dad came almost every day of the week I was in the hospital, but he only remained for five to ten minutes. Which for him was more than enough. I think he probably felt both guilty for not seeing more of me, and also irritated at having to go there every day. Not to mention that he always hated hospitals. With his usual candor, he admitted to being a fair-weather father, and expected me to understand.

It didn't bother me. I was happy to be taken care of by the women in my life. And what a great team! Grandma Fanny brought goodies I could eat, like tapioca and rice pudding. Aunt Barbara brought me Kurt Vonnegut's novel *Slaughterhouse Five,* which had recently come out, and read me a chapter or two a day. Mom took charge, talking to doctors and arranging for a night nurse to come after she left in the evenings. Who needed Dad?

~

Eric and I had bought charter plane tickets to tour Europe that summer. We were supposed to leave at the end of May, but my father had decided to run for mayor again and wanted me to stay until the end of June to help him in the Democratic primary.

"Why me?" I saw my plans with my boyfriend evaporating.

"Because you'll be a great asset in Spanish Harlem."

"But I'm going to Europe with Eric. We already have our tickets and can't change them!" I sputtered.

"I'll pay for your new ticket," he said forcefully. "This is very important to me, and I think you might even be surprised. It could turn out to be an interesting experience. You'll go to Europe anyway, and meet up with Eric later."

I wasn't at all happy about this new, unwanted arrangement. Though I was mildly curious about Dad's quixotic runs for mayor, I resented his dragooning me into a new campaign I figured he'd surely lose. And I was sore that, as usual, Dad's needs and desires came first. I was also annoyed at myself for being such a wimp and not standing my ground. Traveling through Europe had long been another one of my dreams and flying there with Eric was part of that dream. Now I had to postpone it, then get there later, alone.

Once my participation in the campaign was decided, I had to look the part of a candidate's daughter. Beverly and I went to Fifth Avenue on a shopping trip. She bought herself some demure, ladylike suits, and got me a couple of Gucci mini-dresses that looked great. The first time I hit the campaign trail with Dad we stood in front of Macy's at the intersection of 34th Street and Seventh Avenue. He was addressing a crowd of about fifty, speaking through a hand microphone. Jimmy Breslin, running for councilman on the same ticket, was by his side.

Norman, Beverly and me during the campaign. 1969.

Beverly and I were standing slightly behind them and I immediately saw there wasn't much for the two of us to do except look pleasant and smile. Still at first, just as he'd said, I felt charged. The emotion was short lived, though. After the speech we walked east along 34th Street, shaking hands, while Dad repeated over and over, "I'm Norman Mailer and I'm running for mayor in the Democratic primaries. I'd appreciate your vote."

The man who was fond of saying "Once a philosopher, twice a pervert," kept repeating himself ad nauseam. *He must really want to be mayor of New York to do this*, I thought.

Every now and then someone would ask him a question or two, though most of the time they only shook hands and took one of the *Mailer for Mayor* or *51st State* campaign buttons. I trailed along, dazed, jostled by the crowd. Also irritated at the seeming futility of my role, for which I'd sacrificed my own plans. I'd hoped for something meatier, but in the end was just part of the scenery.

A few days later the three of us went to Spanish Harlem. We stood behind my father, while he outlined his platform. Then we walked the streets again, shaking hands. Everyone looked impressed to hear the candidate's daughter's perfect Spanish. At last, I had a role.

At the end of the week Dad said, "Hey kiddo, you might've gotten me a couple of votes there."

Nothing to sneer at, considering Herman Badillo, a Puerto Rican, was one of his opponents.

During the 1960s New York was in bad shape from the lack of public funds, high crime rates, pollution, and severe traffic congestion. In fact, the city seemed to be falling apart. Dad knew drastic change was needed, and his solution was a proposal to turn it into the 51st state. That way all the money the city generated would go back into it, instead of to Albany.

He also argued for strong community action, and for self-rule in each borough. Creative thinking was evident in many of his projects, including a farmer's market, and a light rail line running around the island. One of his most far-sighted ideas was for "Sweet Sunday," a once-a-month holiday from all but essential car and truck travel in Manhattan.

But I didn't really care about any of that. I was merely obeying orders, biding my time until I could split for Europe and begin my own adventure.

At the time most people wrote off the campaign as just another one of Norman Mailer's crazy, egotistical ideas. But he truly believed he had a fighting chance in the primaries. He stopped writing and put all his energy into the campaign. After the election he came in fourth out of five contenders, garnering only 41,000 votes.

He wasn't happy about losing, but certainly was relieved. In later years, he always said that if he had won, his career as a writer would've have been over. Still, in recompense, he would have had his hand "on the rump of history," as he characteristically put it.

CHAPTER 18

Summers in Maine

THE FOLLOWING SUMMER, IN 1970, I TOOK ANOTHER TRIP TO Europe. But first I went up to Maine for two weeks to spend some time with my father and siblings. We hadn't all been together since the summer of 1967, and on this occasion, for the first time, we would be staying there alone with Dad, no stepmother in charge. As an experiment, he was taking off a month from writing to be with us solo. A rare hiatus, one I thought was worth the trip up to Maine. He would be the one planning meals, distributing chores, and organizing activities from hiking to sailing. Aunt Barbara was to come for a week to help out, but we were basically on our own, with him at the helm.

The place we stayed, Mount Desert Island, was one of those New England enclaves for the American upper class. Most seasonal residents had spent their summers in the area for generations; playing golf and tennis, sailing and hiking, all of which were new activities for us. Dad had bought a small sailboat and lots of books on sailing, and joined the yacht club.

Once we were there, he created a summer routine.

Early on sailing mornings he marched into our rooms blowing an old bugle, rousting us from bed, his deep army-sergeant voice bellowing, "Drop your cocks, pick up your socks, and get out of your fart sacks, you bastards!"

On our first day out there were six kids, from age nineteen to four. After he'd assigned each of us a specific chore, we cast off. Only to immediately find ourselves stuck in the middle of the bay with no wind. On the dock, several yacht club members, expert sailors all, watched and shook their heads. My father was beyond exasperation. We *were* inept, of course. The younger siblings were frightened and wanted to get off the boat; Stephen had just turned four a few months earlier.

Frustrated, I asked, "Hey Dad, do you know what you're doing? Do you have *any* experience in sailing?"

He snapped, "Of course I know what I'm doing. I've done my research!"

From then on Danielle referred to us as the Polish Navy. It became a family joke. Undeterred by the failure of our maiden voyage, we kept going out on the boat twice a week.

Dad also insisted we take tennis lessons. He, of course, had no intention of learning the sport, much less getting out on a court. He had decided it would be good for our future prospects. A way of making friends and being accepted in "society." We didn't take him too seriously. After a few ill-fated lessons, we decided we would just have to get by on our good looks.

My father had rented Fortune Rock, a spacious modern house built by Wells Fargo heiress Clara Fargo Thomas. It had a breathtaking view of Somes Sound, the only fjord in North America. *The Hunt for Red October* would later be filmed in those waters. One slope of the island's Green Mountain ran right down to the water over which the house was perched. A ledge jutted out from the side of house into the fjord, and we used it as a diving board. The drop was scary, so we dared each other to jump into the ice-cold water. It was terrifying to "walk the plank," about eight feet above the water. Looking down gave us vertigo, but eventually everyone stepped up to the challenge.

As always, my father insisted it was healthy to face our fears, and in this instance, we all did.

Dad fell in love with Maine and continued to take the family for one month every summer over the next ten years. We were not allowed to bring friends because Dad wanted us to bond as a family. For him, though, the "solo" part of the experiment lasted only the first two weeks of that first month. He decided he'd had enough and asked for help. Carol Stevens, his now-official girlfriend and our stepmother-to-be, arrived the last week of that vacation.

After two weeks I had to depart for Europe, leaving my siblings to stay for the rest of the month. I left Maine shortly after Carol arrived and headed back to New York to board my flight.

Even though I only went once to stay in the Thomas house, the experience remained crystal clear. For years we talked about our summers in Maine, and I reminisced with my siblings as if I'd been with them every time. They would say, "Hey Sue, remember when we climbed Mount Katahdin and Dad forced us to cross the Knife's Edge?"

And every time they asked me, I answered, "Of course I do." And actually saw myself climbing up the trail with them. Those two weeks I spent with my family became engraved in my mind as "our summers in Maine."

CHAPTER 19

Town Bloody Hall

At the end of the summer of 1970, I got back from Europe and went over to see Dad. While I was there, with a sheepish grin he informed me Carol was pregnant. I would soon have another sibling, a seventh Mailer child.

Carol and Maggie, 1975.

I was stunned.

Not that I didn't like Carol. She was calm and soft-spoken, a nice change from Beverly, whose temper could rattle the china. And, as with previous wives, so far Carol had been on her best behavior. She had tried to get to know us, to maybe even like us. Obviously, she wanted to be accepted by Norman's children.

A few years later, Dad confessed he had actually met Carol first, even before he had encountered Beverly. The day before, to be precise. And that he had conducted an ongoing affair with Carol for years. When he told me this, I realized I did have a faint recollection of meeting her, briefly, when I was thirteen. She and Dad had appeared one day at the apartment in Brooklyn Heights. I don't recall how long they stayed, but later they had gone out together.

Now, it seemed it was her turn to be the official consort.

I accepted the change but then again, expected the impossible. I assumed Carol would slip into the role of Dad's wife, and *this* time, we would have a quiet stepmother instead of an angry one. Now that he and Beverly had split up, Dad was definitely more available. Relaxed and easier to approach. He seemed contented.

Now I can have some quality time with him, I thought.

I should've known better.

At twenty I was about to begin my last year of college. I had an adult life of my own now, but still desired my father's attention. When he and Beverly broke up, of course I knew there would be more women. There always were. But I hadn't imagined I would have to share him with even more siblings. The six of us already knew each other; we'd settled into a comfortable relationship.

I had been anticipating going on walks with my father. Having interesting conversations. I'd also assumed that Carol, who had a teen-age son from a previous marriage, would not be interested in more childbearing, so there wouldn't be any sudden post-partum personality changes. She would remain the friendly stepmother.

When Maggie's impending arrival was announced, I sizzled. All my suppressed resentment and jealousy, which had begun building back in Mexico with my brother Sal's birth in 1955, finally exploded. I'd learned to hide my feelings so well over the years, by now I almost didn't feel them. Once in a while I had gotten a twinge of anger, or felt competitive, but I'd squash these emotions as soon as they appeared. And on the rare occasions I'd expressed jealousy or envy towards one of my sisters, Dad would say, "Rise above it."

But this time I simply couldn't. I'd had it with the Mailer Baby Parade. "What! Are you kidding me?" I shouted. "You must be totally nuts!" And with that, I stormed out of the room.

After that blow-up I didn't call my father or see him and Carol for three months. Once in a while he'd phone me, but I was never very communicative. Finally, I calmed down enough to go out to lunch with him. Alone.

I'm sure Carol must've been surprised and hurt, but for the first time I didn't care how a stepmother might feel. In earlier years, I had always made my best effort to be pleasant; it was expected of me. Now I was old enough and enraged enough to let it all hang out. Later Aunt Barbara told me Dad had privately been tickled by my reaction because, he had told her, "It shows how much she loves me."

I'd had to express a jilted lover's reaction for my father to feel loved by me! At the same time, what he'd said opened a window. It hadn't ever occurred to me that he might feel insecure about my feelings towards him. Yes, there had always been a faint undercurrent of anger which made me sometimes act detached or indifferent. But wasn't it obvious I loved him? I realized now, for him, maybe not.

But my outburst created a rip in my relationship with Carol. I don't think we ever repaired what was torn that day. When Maggie arrived in March of 1971, I went to the hospital to get a look at my new baby sister. Carol and I exchanged pleasantries, and I congratulated her on the beautiful baby, but not much more was said between us.

A month later, on April 30, I went to Town Hall to view an important event, "A Dialogue on Women's Liberation," hosted by New York University and the Theatre for Ideas. The four women panelists were Germaine Greer, Diana Trilling, Jacqueline Ceballos, and Jill Johnston.

My father had been asked to be the moderator.

Danielle, Betsy, Aunt Barbara, Grandma, and I sat together near the stage, expectant and excited. Everything indicated it would be a memorable evening. Dad had already been flagged as the male chauvinist who had recently said on The Mike Douglas Show, "I don't hate women, but I think they should be kept in cages." An unfortunate choice of words, in an even worse attempt at humor. The Women's Movement was gaining momentum, and now his face was on their dartboard. With the considerable media coverage, we already knew this Town Hall would be a charged evening. But we certainly were not prepared for the pummeling Norman received that night.

A year before the Town Hall event, Kate Millett's book *Sexual Politics* had been published. It was an analysis of the novels and ideas of D. H. Lawrence, Henry Miller, and Norman Mailer, in which she argued that the literary trio's treatment of female characters was blatantly sexist. Though my father probably enjoyed being placed in the company of those writers, he was incensed by Millett's analysis. His response was to write a long essay, "The Prisoner of Sex," published first in *Harper's* Magazine. Before the Town Hall event took place, it had also come out as a book with the same title. By the time of this public dialogue, the Women's Liberation Movement had declared overt war on Norman Mailer.

Town Hall was packed. Susan Sontag, Betty Friedan, and other well-known feminists were in the audience. From the moment the evening began most women in the audience seemed ready to pounce on Norman. They hissed whenever he spoke, they booed and heckled. The men were notably silent. It was not a dialogue; they were out to draw blood and I felt overwhelmed by the energy they put into it.

At times, exasperated by the treatment he was getting, Norman deliberately provoked the audience. At others he tried to initiate what he considered an interesting discussion.

It was simply not possible.

Recently on YouTube I watched Pennebaker's film *Town Bloody Hall*, which documents that night. At the outset, Mailer turns to the audience and says, "Good evening, I'd like to welcome you to what might turn out to be an extraordinary evening." He then introduces Jill Johnston as "the master of free associational prose from the Village Voice."

Cheering erupts from the audience. Jill rambles through a range of topics, most of them dealing with gender and sexuality, for more than fifteen minutes. Norman says her time has run out, but she replies she wants to read a poem. Mailer insists she must respect the other speakers on the panel. Instead, she begins to recite her poem.

Norman says, "C'mon, Jill. Be a lady." Jill keeps reading. Norman looks irritated, and adds, "Jill you wrote your letter, now mail it."

Loud booing erupts from the crowd. A voice from the audience yells, "Hey, Norman! Feeling threatened 'cause you can't fuck her?"

He answers, "Hey cunty, I've been threatened all my life. If you don't believe me you can come up and try to take my mic." Jill looks unsure then; she smiles, her expression a question mark. Then a woman jumps onstage and starts making out with her. Another soon joins them, to cheering and laughter from the audience.

Norman says, "Hey, Jill. Either play with the team or take your marbles." Jill ignores him and continues making out with the two women. He proposes a vote. "Those who are in favor of letting Jill finish her poem, say Yea." A loud yea echoes through the hall. "Those not in favor, say Nay." A slightly louder nay is the result. "Jill, you lost by a squeak. Now I will introduce Diana Trilling from the podium."

Norman stands and with shoulders swaying, swaggers past Jill and the two women, who are still locked in a passionate, semi-comic embrace.

Finally, she and her entourage leave the stage, and Norman says, "I am pleased to introduce my good friend Diana Trilling, one of the best lady literary critics of our time."

Germaine Greer is quick to ridicule Diana and Norman, or anyone else who dares to disagree or question her ideas. She gets lots of laughs and cheers and is the audience's pretty baby. But Diana is having none of it. She turns to Germaine and says, "Eight times you referred to the

Oedipal family, saying that the family that rejects a child is the Oedipal family. If you are going to read Freud like that it treats him like a fool."

Germaine denies she said that, to which Diana answers, "I have the actual quotes." Germaine shoots back, "I do the same as you, I quote him where it suits me and don't where it doesn't." Diana replies, "No, I said that I take from him what suits me. I don't misquote him."

Laughter from the audience.

Looking unhappy with Diana's rebuttal, Germaine leans into the microphone and says, "One of the characteristics of the oppressed is that they fight among themselves."

"I don't feel that I am oppressed, and I can't let other women speak for me," Diana replies in a calm, self-possessed voice.

During the question-and-answer period, Susan Sontag is the first to raise her hand. The question is for Norman and Diana. "I don't know about you, Diana, but I find the way Norman speaks to women patronizing. I don't like being called a lady writer. Norman, you would never introduce James Baldwin as our foremost Negro writer."

The audience erupts in loud applause at that.

Norman says, "Susan, I will never use the word 'lady' in public again. What I meant was that she was the best in kind."

Now the booing is very loud. Diana says she would like to answer as well, since the question was addressed to both of them. "I don't like it either, Susan, and I recognize the point. But it has a quality. It's like saying a lady jumper, or a lady runner."

Then Cynthia Ozick asks a question. "Mr. Mailer, I've always wanted to ask you something. In *Advertisements for Myself*, you say a good novelist can do without anything but the remnant of his balls. I've been wondering, Mr. Mailer, what color ink do you dip your balls in?"

After peals of laughter die down, Norman replies, with an impish smile, "I would have to think about it, but my first guess would be yellow. Hey, I don't pretend to have never written an idiotic remark, and that's one of them."

A roar of laughter comes from the audience on my computer screen. His now sixty-year-old daughter smiles as she watches, a nod to his witty sense of self-deprecation, and to his courage.

Forty years earlier, in the audience of that Town Hall, I'd been devastated by the way my father was treated. I was also unable to fathom why he had put himself in the eye of that storm. Powerful, conflicting emotions washed through me; my loyalty to him clashing with my feminist sympathies. Even though he had invited the audience and the panelists to an open, civil discussion, his tone was provocative; it ended up sounding more like an invitation to a skirmish. His voice was tight, his shoulders tensed and ready for a swing, his demeanor on high alert. The audience was belligerent, too. They interrupted, hissed, and booed. It was a battle, and he stepped into it without hesitation.

He'd already explained his willingness to throw himself into the fray in *The Prisoner of Sex*, but I had not yet read it. Speaking of himself he had written: *To be the center of any situation was . . . the real marrow of his bone—better to expire as a devil in the fire than an angel in the wings.*

More than at any other time I could remember, at Town Hall there was no protective shield between the public and private personas of Norman Mailer. During most of my life I had tried to erect and maintain a barrier that kept those two aspects of my father's life separate. I had often seen him slip from one persona to another, and he had many. But it always left me uneasy. I much preferred the father of our family dinners; the sage counselor of our one-on-one talks. I needed the father. I tolerated the writer/character/provocateur.

In the past when I'd seen him speak in public it was usually in a more protected environment: a university, a lecture hall, a talk show on TV. I could sit in the audience, feel detached from the character Norman Mailer and just listen. But that night my private father merged with the very public Norman Mailer, the celebrity. He belonged to the audience. Yet he was also still my dad. I knew him, recognized him, and at the same time he was a stranger. I wanted to protect him from the rage whirling in the room, even while hating him for the demeaning and provocative comments he made about women.

That night in Town Hall, I too was swept into the storm. The one raging in the Town Hall venue, and the one taking place inside me.

When he said, "We must face the simple fact that maybe there's a profound reservoir of cowardliness in women that had them welcome this miserable slavish life," I thought, *Norman, stop! How can you say these things! Do you really believe what you're saying??"*

I was furious then, and felt he deserved all the heckling he got.

But next he'd say something I thought was well tempered, and I could agree with him. *Yes, Dad! This should be a dialogue. Do we think biology is destiny? Let's discuss this.* And then again, when the audience heckled, trying to drown out his voice, I'd feel protective. *Oh, God! I wish these women would just stop booing at Dad.* A few minutes later I'd feel an affinity with one of the women's positions; for example, Diana Trilling's calm critique of Norman's depiction of female characters. I also thought Germaine Greer made a few good points, even though to me she felt like a female Norman Mailer.

By the time the evening ended, I realized I didn't like my father much. I had also felt no kinship with those angry, aggressive women.

Even over forty years later, as I watched *Town Bloody Hall* on You-Tube, I felt the sting again. But it was less stressful now. I knew now which Norman Mailer I was watching. I could relax and observe the way he slipped their punches, then gave back some good jabs. Most important of all, I realized he was enjoying the fight. Not only that, he was both villain and the star of the evening! All the booing and the applause had made him the center of everyone's attention, "the devil in the fire."

Dad always said a boxer loves taking a good punch.

A year before he died, my 19-year-old daughter Antonia and I spent a pleasant afternoon with him in Brooklyn Heights. By then the old fighter was thin and frail. He drew each breath with effort. Laboring up the four flights to his apartment was an ordeal. Once he got there, he usually didn't venture out again until it was time to go back to Provincetown, where he lived most of the time from the mid-1990s on.

Antonia was studying at Hampshire, a left-wing college that prides itself on supporting freedom of sexual expression. As we chatted in the living room, looking out at the beautiful view of the East River and the New York Skyline, she asked, "Grandpa, is it true you once said that women were obedient little bitches?"

He smiled. "I was in Berkeley giving a lecture, back in the early 70s, and said a few things that riled up the women in the audience. They hissed at me. I said, 'Louder!' And they hissed louder. Then I looked over at the moderator and said, 'Obedient little bitches, aren't they?' "

The three of us cracked up.

Antonia knew she had a good story to take back to her friends. And for a few minutes, the old twinkle in Dad's eye returned.

CHAPTER 20

Rocky Mountain Crash

AFTER TOWN HALL, THE FAMILY WENT TO SOUTH LONDONDERRY, Vermont for the summer. My father rented a large, sprawling country house that came with five horses, and hired a young riding teacher. The highlights of my summer were learning to drive a car and to ride a horse. Bobbi, our funny, energetic 27-year-old housekeeper, took me out on country lanes in her Volkswagen Beetle until I learned the rules of the road. I got a Vermont license after the second attempt at the test.

Scott, the equestrian instructor, taught me how to properly sit and stay on a mount. By the middle of the summer I could ride a galloping horse without falling off, erasing my earlier trauma from the ill-fated outing in San Miguel Allende almost a decade earlier. Near the end of that summer, Danielle, Betsy, Bobbi, Kate, and I rode up into the Green Mountains to camp overnight. Scott taught us how to build a fire and care for the horses; then we watched shooting stars and cooked baked beans and franks for dinner.

We hardly ever saw Carol or the baby. Myrtle, who would be with our family for the next fifteen years, was Maggie's nurse and Carol's companion. As with the earlier babies, we had to be quiet around the house. Again, we had a sensitive infant sibling who needed a calm atmosphere, which was very hard to come by considering there were six older kids in the house. I suspect we were pretty tired of catering to babies, no matter how cute, so we simply went our own way, steering clear of Carol's and Maggie's room in the left wing.

My recollection of those two months is that, except for dinner, Carol rarely appeared, and except for a couple brief glimpses, we rarely saw Maggie. This strengthened our bond as siblings. Stephen could make believe he was the youngest for a few more precious months, while Bobbi, Danielle, Betsy, and I organized the housework, cooking, and food shopping.

We all went riding, taking turns on the best horse. Kate was already a good rider, thanks to Jeanne. Betsy and Michael were afraid of horses, so of course Dad made sure, with not-so-gentle coaxing, they learned enough to join us for long, leisurely rides in the Green Mountains. Even Grandma sat on a horse. Aunt Barbara came for a week, yet still we hardly ever saw Carol. I was relieved. This time I let my resentment have an inner voice, at least: *Another wife with post-partum depression*, I thought, and left it at that.

Grandma on a horse in Vermont, 1971.

~

I went out on a few dates with the riding teacher. Late one night I arrived back home to see Dad sitting in a rocking chair near the front door. He looked tired, but his tight-lipped expressions showed he was also upset.

"Hey Sue, where've you been?"

"Out with Scott, why?"

"Do you think this is a good time to get home?"

"What! What do you mean?" Was he really trying to be a protective father now, at this late date?

"I mean this is a bad example to set for your sisters," he growled.

I couldn't help smiling. *He* was giving me lessons on good examples! What he didn't say was that like any father he'd been concerned about me, and maybe unable to sleep until I was safely home.

Near the end of August Dad took me to the airport. I was wearing a Danskin top and bell-bottomed jeans. He put an arm around my waist and said, "You have a tiny waist. I used to wrap my fingers around Bea's waist. You remind me of your mother."

This time the reference was a compliment; a loving going-away gesture. In a few days I'd be heading off to Boulder to attend the University of Colorado's graduate school, in an Archeology/Anthropology PhD program. I was leaving behind my college boyfriend, Eric, and four years of university life in New York City. It had been the longest, most uninterrupted stretch of time I'd ever spent with my father and the rest of the Mailer family. But I was too excited at that moment about my new adventure to stop and feel what all these changes meant.

~

Boulder was certainly different from New York City. Everyone seemed beautiful, athletic, and blond. When I walked down the street strangers would stop to say hello and wish me a nice day. What a difference from Barnard and Columbia, where so many averted their gaze so as not to have to speak to anyone. No intellectual Woody Allen types here! Everyone hiked, swam, skied and played basketball. In Boulder football was considered a serious endeavor; the players were idols who got all the prettiest girls. At Columbia we had only gone to football games to enjoy the band and laugh at the players. We wouldn't have dreamed of belonging to a fraternity or a sorority. Yet here, it was the thing to do.

Soon I found a lovely small house to share with a couple grad students. And quickly found my niche with the chill and easy-going students and faculty of the Anthropology Department. The first year I skied and hiked and sometimes studied—life in Boulder felt like being on a long vacation. Sal, who was living in Worcester with our mother, was having a hard time adjusting to living in the States. I invited him to Boulder, thinking he'd enjoy the change. He was a natural athlete, so I took him skiing. After a couple of runs down the baby slopes we were off on the expert runs. A month later my sister Danielle arrived, and I took her on the same tour. By then, I was in love with Colorado and wanted to share it with all my siblings.

After I had been in Boulder for about a year, in October of 1972, I got a call from Dad. He'd been invited to speak at the University of Colorado. I was thrilled. The people who were organizing the event approached me to discuss some sort of social gathering after the conference. I told them I'd be happy to host it at my place.

However, when he got off the plane in Denver, Dad was not alone. As he approached, I saw he was with a young woman I'd never met, a brunette, slightly older and taller than me. He introduced Suzanne as his assistant, but I didn't buy it. What chutzpah! Even for Norman. Still, I put on the blandest face I could muster, led them out to the parking lot, and put their luggage into my new-old BMW.

As a graduation present Dad had given me two thousand dollars to buy a car. With the help of some automobile-savvy friends in Boulder, I settled on a seven-year old BMW model 1600 with a hundred thousand miles on it. I paid eighteen hundred dollars, which left just enough for insurance. I loved my car. It was certainly well travelled, but it had spunk, stuck to the road at high speed, and the steering was nervous and precise. A great vehicle for navigating mountain curves and icy streets, which was fundamental in Colorado. I drove it to Aspen, then cross country to New York and back, adding another ten thousand miles without so much as a sigh from the vehicle.

I proudly showed it off to my father. Then, with Dad in the front and Suzanne in back, I started off for Boulder, feeling nervous about how he might be evaluating my driving skills. Dad was actually a terrible driver himself, although I wasn't aware of that. As he did with almost every other skill or activity, my father gave off the *aura* of an expert driver. So, I was on tenterhooks, waiting for his verdict. Surprisingly, as we proceeded, he made no comment about my driving.

That would come later.

We decided to go out for an early dinner so we would not be late for his 7:30 appearance. I took them to a quaint place tucked away in the mountains, about twenty minutes from Boulder. I was still trying to swallow my shock over Suzanne coming along. What about Carol? We might not be best buddies, but Dad had put me in the uncomfortable role of an accomplice to adultery. A part I had not chosen to play. I'd always assumed he secretly had affairs, but now he was throwing one of his girlfriends in my face. *Why bring her on this trip, anyhow? Could this new* development *be a serious relationship?* Very upset, I was unable to stop ruminating.

We had cocktails, then wine with dinner, which certainly helped my mood. The alcohol created a pleasant buzz and relaxed me. Soon I stopped worrying about Carol. Dad, for his part, was engaging. He told Suzanne with obvious pride about how tough I had been as a kid, going into detail about taking me to the bullfight, the old *angelitos* road-trip anecdote, even the "Poor man, his woman left and took the dishes" story.

Then, slightly tipsy, but still believing myself to be in control, I got behind the wheel to drive us back to Boulder. The winding mountain road had a sharp drop to the right, and a sheer rocky face to the left. Again, Dad was in the passenger seat next to me, Suzanne in the back.

It was already seven, and we had to be back on campus by seven-thirty, so perhaps I was driving faster than I should've. Certainly my reflexes were muddled.

At that moment, Dad decided to give me a driving lesson. "Sue, when you're driving on a narrow, winding road you should . . ."

Annoyed, I turned my head to look at him, inadvertently moving the steering wheel sharply in his direction as well. The same direction as the drop.

The high-strung car immediately veered toward the ravine, so I jerked the wheel left to compensate. But too fast, and with too much energy. The car did an about face and smashed into the mountainside. I felt the jolt in my neck and through the rest of my body.

A few seconds later I heard my father say, "Woohoo! Susie, are you ok? Suzanne?"

Yes, we were all fine, no breaks or bruises, just shaken up. But the car was totaled. We decided to leave it there and stood at the side of the road, hoping someone would give us a ride. The first car that passed us stopped, backed up, and took us straight to the University.

We arrived at the theater a few minutes late, and rushed backstage to get Dad ready to go on. Then, Suzanne and I took our seats. After what had happened on the mountain I was distracted, though, and couldn't listen to most of his speech. I later heard it was pretty good, which wasn't a surprise, since Norman was always energized by danger.

Later, at the party at my house, I acted hyper, speaking loudly and laughing too much. The accident was the main conversation piece. We were in the midst of quite a merry gathering when a police car pulled into the driveway. Two big uniformed officers knocked on our door, and someone opened it.

"Does Susan Mailer live here?" one policeman asked.

I rushed over. "Yes, officer. Here I am."

"Are you the owner of a 1965 BMW?" he asked, and read the license plate number from a notepad.

"Yes, that's my car."

"Are you aware it's been in an accident and is now sitting abandoned on Arapahoe Mountain Road?"

I explained what had happened and why we'd had left it there. They didn't act sympathetic. I was nervous, wondering if I'd broken the law, not knowing what would happen next.

Dad came up then, a glass in each hand. "Officers, I thought you might enjoy a drink."

"Thanks very much, but we're on duty. We could accept a Coke."

After that their attitude improved. They said I had to have the car towed tomorrow, at the very latest, then stayed for close to an hour talking to the rest of the guests.

The next day I had my poor old BMW towed to a garage, only to find out my insurance had expired the week before. To get it back in working condition would cost at least a thousand dollars. So, after much deliberation I sadly sold it to the garage for $450.

I was heartbroken to lose my beloved car. I blamed Dad for the crash, and at the same time felt ashamed I hadn't been up to the test. I wanted him to say something to make me feel better. I also wanted him to offer to pay for the repairs, but that never seemed to cross his mind. Most of all, I was still angry and upset he'd brought Suzanne with him. Once again, he had disappointed me by putting me in a situation in which I believed I had to act nice, when what I really wanted to do was say, "Go fuck yourself!"

As usual, I didn't dwell on the anger. Instead I transformed his trip to Boulder, and the accident, into a funny anecdote to tell friends at parties.

But the real effects of the crash lay dormant within me. A sleeper, waiting to be awakened.

~

Not long afterward I left graduate school. I'd finally realized the kind of work it took to earn a PhD. I'd have to write many papers and do loads of research, and I didn't see myself staying in academia for the rest of my life. For some time, I had been considering going to medical school. It seemed a good and practical profession. I wanted to become a psychiatrist, like my mother. So, soon after Dad's visit, I signed up for pre-med courses.

I quickly found out I didn't understand calculus at all. It was a mysterious, abstract language to which I didn't have the key. To make matters worse, I wasn't the least bit interested in organic chemistry or physics. Except for that first depressing year at Barnard, I had always done well academically. So not being able to understand calculus was a huge blow to the ego.

I crashed again, this time emotionally.

First, I couldn't sleep, and started having a couple of drinks in the evening. That relaxed me enough to nod off, but I would wake at 4 AM feeling confused and anxious about my future. Med school was clearly out of the picture. I was out of wind, with no projects looming on the horizon.

I knew I was depressed. This terrible heaviness had hung over me before, only this time it was much worse. I drove to Denver to see a psychiatrist a friend had recommended.

I walked into her neat office, sat down, and began to cry. I told her about my father and Suzanne, my wrecked car, the failed attempt to go to medical school, and my drinking at night. She listened, and I felt understood. Then she prescribed antidepressants.

"I don't approve of them. I'm not sure what they'll do to my mind." Out of the mouth of Norman Mailer.

The doctor looked at me seriously. "So, you think drinking yourself to sleep will be better for your mind?"

She had a point, but I didn't budge. Instead I got a job waitressing at a bar in town. I went out with friends. I drank and partied, trying to brighten the darkness with excitement.

A couple months later I took a trip to Mexico to attend Carina's wedding. I would end up staying there for seven years.

CHAPTER 21

Sleeper Cell

LESS THAN A WEEK AFTER I ATTENDED MY FRIEND CARINA'S WEDDING, I met Manuel at a party. Even though I was not physically attracted to him at first, the intensity of his feelings seduced me. He was a good talker, and very smart. We enjoyed dancing and going to bars; before long we were out together almost every night.

Nothing important waited for me back in Boulder. I decided to stay in Mexico, and soon moved in with Manuel.

One of his favorite spots was a decaying cabaret; a dive bar, really. One of many in downtown Mexico City that had probably never seen better days. It was dimly lit, crowded with small round tables, and had a good dance floor off to one side. The patrons were mostly single men who went to pick up women. These were dressed in provocative miniskirts and tall stilettos, and wore lots of makeup. Their hair was usually dyed in shades of blond or red, and teased to make them look taller. What they lacked in beauty they made up in high spirits, while hanging around the bar waiting for customers to approach. After each dance the women ordered a round of drinks. The more a customer drank, the higher the cut she would get later from the bartender.

I'd never been in such a place before, yet it seemed oddly familiar. I could easily imagine Dad and Salvador at the bar, joking with the ladies. I could just as easily see my mother dancing, drinking, and becoming the women's confidante. As I soon did.

Manuel and I went there often with a group of friends. We met Margarita and Elsa, who liked to stop at our table on their breaks and have a drink with us. I was curious about them, eager to hear about their line of work. They didn't have sex with most of their customers; mainly they danced with them and encouraged them to drink a lot. Once in a while, if they were especially turned on by a man, or at least very well paid, they might spend the night with him.

In the 1970s bars in Mexico City closed at 2 AM. When the lights went out in the dance hall, we walked over to an afterhours bar that was camouflaged as a *salon familiar*, a family restaurant. As long as there was no sign out front with the word *bar* or *cabaret* on it, and the police got their cut of the proceeds, a joint could keep its doors open 24/7.

We'd order a bottle of rum, several Cokes, sliced lemons, a bucket of ice, and spicy snacks. Sometimes we danced until dawn. I'd manage to get couple of hours sleep, then shower, have breakfast, and go to work. Often, that same night after I got off, Manuel and I would go out again for another round of dancing and drinking. I felt like a character in a movie my parents had produced and directed.

But the fun didn't last. Soon Manuel and I were fighting. He was jealous about my previous relationships and kept questioning me. He wanted all the details. If I answered, he'd get furious. If I didn't, he'd get paranoid, step up the pressure, and claim I was holding back something important.

Our good times together dwindled. At the same time the drinking and our fights escalated. We were spiraling into a dark place. Even though the scene was all too familiar, I couldn't let go. I knew I had to leave Manuel, but at the same time felt a force pulling me back, not allowing me to escape. It felt like falling into quicksand. I kept sinking.

I love him, I'd tell myself. *He's so smart and interesting. He can be so sweet. Who cares if we fight? I don't need a normal relationship.*

But underneath the rationalizing, I felt ashamed of myself. My closest friends kept asking, "What the hell are you doing with this guy? He's bad news!"

And I knew they were right.

One day, after a horrendous row, I kicked him out of my apartment and threw away all his stuff. His clothes went into the garbage, his records and his books I gave to local schools. Soon no visible traces of him were left in the apartment.

He came by a few times and tried to mend things between us. But I turned him away, hung up when he called, and finally over coffee told him I never wanted to see him again. By then I knew I would never let myself drift into that emotional sewer again. Whatever romantic fantasies I had ever cherished about the glamorous-looking lives my parents had led in the 1950s and 60s, I was also well aware of the grand finale. Norman and Adele's.

I didn't want that. I had finally woken up.

Instead I rekindled my old friendships and made a serious effort to get a good job. I also stopped drinking, except for an occasional glass of wine.

Those first few months in Mexico I had worked as an English teacher in a Berlitz-type institute. After the break with Manuel, I decided I needed a change of career. I swallowed my pride and for the first time ever enlisted my father's help to get work.

He called his friend, the writer Carlos Fuentes, who invited me to tea at his house in San Angel the following day.

I arrived in the late afternoon. His housekeeper showed me into a beautifully decorated living room. On the walls hung paintings by Tamayo, Jose Luis Cuevas, Jose Coronel, and other famous Mexican painters. The fine art, the rare Mexican crafts, and Pre-Colombian figures combined perfectly with sleek modern furniture.

Fuentes came out to greet me impeccably dressed in a shirt and sweater, khaki pants, and comfortable-looking moccasins with no socks. He was tall, very handsome and friendly.

I was totally impressed.

First, we spoke in English, then switched to Spanish. He asked after my father and told me how much he admired Norman. He also asked what I was doing in Mexico, and how I came to speak such excellent Spanish. I explained about my geographically-divided childhood.

He listened, then graciously said, "We are kindred souls. My father was a diplomat, so I grew up in many places. Argentina, New York, and Europe."

By this time, I was floating on a cloud.

Then he posed the question. "So, Susan, Norman said you were looking for work. What would you like to do?"

"Oh, I don't know. Something interesting," I said carelessly, as if I were totally laid back about the issue. When in fact I felt desperate.

"Would you be interested in working for Televisa?"

Work for Televisa? Only the largest television network in Mexico! I thought. Still trying to sound cool, I murmured, "Of course, but in what capacity?"

Right then Fuentes picked up the phone and called Emilio Azcarraga, the owner and CEO of the company.

The next day I was ushered into an elegant office and greeted by one of Azcarraga's business partners. He offered me a position as public relations liaison and associate producer for *Encuentro,* a cultural program that was just about to go on the air. The plan was to invite important figures in the cultural scene like Borges, Sabato, and yes, Norman Mailer. So, you could say I fell into their laps. It was a relationship of mutual convenience.

When my father was invited to appear on the program, once again he showed up with Suzanne. I wanted it to be a memorable visit, yet I was still resentful of her presence. It colored all the choices I made.

Before they arrived I searched for the perfect hotel, something old and grand like The Plaza in New York, only in the heart of Mexico City. The Hotel Cortez looked great from the outside and its courtyard was charming. But I failed to check out the rooms. They turned out to be slightly run down, and the noise level from the street was considerable.

Televisa also paid for them to spend three days in a resort. Instead of the usual five-star tourist attractions, I thought Dad might enjoy visiting a real Mexican pueblo by the sea. I decided on Puerto Escondido in Oaxaca, because even though I'd never been there, I had heard about it for many years. And it might have been a good choice for my friends and me, but as a special place to take my sophisticated, worldly father it turned out to be a disappointment. Back then, in 1973, Puerto Escondido was a hippie town; its one presentable hotel had bad air conditioning. There was very little to do beside sitting on a beach chair under the *palapas* with a drink.

That could have made it a good opportunity to have a long talk with Dad. But with Suzanne in the picture, I didn't feel like we could take off and leave her alone. So instead of relaxing and enjoying the beach, I felt stressed and uneasy. I kept observing them, especially my father, trying to figure out if he actually liked Puerto Escondido. I worried I had screwed up a golden chance to show him the wonderful Mexico I so loved.

All things considered, he and Suzanne took the side trip with good humor. No complaints, no harsh remarks. The problem was in my head.

After three days, the beach trip came to an end and we returned to Mexico City. As soon as we arrived, we received an invitation to meet the President of Mexico, Luis Echeverria.

At the appointed hour a black limo car with tinted glass came to the hotel to take us to Los Pinos, the president's residence. We arrived in Chapultepec, and drove down Calle Lira, where two guards stood at the entrance to the place. The car went past them and down the road that led to the big house. We were met at the top of the grand steps by Echeverría's chief of staff and a couple government ministers, who escorted us to an informal living room. Its large windows overlooked a garden and also gave a panoramic view of Chapultepec Park. The room was decorated with exquisite Mexican arts and crafts. Two large couches faced each other, with comfortable armchairs positioned on both sides.

We sat and chatted about the weather, the beach, Oaxaca, and Norman's impressions of Mexico. Echeverria arrived a few minutes later and after a round of introductions I acted as the official translator.

We sat facing each other. My father, Suzanne, and I on one sofa and the President on the other. His minister and chief of staff took the side chairs.

That day I was inspired. In good form. The conversation flowed in an easy stream of Spanish-English-Spanish-English. From me! Who was always uneasy about translating, and had always felt at a loss for the correct word. My father's pleased expression said he was proud of me. And everyone else looked impressed too. I don't remember many details of their conversation. Echeverría asked Dad what he had thought of *Encuentro,* and the Argentine writer Sabato. They also discussed Latin American literature, and though Dad was pretty ignorant on the subject, he'd read Borges and Garcia Marquez, and was of course friendly with Fuentes. All of which probably made him seem well informed.

Echeverria gave my father a beautifully handcrafted chest from Olinala, Oaxaca. Then we posed for the official photograph, and the meeting was over.

As we were walking out, one of the president's collaborators, a young man who was also the head of a government-owned publishing company, asked me, "Why don't you leave Televisa and come to work with us at *Fondo de Cultura Económica.*"

"I'll think about it and let you know later," I answered, playing hard to get.

Actually, I was tickled by the offer. I felt reasonable happy in Televisa, but I didn't see much future in my job. Also, working there required a rather demanding dress code, working the social scene, and often going out for dinner and drinks. The routine was getting old. On the other hand, there was something appealing about working for a publishing company, probably due to my lifelong kinship with books. And *Fondo de Cultura Económica* was very well known throughout Latin America.

I quit Televisa, and a week later I sat in the publisher's office, listening to the terms of my contract.

A few months later, I met Marco.

Official Photo of Echeverria, Norman and me.1973.

Marco had the romantic aura of the political refugee. He had arrived in Mexico in 1974 from Chile, via Amsterdam, five months after Pinochet's military coup. An economist, he had lived in Paris with his wife and oldest child during the late 1960s. When he returned to Chile in 1970, he worked for Allende's government as head of foreign trade at the Central Bank of Chile. The day after the coup, his name appeared on the military's wanted list. Instead of turning himself in, he asked for asylum at the Dutch Embassy and remained there for three months. Once his safe-conduct papers arrived, he flew to Amsterdam, where he lived for another three months. He arrived in Mexico in May and was offered a job at *Fondo de Cultura Económica*, in the same building where I would soon be working.

For months we were simply friends. During that time, we had many conversations over coffee. Until one day it dawned on us that perhaps there was something more than a collegial friendship between us. He had recently separated from his wife, and with three small children was having a hard time of it. He missed them and fretted about his absence harming them.

I had no qualms about entering an intimate relationship with a still-married man who had just separated from his wife. My parents' track record of separation, divorce, and jumping immediately into new relationships, had made that seem natural. But for Marco it wasn't as easy. He came from a large, traditional Sephardic Turkish family. His parents had nine children, and a good, long-term marriage. Divorce, consequently, was a hard decision, and it took him a while to come to terms with the idea.

CHAPTER 22

The Last Wife

I MET BARBARA DAVIS NORRIS, SOON TO BECOME NORRIS CHURCH Mailer, in the late fall of 1975. A little earlier Dad had told me he and Carol were separating and he was no longer with Suzanne. "I want you to meet a friend, someone special," he said.

And I thought, *Oh no. Not another girlfriend.*

The family met at Aunt Barbara's for dinner. All of my father's children were present, including Maggie, who was then four.

A very tall redhead with a page boy haircut, wearing a white wool short dress, walked in. Barbara Norris was just beginning a career as a fashion model, so she'd been at a photo shoot and was late.

When my father asked about it, she said, "Wilhelmina was very nice. She wanted me to try a different hair style, so she sent me to the agency's stylist. I had no choice. But I just don't know if I like this haircut. What do you think, Norman?"

Throughout the evening she kept looking at her reflection in the dark window of the living room, moving her head, trying to find her best angle.

The family at Aunt Barbara's apartment the day I met Norris. 1975. In back:
Norris, Dad, Grandma, Stephen and Michael. Sitting: Al, Aunt Barbara.
Floor: Kate, Peter, Maggie, Betsy and Danielle. I took the photo.

She also asked each one of us what we thought of the cut. "Norman, do you prefer my hair short or long? What about you, Danielle? Barbara, do you think this short dress is becoming? My legs are so long, I look like a grasshopper."

I remembered one of Dad's favorite phrases, *You wrote your letter, now mail it.* I made no comment, just silently listened to all of this, with a faint smirk.

Barbara was indeed a beauty, and just twenty-five. My age. I thought she was too young to be Dad's type, but by then I had to admit I hardly knew for sure what his type was. He had married and had affairs with women who were closer to his age. But then, judging from Suzanne, who was only about three years older than me, he also liked younger women. Yet Barbara was far too young for my comfort zone. I was not going to help her join the family. I definitely did not want some six-foot-tall-in-heels Southern Belle as the new stepmother.

From Arkansas, she had a noticeable Southern accent, did not appear to be an intellectual, and seemed overly concerned with her looks. Dad was playing Pygmalion to her Eliza Doolittle: commenting on her attire, telling her how to get a photo shoot at the agency, and what kind of attitude to strike to make a powerful impression. He even suggested she change her name to Norris Church because it sounded more sophisticated than Barbara Davis. I stared at him, thinking, *But Norris is her ex-husband's last name, and Church is Carol's stage name!*

I could not quite believe what I was seeing and hearing. I figured he would tire of her soon enough.

Barbara was eager to please, attentive to all of us, and clearly hoped she and I could become friends. I had no interest in yet another relationship with another one of Dad's girlfriends. But when she said, "Why don't we go shopping soon?"

Dad jumped in with, "Sounds like a good idea to me."

I wasn't quick enough to come up with an excuse.

A few days later Barbara and I went to Bloomingdale's, to buy me an outfit for a cocktail party the three of us were going to the following evening. Everything she tried on looked fantastic. Nothing I chose fit. What made the outing truly painful was Barbara's attempt to be nice by picking out a few outfits for me to try on. All of them had been designed for six-foot slender model types like herself.

I felt my "ugly self" was on full display in that fitting room. I couldn't figure out if she was being nice, or nasty, or simply didn't *see* me. I was petite, only 5' 2". If she had only taken the trouble to actually look at me, she might have noticed that the outfits she chose were obviously not meant for someone like me.

Barbara walked out of the store with a beautiful black-velvet jump suit. I left empty-handed. By that time I was in a funk and just wanted to go home. But we'd already agreed to go see the new film *Saturday Night Fever*. So we headed to the theater. I thought the movie was fluffy, unimportant, and full of clichés. Barbara loved it.

She kept trying, though. On the walk to the subway, afterward, she confided in me about her problems with Norman.

Really? I thought. *Do I need to listen to this?*

"He wants me to be a successful model but won't let me go to Europe for shoots. It's so frustrating 'cause I don't want to fight with him, but Wilhelmina, my agent, says if I don't do as she says, I'll never make it. What would you do, Sue?"

Oh please, spare me your tough decisions.

I said in a definitive tone, "I wouldn't be with someone like Dad."

She blinked as if surprised, and in that honey-flavored voice exclaimed, "Oh, Sue, don't be mean! Your opinion is important to me. Really!"

Her eagerness to be my friend finally punctured my armor. Granted, I had good reason to be annoyed at my father for once again putting me in this awkward situation. I was also jealous of her drop-dead gorgeous looks. But it wasn't easy to keep up the smart-ass attitude. At heart, I was a pushover.

Barbara, like most beautiful women, was aware of the effect she had on men and the envy she provoked in other women. She was smart, cultivating a soft, friendly, caring personality that actually was quite appealing. It won me over to her side.

But being Barbara's friend was no easy task. She now went by the name Norris Church, as Dad had suggested. And when five-feet-two me walked down the New York streets beside a five-foot-ten fashion model in six-inch stiletto heels, all eyes went to her. I became invisible. I tried to practice a form of Zen, a letting-go of the ego. I would look straight ahead and convince myself I didn't care. Or at least pretend I didn't notice.

When we went to cocktail parties with my father, people politely shook my hand, then immediately turned to Norris and Dad. If someone did happen to strike up a conversation with me, their roving eye was usually looking for the glamorous and beautiful Norris.

I sort of got used to this, but it never stopped being painful. And it was always the case, except at one memorable party.

It was a fund-raiser for Ted Kennedy, who was running for senator again. I noticed Dad making his way to the candidate, so I grabbed his arm; Barbara was already on the other one. After introductions, Kennedy asked me politely, "What do you do, Susan?"

Norris Glam photo, 1976.

Before I knew it, we were deep in conversation about Chile. I told him about my exiled Chilean boyfriend back in Mexico. About the coup and the military dictatorship.

He nodded somberly. "I'm working hard in Washington to help uncover the U.S intervention in Chile. We've managed to get a good group of people on our Chile Desk."

He was about to go into more detail when he was summoned by

an aide and went off to make his speech. I could see from the corner of one eye that Dad was beaming, proud of me, while Norris looked ruffled. Kennedy had paid no attention to her.

But what came later was even more surprising. Once he finished his speech, Kennedy managed to make his way back over to me, shaking all the outstretched hands in his path. Then he resumed where we had left off. "Let's see. I was telling you about the Chile desk in Washington...."

We talked for another few minutes, until it was time for him to leave. He shook my hand and said, "Susan, if you're ever in Washington for some time, please consider the idea of working for us."

This time, when I turned back to Dad and Norris, it was me who was beaming.

But that was definitely an exception. Usually, going to parties with them was a source of escalating anxiety. I would first obsess about what to wear, what to do with my hair, what I would say at the party. Then my father would invariably have something critical to say about my outfit, usually suggesting I should take some hints from Norris. Eventually, I not only stopped going to such affairs with them, I actively avoided social events with the rich and famous altogether.

Every New Year's Day Aunt Barbara and Al, her husband, threw a party that had become a tradition among their many friends and relatives. It began around 1 PM and lasted late into the evening. Marco arrived from Mexico just before the 1976 party, and after settling into the Warwick Hotel, we dressed to go to Aunt Barbara's. He wore a blue suit, which set off his gray hair and unruly curls. He looked terrific. Though Marco barely spoke English, he turned this to his advantage by conversing in French. And he was a hit! This thirty-five-year-old Chilean political refugee who seemed incredibly self-possessed impressed everyone there, including my father. All the women at the party suddenly rediscovered their rusty high school French. They kept congratulating me on my great catch. By then I was already sure Marco was The One. This party had only set it in bold print.

Later in the evening Dad winked at me, as if to say: *He's OK!*

∿

When we went out for our next "one-on-one" dinner, Dad asked what I thought of Norris, adding, "I think this is a serious relationship. It won't be easy, though, because she left her son Matthew back in Arkansas."

He was concerned she might not get used to New York. There were other considerations: his writing, the busy engagement schedule, his own seven kids. All of these important pieces to fit into a complex puzzle. But he had high hopes for Norris.

"You know, I think she has a good chance to make it here," he concluded. "If all this works out, I have a feeling we could be together for a long time."

I suspect no one ever imagined that "a long time" would turn out to be thirty-two years.

CHAPTER 23

How Can Someone
So Smart Be So Stupid?

IN THE LATE SEVENTIES, I RECEIVED A LETTER FROM DAD, IN WHICH he wrote:

> I have some ideas about the psyche that might interest you, so next time you come to New York let's set some time aside for a real discussion.

At the time I was working on a master's degree in clinical psychology at the University of Mexico. I knew he'd always been interested in psychoanalysis, albeit in a critical way, so I assumed he wanted to discuss Freud's ideas.

We sat down in the living room of his apartment in Brooklyn Heights on a cold winter day in 1978. I was nervous, but also excited by the idea of being treated as his equal; of discussing important matters with him. It felt like a special occasion. I already had an image of the two of us locked in a profound *tête-à-tête*.

A tape recorder sat before us on the coffee table.

"What's this for?" I asked.

"I thought I'd tape our conversation. Some interesting stuff might come out of it that I can use in something I'm writing."

Talk about pressure. My God, now I really had to be smart.

He added, I suppose to make me feel better, "You might be nervous at first, but soon you'll forget we're taping this. You'll see."

Dad opened the dialogue. "How much do you know of these ideas of mine, what we are going to talk about tonight? You know, about the notion that the normal situation of the psyche is not that it is the possessor of one soul, but rather that it is a house which encloses two souls who live in a relation to each other that's analogous to marriage."

Immediately Freud flew out the window, as did my other ideas about the sort of conversation I would be having with my father, concerning psychoanalysis.

What! Soul in the psyche? What the hell is he talking about?

By then I'd heard his theory of the two personalities in the psyche, but the word 'soul' unsettled me. I was, and have been for most of my life, a non-believer. So, the idea of a psychoanalytic discussion using the concept of a soul did not sit well with my own psyche. But that wasn't the only problem. Dad had started off with a bang, and it would be hard to keep up. I could only hope once in a while I'd be able to say something that would catch his interest, and thus add to the conversation an idea or two of my own.

I was anxious, of course, and as usually happened when I felt nervous, Spanish words popped into my head instead of English ones. To hide my distress I stalled, using phrases like, "How can I say it?" or "How can I explain it?"

Dad was nothing if not a brilliant speaker and he turned his rhetorical powers full force on me. Next to his performance, my ideas seemed basic and unbearably simplistic. I was twenty-eight but sounded like a twelve-year-old.

What's more, we were at cross purposes. He wanted a philosophical discussion about the nature of the psyche, while I was eager to engage him in a dialogue about Freud. I couldn't switch gears quickly enough, so I tried to hold my ground and talk about concepts I understood.

Soon, however, the conversation evolved into a Norman Mailer monologue. Pretty close to a disaster for my ego.

Recently I re-read the transcript of that taped conversation. I could hear even on the written page his slightly irritated tone, forceful and impatient, which at the time only added to my discomfort. I was on guard, entirely focused on rebutting him. I'd sought, and failed, to find quick, smart answers. On the other hand, he was so intent on elaborating his ideas to a captive audience—me—he didn't notice how upset and pathetic I felt.

It wasn't a conversation, it was a one-sided debate. And of course, I lost.

There were some bright exceptions to my general feeling of malaise. At one point we discussed the process of conception and chromosomes.

Dad said, "You're speaking of one committee meeting another committee. I'm speaking of one entity meeting another entity. We don't have to argue over this. I don't have to say there are no chromosomes. All I have to say is that when you say the word 'chromosome,' you don't say any more than you did before you knew the word 'chromosome.' You should stop thinking about it because you don't know a damn thing about chromosomes."

He was engaging in his usual debating technique, which consisted of expressing apparently interesting concepts in such a forceful tone it left no room for discussion. He then cut off any coherent rebuttal with judgmental phrases that implied the other person was ignorant on whatever topic had just been introduced. Chromosomes, for example.

My mind was stuck on one word he had used: *entity*. I couldn't stop thinking, *What the hell does he mean by entity?* But when I heard him bluster, "…you don't know a damn thing about chromosomes," that pissed me off.

I lamely replied, "Yeah, so you're right. As usual."

My attempt at a jab was too weak. He ignored it and went on to elaborate on chromosomes for another ten minutes, only to veer off and delve into a theory about the egg and the sperm. His hypothesis was that the female egg had the power to choose what sperm it wanted.

"I don't know about that," I said.

"Are you going to say the egg has *no* such power? That it's there as some passive blob of femininity, incapable of making up its own mind? Is that in accord with your own experience?"

"I don't know if it has a mind."

"Do you have a mind?"

"*I* do. I don't know if the *egg* does."

"Why do you ascribe more power to your mind than to your egg, when your egg has more importance—will determine the future of your life more than your mind, or at least equal to it? The child you have is going to determine far more about your life than yourself."

"I'm not so sure about that either."

"Well, it may not be true at all. But at the very least will you admit that it's a little frightening to ascribe no intelligence whatsoever to your egg—no power to choose?"

"I think you need a stronger argument."

"You think *I* need a stronger argument?"

"I think you do. Something stronger than, 'Don't you think it's a little frightening not to ascribe more power to your egg.' I'm willing to ascribe *no* power to my egg. I'm okay with the thought that this little sperm comes up and gets in. And that's it."

Yes! That felt good. But it didn't last long. I still had to fight my way uphill another few miles.

Our dialogue had two parts. During the first, with the exception of a few moments like the one I just described, I felt stupid. Verbally inept, and in the company of an intellectual bully who'd cornered an easy mark.

During the second half, our conversation gradually did turn to Freud, and his concepts of femininity, castration, and power—the irony of which was not lost on me, considering I felt castrated and powerless at that moment.

But by then I had given up. I wasn't trying to prove anything and had stopped caring that my father was taking up at least 85% of our so-called exchange. I interjected a few more short sentences, some good, some pretty bad—while he spoke in full paragraphs, almost stream-of-consciousness elaborations.

I'd thought Dad had wanted this conversation to be an intellectual exercise. I knew he wanted me to think quickly, to debate intelligently. His tactics, however, made me feel slow and out of breath—I was a petite runner trying to keep up with someone with long legs in a one-hundred-yard dash. After a while I gave up trying to debate at all. It was easier to fall into step, agreeing when it was expected, or asking a question when I sensed he wanted to expand further on a theory. My way out was with one-liners, which he enjoyed, especially when they caught him off guard.

This had always been my version of our encounter. Up until recently.

Every time I remembered that old conversation, I'd had the uncanny sensation my father was talking to me as if I were someone else; that he was trying hard to get something out of me which I simply couldn't deliver. Why had he been so vehement? Who was he trying to impress?

When *The Selected Letters of Norman Mailer*, edited by Michael Lennon, was published in 2014, I learned that in the mid-1950s, when Dad was in his early thirties, he'd had a close friend named Robert Lindner. Dr. Lindner was a psychoanalyst and author of several psychology books, including *Rebel Without a Cause* and *The Fifty-Minute Hour*, two of the most successful. Both my father and Dr. Lindner were rebels and kindred souls. Together they'd questioned the turn American psychoanalysis had taken toward conventional values. Their correspondence had included a lively discussion on Freud, Marxism, sex, language, and philosophy which was evidently stimulating for both.

During this time, in early 1954, my father had kept a journal in which he recorded his experiences with marijuana and the psychological depths he discovered when he was high on weed. Really a manuscript of 250 single-spaced pages, which he called *Lipton's*, since in those days weed was sometimes referred to as 'tea'. In this experiment, Robert Lindner became his intellectual companion and at times, his informal therapist. Over a four-month period, my father kept this journal and

Robert Lindner.

mailed the carbon copies to Robert, who read the pages and discussed them with him. Sometimes by phone, other times by mail, and many times in person, either in Baltimore, where Lindner lived, or in New York.

My father stopped writing *Lipton's* in the spring of 1955 and went back to revising *The Deer Park*. He stuck the journal in a folder and stashed it in his files. Yet the insights he'd had and recorded during this time were seminal for the themes he developed in his writing over the rest of his life. Cancer, the saint and the psychopath, the rhythm of words, and bisexuality are among the many topics he touched on in the journal. His endlessly reprinted essay, "The White Negro," also came out of it, as well as from his discussions with Lindner.

Their relationship continued for another year until Lindner died of heart failure in February 1956 at the age of 41. My father was just 33. It was a profound loss for him.

While I read the journal and his letters to Lindner, I thought of our failed attempt several decades earlier. Had my father, perhaps without realizing it, wanted to reenact his past experiences with Robert with me, a future psychoanalyst? My initial fantasy of the two of us in deep conversation was not that different from the dialogue that comes through in those old letters. But *our* conversation was doomed to fail because I was his daughter, not his psychoanalyst friend. And he was no longer that thirty-two-year-old trying to discover the secrets of the psyche.

One of the sad results of our experiment was that, from that moment on, I shied away from intellectual dialogues with my father. Every time I was in town Dad would take me out to lunch or dinner. On those occasions, which were always important to me, we'd talk about the family, Marco and the kids, myself, what Dad was working on. But we never again made a serious attempt to discuss his philosophical concepts. Or mine, for that matter.

Toward the end of his life my father suggested we have another conversation about the psyche. I shook my head. "Once was enough, Dad."

He sighed. "Yeah, I read the transcript the other day. I was awful, I'm sorry. That's why I'd like to do it again, this time better."

But it was too late for a retake; he died a year later. Now it strikes me as a missed opportunity. By then I was wiser, more knowledgeable, and could've remained calm and self-assured, able to think about what he had to say, and how best to respond. I might've even had some ideas of my own to capture the interest of the 33-year-old Norman Mailer, who was still searching for answers.

CHAPTER 24

Dancing Leaves

A FEW MONTHS LATER, DAD AND NORRIS VISITED US IN MEXICO for a few days. Marco and I picked them up at the airport and drove straight to Cuernavaca, to escape the big-city air pollution. We'd rented a pleasant house with a large garden and a small swimming pool in one of the old neighborhoods. On the way Norris told me she was upset. Matthew, her young son from her first marriage and our ninth Mailer sibling, and my baby brother John were both being cared for during this trip by relatives in Arkansas. But John was just over a year old, and they'd never been separated before.

"He cried when we left, and so did I," she said.

Norman, acting as the cold and practical father, said she shouldn't make a big deal out of it. "John is my eighth child, I know about these things."

But Norris didn't look convinced.

Not having children of my own yet, I wasn't much help. But something did stir in me. I knew, even if I didn't actually remember, what it felt like to be left with Grandma while your parents went off somewhere.

We got lost on the winding, circular roads of the old section of Cuernavaca. When we finally found the house, we dropped our luggage on the bedroom floors, and went to El Centro for lunch. Rick Stratton, an old friend of my father's, joined us there. After the meal, the two of them went off to another table to discuss something privately, while Norris, Marco, and I took a side trip to the market near the Palacio de Cortez, to check out the local arts and crafts.

After dinner the next night we smoked a joint, although Norris declined. Next door a party was in full swing, blasting salsa, mambo, rock n'roll, and more salsa. The loud music beckoned Norris and me. We walked to the corner of the garden closest to where the party was roaring and crouched in the bushes to watch. As we were leaving, she noticed something strange about one of the plants in our garden border. Tall and green, with large thick leaves, it was swaying to the rhythm of the music. Or so it appeared. We looked at each other and exclaimed in unison, "No, this is not possible!"

At first, I thought it must be an aftereffect of the pot. Then I remembered Norris hadn't smoked any, and she'd been the first to notice the dancing leaves.

"Let's walk back to the house, and check it again in a few minutes," I said.

Five minutes later we returned, and lo and behold, the partying plant was still undulating to the salsa. And now it wasn't just that one, but a whole row, all moving rhythmically and in unison—I swear!—to the music.

Astonished, we called Norman and Marco to come out. "You have to see this!" we insisted.

They did, and were not impressed. The men thought it had to be a coincidence: the sound waves from the music, or perhaps there really was a breeze, and we just hadn't noticed.

We went inside for a bit. But soon Norris and I headed back to our corner, to watch the plants enjoying themselves. The dancing leaves kept swaying to the beat. Each time the music stopped, they stood still again.

The men were never convinced, or at least never admitted to it. But Norris and I were captivated; true believers. The experience became another turning point in our relationship. Sure, it might have been a coincidence, a breeze, or a sound wave vibrating the air. Anything's possible. But Norris and I were sure those plants had danced *for us.*

The next day their visit came to an end. We drove to the airport—so they could go back to the States, and pick up Matthew and baby John from temporary exile in Arkansas.

Me with John eight months old. 1978.

CHAPTER 25

The Engagement Party

By 1979, Marco and I had been together for more than three years. His kids were now living in Chile with their mother, and the year before, he had been permitted to return to the country, as well. We thought it might be time to consider moving there as well, at least for a while. But first, we decided to get married.

As soon as I informed my parents, a quiet struggle broke out. My mother wanted her sisters, close cousins, and aunts and uncles at the event. Grandma felt the same about her side of the family. Dad thought all the details about planning a wedding a huge bore and didn't want to get involved. Instead he offered the apartment in Brooklyn Heights as a venue and let the rest of us iron out the details.

Marco and I also wanted to invite our friends from Mexico, and his brothers and sisters, who all lived in Chile. I planned to include the few friends I still had in New York, as well. All too quickly the wedding had turned into a big production, something neither of us wanted. In addition, Mom and Dad were already sending nastygrams to each other through me. The idea of having them in the same room at this event was not a notion I cherished.

For a while Marco and I considered simply having the wedding in Mexico, but this was before destination weddings were a thing. We figured it would be too burdensome for everyone in the U.S. and in Chile. So, we postponed the whole affair. Then Dad offered to simply throw a party for us, a big engagement bash, to which he would invite his friends and acquaintances. We agreed and I invited my own friends in New York as well.

Norris and Dad's secretary Judith were actually organizing the event, so everything seemed to be under control. But the big issue for me, as usual, was what to wear. Norris would obviously look stunning in some incredible outfit. I couldn't compete with that, even at my own engagement party, so I settled for *chic:* a black silk blouse with a sexy V-neckline, a red Italian crude silk tube skirt, black suede heels, and a touch of makeup.

Marco and I arrived early to help with the preparations. All the lights in the apartment were turned on, giving it a festive air. A coat rack had been set up on the third floor, and the street door was left open to let in the constant flow of people. A punk band livened the party, and there was a great spread on the dining room table: an assortment of cold cuts, all kinds of cheeses, crackers, and bread, Aunt Barbara's famous paté, a smoked ham, and a beautiful platter of fruit. The bar was set up on the kitchen counter with a bartender behind it.

After climbing up four flights of stairs, breathless guests were greeted at the apartment's entrance by my father and me and Marco, who stood next to me. Norris was by turns at Dad's side, and busy overseeing the bar and the food.

Aside from my family and relatives, I'd never seen most of the people who shook my hand and wished me well, but I smiled at everyone and thanked them for their good wishes.

I was just beginning to wonder how much longer I could stand in my heels when Woody Allen appeared, escorted by two tall women. I pumped his hand with a big smile and gushed, "I'm so happy you could make it! And thrilled to meet you! I enjoy your movies so much."

He looked uncomfortable, even slightly embarrassed. I could tell he wanted to move on but, at the same time, he seemed reluctant to enter the next room, which was swarming with people. After he'd gone inside, I obsessed about my gushy, totally uncool display. I was rescued from my embarrassment by more arrivals, more handshakes and good wishes. I was hoping John Lennon and Yoko would make an appearance. The year before I'd met them at a book party for my father and had actually had an interesting conversation with Lennon, while Yoko smiled beside him and remained silent. But my father told me they were out of town.

Finally, someone I knew well appeared making his way up the stairs. It was José Torres and his wife Ramona. José gave me the usual bear hug, smothering me against his huge, hard prizefighter's body. Then he turned to Marco, shook his hand and gave him a hug, slapping his back, Latin style, and said, *"Así que te la llevas, cabrón."*

Many of Dad's well-known old friends came: the Trillings, Steven Marcus, Dan and Rhoda Wolf, Barbara Probst Solomon. I spotted Kurt Vonnegut sitting on the sofa and sauntered over to introduce myself. I did my best to interact with as many guests as possible and worked hard at circulating.

The gathering at the apartment was quite an event. The trouble was, it had nothing to do with the kind of engagement party I'd actually wanted. Instead it felt like one of Dad's notorious bashes, a Norman Mailer affair, only this time the excuse to throw it was his oldest daughter's engagement. I felt let down and frustrated with myself for not enjoying it more. I wanted to feel grateful, but actually felt disappointed. And I knew that I was partly responsible for that feeling. I had stepped off and let other people handle the details, choosing not to participate during the planning. I hadn't really taken the time to think about what kind of party I wanted. Or if I did really want one. I was too dazzled by the idea Dad had presented; excited about the fact that he actually wanted to celebrate us. So I had left it all in Norris's hands. And now there was no room to complain, even to myself.

After the party Marco and I were more certain than ever that we wanted a simple wedding. We flew to Chile a few weeks later. And on a late summer day in the Southern Hemisphere, in late March we walked over to the office of the Justice of the Peace and got married.

That night one of Marco's sisters threw a barbecue for the family. But my father and mother, my grandmother, Aunt Barbara, all my siblings, my friends? None of them were there.

At the time I had thought nothing of going to another country to get married, without a single known friend or relative in attendance. In fact, I felt the choice reflected the independent image I had of myself. The next day I called my parents and informed them we were officially united. Almost everyone congratulated us. Only my mother was upset. She hadn't been invited to our engagement party in New York, either, so she was unhappy she hadn't had a chance to celebrate us and our union. But at that moment I was oblivious to the pain I had caused her.

Marco and me. 1980.

Part III

CHAPTER 26

What is Norman Mailer's Daughter Doing in Chile?

I'D ALREADY VISITED CHILE ONCE, IN 1978, TWO YEARS BEFORE WE got married. I had expected to see military police and tanks on the streets of Santiago. Instead, I was welcomed at the baggage claim area by some lovely young women dressed up in *huasa elegante* costumes who were dancing the *cueca* with male partners. Once the music stopped they offered us, the weary passengers who had flown all night, a pisco sour and an empanada.

This was in mid-September, close to Independence Day, so the airport was decorated with Chilean flags. I drank the pisco, ate the empanada, and passed through customs; my documents were received by smiling customs officers. Outside immigration Marco was waiting. This was an important trip for me in many ways—not just my first visit with his large extended family, but also, more importantly, the first time I would meet his children.

As soon as I stepped out of the terminal, I noticed the air in Santiago had a distinctly different smell. I couldn't pinpoint what it was, precisely, until I realized the exhaust fumes here were far less pungent than in Mexico City. That, together with the crisp mountain air, made me realize I had definitively arrived in another country.

On our drive into the city we passed through several poor neighborhoods, actual slums. As we reached the center of town and the main artery in Santiago, La Alameda, I noticed old, gray, dusty buildings on either side of the street were punctuated by a few grand French-style mansions, one of which was the Universidad de Chile. We also drove past La Moneda, the presidential palace; it was still being repaired.

The first time I'd ever laid eyes on La Moneda was as an image on a television screen. The date was September 11, 1973, the day a military coup overthrew Allende's socialist government. I was in Mexico, watching as planes flew over the palace and bombed it. Later that afternoon, still riveted to the screen, I saw four Chilean generals, all sitting in a row. Commander of the Air Force, General Leigh; Commander of the Armed Forces, General Augusto Pinochet, wearing dark glasses; Head of Police, General Cesar Mendoza; and the Navy Commander, General Toribio Merino.

"We will remove the Marxist cancer that has had this country under siege," said Air Force Commander Leigh. "*Extirparemos el Cáncer Marxista.*" A premonitory glimpse of the murder and repression that was to follow.

For me, as for most of Latin America's progressive youth, Salvador Allende was a revered icon. As the first socialist President to be democratically elected in Latin America, he was a symbol of the "new socialism" to come. The coup and his death were a shock that left many, including me, in a state of anxiety and disbelief.

That had all happened five years before my arrival, and the country was still very much under military rule. But everywhere cheerful street vendors were selling Chilean flags and multicolored balloons. Music in the streets created a festive air. I saw no soldiers and hardly any police. All of this, of course, was a façade, like a scene from *The Truman Show*.

We arrived at the home of Salvador, Marco's older brother. Here the snow-capped, blue-and-pink-mineral-streaked Andes made an impressive backdrop. It was early spring in the Southern Hemisphere, so the flowering shrubs and trees were bursting with colors. The characteristic aroma of *jazmin* from Salvador's garden filtered through the open windows to settle in the living and dining rooms. Marco's family welcomed me with open arms and a table set with all the delicacies of the Chilean coast: clams, *machas, erizos, locos,* fried fish and rice cooked in the Sephardic style, and many salads. Also, more pisco sour and some Chilean wine. The first dessert was *Chirimoya Alegre,* which is the *chirimoya* fruit soaked in orange juice; for the second dessert, an assortment of pastries. Altogether a feast for the eyes as well as the palate.

The Colodro clan had nine brothers and sisters, just like the Mailers, though all from one set of parents. Marco was the youngest brother, while Salvador, our host, was the oldest. Along with so many siblings and their spouses, Salvador's three teenage children were present. After lunch a stream of adolescent nieces and nephews also arrived. In the evening we went out with Marco's kids: Max, 11; Daniela, 7; and Ivan, 5 years old. They were quiet, but seemed curious about their father's girlfriend. Even though I usually felt stiff and awkward around kids, I tried my best to charm them, remembering all the times I'd been in the same situation, only in the child's place.

I returned to Chile in 1980, when we moved there from Mexico City and got married. We were convinced by then it was important for us to live near Marco's kids. He also felt he needed closure with the failed experience of Allende's government, and the trauma of the coup.

And me? I was ready for a change, but didn't really consider all the pros and cons of moving so far away, and to a country under martial rule, to boot. Actually, I thought of it as a new adventure. Besides, I figured we could simply move back if we didn't like living there.

We bought a small white house in the foothills of the Andes, perched on half an acre of land. The high ceiling and large windows framed the magnificent mountains. We bought the place at the end of summer, so we didn't consider mundane issues such as heating and insulation. Those problems would make themselves evident later, with the chilling onset of winter. We didn't have a phone, either, since no lines were available in the area at the time. Yet it all seemed lovely and bucolic; just perfect.

The feeling was short-lived, once it hit me just how far away I was from everyone, literally at the end of the world. And then I felt incredibly lonely.

The country which had seemed so cheerful and bright on that first trip turned out to be gray and depressing. Soon, so was I. For one thing, there was little for me to do, so I took long walks with Hamlet, a beautiful Siberian husky we'd brought from Mexico. After crossing several valleys, we'd reach a small farmhouse that sold almonds and jam. I'd chat for a while with the farmer, then walk back. By that time half my day was over. Only a few more hours to go before Marco arrived home from work. Or sometimes after our walk I'd go to Mary's, my sister-in-law, for lunch. We would settle into an afternoon of Brazilian soap operas, both lying on her bed, watching the onscreen drama.

Yes, we were definitely at the very end of the world. The Big Dipper was upside down in the southern skies. And the seasons had reversed for me: it was hot, so very hot, during the Christmas season. Most of my life I'd spent that holiday with the Mailer clan, so I was used to the New York City holiday scene: the frosty winter air, the amazing, animated Fifth Avenue holiday window displays, followed by lots of presents and an early dinner at Dad's apartment in Brooklyn.

Marco's family didn't celebrate Christmas, though; they were Jewish. Of course, so was I—but an assimilated New-York type of Jew who'd celebrated a secular holiday all her life, with plenty of gift shopping, Christmas carols, eggnog, and snow. That first December in Chile I felt disoriented. I was seven months pregnant, without any friends or my own family. On Christmas Day the temperature hit 90 degrees.

Memories of Mexico were also a constant ache. I walked through the streets of Santiago feeling lost; everything reminded me I had no history in this city. Some afternoons I'd see teenagers leaving school and recall my friends at Secundaria Albert Einstein. In Mexico, so many streets, corners, or neighborhoods held childhood memories or had exciting adolescent experiences attached to them. Now I yearned for those days and my old friends. I hungered for the scent of cilantro and avocado, of fried *carnitas* and fresh corn tortillas. I missed everything from the colonial landscape to the pre-Colombian presence. I pined for bold Mexican colors: shocking fuchsia, golden yellows, indigo blue, bright reds, deep purple, turquoise, and deep greens.

Chile was unremittingly, depressingly gray, with an unspoken threat hanging in the air. That first year we noticed a white Peugeot always parked right outside our house. At first, we paid little attention. But seeing it out there day after day, always in the same place, finally took its toll. We figured it was the CNI; the secret service called *Central Nacional de Inteligencia,* doing surveillance on Marco, since he'd only recently returned and was still considered a possible "enemy of the state." The CNI obviously *wanted* us to know they were watching, and I was spooked. Sometimes I'd wonder what would happen if they took him away. We didn't have a phone, lived in the foothills, far from the rest of the family, and we didn't know our neighbors. Marco instructed me on what to do and where to go if they did come one night.

They always came at night, he said.

For the first time in my life I didn't feel secure in my own home. I walked around with a knot ever-present in my stomach. Many times during the day I'd catch myself turning around to look behind me. Just in case.

Chile also had a curfew. By 1 AM everyone had to be home, or at least indoors, unless you wanted to be picked up by the police and put in jail. When we went out to dinner everyone spoke in low tones, almost whispers, so as not to be overheard. Except, of course, if one was pro-Pinochet; then there was nothing to fear. I could always tell who was in favor of the government, because they acted as if they were the Masters of the Universe.

Finally, I made a couple friends, Memu and her husband Juan. But he died of cancer just a year later, adding to the overall darkness of life in the country.

Around this time I was introduced to a psychoanalyst who worked in the psychiatric hospital. He invited me to attend the Thursday clinical meetings he chaired, and to work pro bono in the hospital's halfway house. Slowly, I began to stitch together a network. Most of the young psychiatrists and psychologists had been students during Allende's government, and most were anti-Pinochet. Their jokes and easy-going style, the neighborhoods where they lived, the schools they had attended, all these small bytes of information told me something about them and their politics.

I was beginning to understand the codes.

Living under an authoritarian government scribed the boundaries between friend and foe very clearly. One could always recognize who was on your team. There was an underground culture not visible in the mainstream of Santiago's everyday life, but noticeable to those who were aware of it. Marco and I were part of that culture. Many of our friends, like my husband, had left Chile and then come back, while others had remained after the coup.

I learned many years later that a few of our acquaintances were in the country incognito and involved in underground activities. We felt like comrades united against the government, even though not all of us actively worked against Pinochet. During those years we felt we were all resisting the regime in one way or another, and this helped us to develop a bond and feel part of an important movement.

My daughter Valentina was born in February, almost a year after we moved to Chile. Mom, her partner Ed, my brother Sal and his new wife Patty all came to Chile to meet the baby. They stayed for a week, except for my mother, who remained for almost a month to share with me the intense beginning of motherhood.

Dad and Norris were scheduled to arrive a week after Mom left, but I asked them to hold off for a few months. I didn't feel up to entertaining, even though they insisted they just wanted to meet Valentina and see where we lived. They said they'd be easy guests, but I knew better. I couldn't imagine the two of them just hanging out with me and a new baby. Dad always enjoyed stimulation, lots of interaction with other people. He also needed a place to work, and my house was too small to provide him with a separate writing room.

Norris was gregarious; she liked going out and shopping. And I'd have to, at the very least, throw a small party to introduce them to the Colodro family. Thinking smart and keeping up with Dad and Norris was beyond me at the moment. My head was full of diapers, burps, and breast-feeding. I wanted to be alone with my baby and my husband.

When I told them not to come just yet, they were disappointed. I could tell by Dad's tone he also felt hurt. But I was relieved.

In April I went to the American Embassy to register Valentina and get her American passport. Marco had to renew his tourist visa, so he came along and filled out paperwork for that. Seven days later, he told me his visa had been rejected. He wanted me to go with him to find out what had happened.

We entered the grand old mansion that housed the American Embassy near Parque Forestal, and asked to see the consul. A young man came out and explained that Marco's visa had actually been rejected higher up. When I asked why, he said Marco was considered persona non grata because he'd been exiled.

"But he's obviously not exiled any more. If the Chilean government doesn't think he's dangerous, why should the American government?" I asked.

"Please fill out this questionnaire," was all the embassy guy said.

The questionnaire requested Marco's name, my name, my nationality, my mother's name, my father's name, my place of birth, and Marco's place of birth. We dutifully filled in all the blanks.

"Okay," said the young man. "I'll take this to the consul." He glanced over the form. "It says here your father is Norman Mailer. *The* Norman Mailer?"

"Yes. *The* Norman Mailer," I said, thinking, *Now we're getting somewhere.*

"You know what, I'm just a *schlep* here. I have to take this to my boss. Please wait."

We sat for a half hour, until he reappeared. "You have an appointment with my boss in a week."

On the appointed day, we were ushered into a large office on the second floor. A middle-aged man in shirt and slacks but no jacket or tie shook our hand and asked us to come in. A thick folder lay on the table next to him. He said, "Mr. Colodro, I see you want a tourist visa. What is the reason?"

"My wife is American. Her family is American. We just had a daughter. My in-laws live in the States and we want to visit in July," Marco answered.

"There seems to be a problem. Would you agree to answer a few questions?"

"Of course."

The man opened the folder and began asking Marco about his past. "Mr. Colodro, you went to Cuba in 1964 when you were still studying at the University of Chile. What was the reason for this trip?"

"It wasn't a personal invitation. The invitation was extended to the whole class. And all students, left and right wing, went to Cuba."

Next the man asked Marco about his studies in Paris. At last he finally came to the main question. "You came back to Chile in 1970 after being in Paris for two years, and you got an important position at the Central Bank. Now why would a 30-year-old man with no previous experience in government get such an important position if not for his political affiliation?"

Marco calmly replied. "At the Sorbonne I studied under Ignacy Saks, a well-known economist, and a specialist in foreign trade. He was my thesis adviser, so when I came back to Chile I was offered a position in the Central Bank as head of foreign trade."

"You are talking about Allende's government."

"Yes."

"And you were a Socialist."

Marco nodded.

"Well, I think we might have a problem with your visa because of that."

"Because he was a socialist, or because he worked for Allende?" I blurted out. "Why would that be a problem, working for Allende's government? Allende was a democratically-elected President. Unlike Pinochet, who is a dictator. And at the time being a socialist was not against the law."

The man turned and looked me straight in the eye. "Let's not get into that."

I was not put off. "I am an American citizen. My daughter is American. My family is American. I don't see why my husband should have a problem getting a simple tourist visa."

"He has a leftist past, which is considered a security risk by the State Department."

"This is ridiculous. If the visa is denied, I'll send a complaint to the pertinent authorities. My father is Norman Mailer. He has connections, as you might imagine. My mother is a member of Amnesty International. My uncle is one of the producers of *60 Minutes*." I figured this guy was CIA, but instead of being cautious, I felt empowered. That, in the Embassy, I was on US territory and therefore had a right to speak my mind. I had suddenly, instinctively adopted my father's combative spirit.

After a pause, he said, "I could offer your husband a waiver visa."

We found out that would mean every time Marco wanted to enter the United States, he would have to ask for a visa. One which might be rejected at any time. The State Department guy also informed us it was the type of visa given to those who posed a potential threat to the security of the US. Like terrorists and drug dealers.

"In that case," Marco told him, "I'd rather never set foot in the States."

As we were getting up, the man said, "Look, I have to confer with my superiors at the State Department. I'll get back to you soon."

A month later, Marco received a ten-year multiple entry tourist-visa to the United States of America. It was authorized by the State Department, and stamped by the American Embassy in Chile.

~

In October, I heard through the grapevine that a well-known Chilean psychoanalyst would be visiting the country to do a group therapy workshop. He lived in Topeka, Kansas and had worked at the Menninger Clinic since the early sixties. He visited Chile every year to collaborate with a Chilean friend and colleague who also would be leading the workshop. Both analysts were highly respected in Santiago.

I decided to sign up.

When I arrived at the venue, I found out that there would be two groups, and that the leader of mine was not the analyst who lived in Topeka. I felt disappointed because I'd been looking forward to the connection with someone who had lived in the United States. I was sure he'd be more sensitive to how I felt now, in Chile.

The session began. Wasting no time, the analyst who led my group asked us to describe our parents and our relationship to them. When it was my turn, I said, "My parents divorced when I was very young. I grew up in Mexico far from where my father lived. I have a complicated relationship with him, even though we do love each other."

I stopped there. The analyst looked at me as if waiting for more. Finally, he said, "It will be helpful for everyone in the group if you can be more specific. Where does your father live?"

Once again the story of my life. "Both my parents are American. After they divorced my mother married a Mexican, so I grew up there while my father lived in New York with his second wife. Later, he remarried a few more times. Four, to be exact. I have one brother from my mother's second marriage, seven brothers and sisters from my father's six marriages, and another brother from his sixth and latest wife's previous marriage."

"You said your relationship with him was complicated. What do you mean by that?" The analyst inquired.

Isn't this scenario complicated enough for you? What more could I say to describe its complexity in a reasonable amount of time? I felt exasperated, but made an effort not to show it. Also, I wasn't sure how much to reveal. This was a weekend experience; I didn't want to open my bleeding heart unnecessarily. And lurking in the background was that inevitable moment when the analyst would ask, "And who is your father?"

I was feeling uneasy at that point, to say the least.

The analyst immediately picked up on this. "You seem to be keeping something back. I know it's difficult to talk about events that may still hurt us." He asked me to continue, nonetheless.

"It's complicated because, aside from all the separations and not living near him, my father has a very strong personality. He's also very well known. Actually, famous, which makes my relationship to him even more complex."

"We all think our parents are important and perceive our fathers as more powerful than they really are."

Do I hear a subtle condescension in his voice? I said, "I know that. But *my* father *is* famous. He's a well-known writer."

"What's his name?"

Finally, the question I'd been expecting. One I hated and at the same time relished, because I enjoyed seeing the effect of my response. Heart beating slightly faster than usual, I said, "Norman Mailer."

To my surprise, in a tone that showed he had made his point, the analyst said, "I've never heard of him."

What! He'd never heard of Norman Mailer? I couldn't believe it! Weren't psychoanalysts supposed to be well-read intellectuals? His answer surprised me. But I responded, in a neutral tone, "Maybe you haven't heard of him, but it doesn't mean he's not well known. In the United States he's a famous writer."

We left it at that. The analyst moved on to the person sitting next to me.

There was a break midway so the two analysts could discuss what had transpired in each group while all the participants chatted over coffee and cookies. Before we entered the room once more, the other analyst, the one who lived in Topeka, Kansas, walked up to me. With a big smile, he asked, "What is Norman Mailer's daughter doing in Chile?"

CHAPTER 27

On the Couch

MY DAUGHTER VALENTINA, BORN IN FEBRUARY OF 1981, WAS TWO months old when I began psychoanalysis. I was in dire need of help, and the analyst came highly recommended, so I was delighted when I called and was told she had an opening. Her office was situated in an old section of Santiago, in front of a park surrounded by lovely French-style buildings.

I rang the bell and was greeted by a slender woman in her early fifties, dressed in a dark, narrow knee-length skirt and a light-colored blouse. Her brown hair was perfectly cut and styled and matched the color of her rather large eyes. Ximena reminded me of Queen Elizabeth: stiff, elegant and poised. I, on the other hand was wearing a flowered skirt, a white cotton blouse from India, and cowboy boots.

Ximena led me into her office, a large, dimly-lit room with high ceilings and French windows. Two armchairs, angled at 45 degrees, had been set before a desk. A good-sized bookcase stood in one corner; it held Freud's complete works in English, and Melanie Klein's in Spanish.

The therapist pointed me to one chair and took the other. "So, what brings you here?" she asked.

And so, I began.

After two interviews, she told me I was to come four times a week.

Four times a week! This is way too much, I thought, and asked if we could start with three.

Ximena politely said, "This is the method I use." Making clear there was no room for dissent. She was basically saying, *Take it or leave it.*

So, I took it.

I left her office apparently feeling grateful, anxious to begin the journey into my mind. Which, I understood at that point, would begin three weeks later.

The following week I got a call from Ximena. In a terse voice she asked what had happened to me. Why hadn't I shown up last week?

I had no idea what she was talking about. There seemed to be a misunderstanding. I was sure she'd mentioned one date, while Ximena was positive she had said we would start the analysis the Monday following our interviews.

This was my in-the-flesh introduction to the unconscious.

Beneath all the gratitude and apparent willingness to begin therapy, I also felt resentful she had been every bit as authoritarian as my father! No wiggle room, no negotiation. Take it or leave it.

So yes, I'd taken it, but at my own pace.

On Monday I arrived punctually. She led me into the sanctum, the room where she analyzed patients. The decor was Spartan: a brown leather couch, a red armchair positioned behind it, and another chair at the entrance where I left my purse and coat and stuff. No books, no paintings on the walls.

Everything in Ximena's demeanor was reserved. She spoke to me in the formal *Usted* manner used in Spanish, and didn't laugh at my attempts at humor. There was nothing warm and fuzzy about her. But on the flip side, she was totally dependable. In all the years we saw each other she rarely missed a session, and always began and ended on time. Her consistency could feel suffocating, though. Many times I thought of bolting out of the office. But Ximena's calm and unwavering stability proved to be grounding. Eventually, through our work together, I became rooted in Chile.

We met regularly for eleven years and covered a lot of ground in that time. The first half of my analysis was spent getting used to Chile and finding my place there. Over those years I also had two more children, Alejandro and Antonia, and was able to get my professional life in order. My goal was to eventually become a psychoanalyst, too. After I entered the Psychoanalytic Institute, I spent many hours with Ximena thinking about the kind of analyst I wanted to be. I also spoke at great length about my life, my parents and siblings, and got in touch with the painful emotions I'd buried during most of my life.

As could be expected, an important focus of the analysis was my parents. I had been born to a man who became a celebrity at the age of twenty-five. For most of my life, I'd felt convinced there was nothing I could ever do that would be worthwhile. Yet I knew I had to excel in something, it didn't matter what. And to keep up with my father, it had to be in New York. Being a writer was out of the question. I didn't have the talent, or perhaps I should say, I didn't have *his* talent. I couldn't begin any project without immediately thinking, *What for?* or simply *What's the use?* Every ambition of my own paled when I compared them to his already-established, intense rock-star persona and fame. So, I always lost the match before it started.

At times I'd despaired, thinking I would never find my niche, never excel in anything.

Then there were my parents' multiple marriages and divorces. For more than two decades my father had left one wife, only to quickly have another appear. Not to mention the nine siblings, all born in rapid succession after I was six years old. I had loved my stepfather Salvador, but he had left. And I barely had time to get used to one new stepmother and baby before another arrived on the scene.

Having my own kids had opened my eyes to the problems with the sort of parenting I'd had as a child. I wasn't prepared for the intensity of my children's love or how much they needed me. I was totally in love with each one, and this made me think of the kind of attachment I had to my own parents. *So, it is normal, natural, expected,* I realized, *to need one's mother, to want to be with her.* To be comfortable and happy with Mommy and Daddy. Instead of always feeling slightly on edge, as I had around my own parents.

What had my mother been thinking when she left me for three months with Grandma Fanny? Why hadn't my father prevented her departure, or at least mine? Why had she been in such a rush to leave the States? It wasn't the first time I had asked these questions, but now the old answers didn't satisfy me.

Of course, it was too late to think of what they could've done differently. I couldn't change any of it. But to realize I simply had not been an important player when it came to their life decisions, that fact, became a hot and constant ache. I walked around in a rage for months.

Being in Mexico as a child had been wonderful, but there were also many things I missed by growing up there. Most likely, it was a blessing to not have been that near my father in the late 1950s and early 60s, his most volatile decades. But living far from him for many months in the year also generated a push and pull in our relationship; a combination of intense closeness and uncomfortable distance between us that we never managed to navigate well.

Old childhood scenes vividly reappeared. One sticks out painfully.

I am five or six; my father is holding my hand. We are walking to the apartment where my mother and Salvador live. After three months with my father in the States, he has brought me back to Mexico and will be leaving the next day. He knocks on the door, and my mother opens it. I hug her perfunctorily, then start walking off, to my room. Mom says, "Aren't you going to say goodbye to Daddy?"

I turn toward him. "Bye."

He says, "Hey, Diamond Eyes, come here and give me a hug."

I let him hug me, then immediately turn away again, and start speaking to the maid in Spanish, cutting Dad off completely.

It had been excruciating. Joining my mother always meant saying goodbye to my father once more, and vice versa. To deal with the pain I'd had to turn off and shut them out. When I was in New York I never thought of Mom and forgot all my Spanish. When I was in Mexico I didn't think of Dad and refused to speak English.

Having dual identities may sound like an asset, and in many ways it is. But for me it came with the price of never totally belonging, no matter where I was. I used to think of myself as a free spirit who could live in any place. In a private crevice of my secret being, I believed I could get by on my own. That no one was indispensable. But often I also felt detached, in a nowhere place, as if I were observing myself going through the motions, acting happy or faking interest, but not totally inside my body. I wouldn't say I was terribly unhappy, but neither was I truly happy. Not unless I was actively pursuing something exciting, like being in love, or traveling, or a frenzied social agenda.

When I was younger, before I had kids, it had been easy to escape longing and anger. But those feelings were always waiting around the corner, waiting their chance to mug me again. After I got married and moved to Chile, and after the birth of my first daughter, all the separations and the jealousy towards my stepmothers and my numerous siblings rose to the surface. There was no place to escape. The recurrent low, spacy moods evolved into deep depression.

Those years with Ximena finally gave me the opportunity I needed to mourn for what I had missed, for the fame I wouldn't reach, for the anger I hadn't expressed, and for the many ways I had hurt myself. During this journey I recovered my love for my parents; a love that had lain dormant and muted for as long as I could remember. I began to see them in a kinder light, once I achieved enough distance to think about my own life, and also about our lives together.

Becoming an analyst marked a turning point. I had found an occupation I was passionate about; I was seriously training my mind. This cemented my sense of belonging in Chile. I now had colleagues who respected me, and I made deep friendships. I realized finally I didn't have to be famous to be seen. Having recognition was more than good enough. I was now part of a professional international community. When I went to New York I began to participate in seminars and conferences, and in so doing, built a bridge between my two worlds. A bridge, which unlike during my childhood, I could now cross with growing ease.

The old sing-song refrain *what for, what's the use* receded into the background. And I remembered something my mother had once said to me: "Men come and go, children leave, but what you do stays with you."

CHAPTER 28

Karmic Vibrations

I N JULY OF 1981, WHEN VALENTINA WAS FIVE MONTHS OLD, WE WENT to the States for a month, to spend two weeks with Mom in Daytona Beach, Florida and almost three weeks with Dad and Norris and my siblings in Maine. This time my father rented The Griswold House, a large sprawling home with a barn and a few acres of land.

It rained for most of our visit, but I still enjoyed every minute. I loved getting up early every morning, nursing Valentina, then having breakfast with Dad before he went off to his studio. Marco and I sat in the kitchen with Valentina in her bouncy chair while a constant stream of siblings appeared for breakfast. It was an old-fashioned kitchen, large and full of light, with a wood stove and a beautiful long oak table; a cozy space and a natural gathering point. By noon, after several rounds of breakfasts, it was time to think about lunch.

When it rained heavily, a mile's walk along the path that led to our mailbox was the highlight of our afternoons. Every other day we went to the supermarket, and once a week we piled into the van and went to Bar Harbor or Bangor for pizza and a movie.

My father grumbled more than once, "I never thought I would rent a van." For him, these vehicles were manufactured without a thought to beauty or class. He much preferred squeezing all his kids into a tiny

Porsche. But that summer, Norris had put her foot down. Despite the van's lack of beauty, we were all relieved to have more space.

I was so excited to be with my family, at first I didn't notice Dad was in a funk. Quiet and withdrawn, he spent more time than usual in his studio, which was in some lost corner of the rambling house. I might have read about Jack Abbott in an earlier letter from Norris, but after Valentina's birth, I was living in Babyland, so it didn't really register.

Mailer kids from youngest to oldest: John, Maggie, Stephen, Michael, Kate, Betsy, Danielle and me. Matt is missing. Maine, 1981.

When I got to Maine, the family filled me in.

In the mid-1970s my father had been writing *The Executioner's Song*, an intimate portrait of ex-convict Gary Gilmore and the events that had led to him shooting two Mormons in Salt Lake City, and ultimately to a cell on death row in Utah.

Meanwhile Dad had received a letter from Jack Abbott, a prisoner at the maximum security federal penitentiary in Marion, Illinois, who was serving a sentence for forgery and armed robbery. Abbott, like

Gilmore, had spent most of his life in prison. He wrote to my father offering to share insights on what life was really like for seasoned convicts like Gilmore and himself. He also claimed to have knowledge of Gilmore's character, obtained through the prison grapevine. The two had never met but had been in the same prisons at different times.

The letters Jack sent to my father over a two-year period eventually became a book, *In the Belly of the Beast*, published by Random House in 1980. Abbott's talent had impressed my father. Dad thought, quixotically perhaps, that art was capable of changing a man's soul. He believed Jack could begin a new life in the outside world, and felt sure that if his book did well Abbott's chances to stay on the outside would be better than that of most ex-cons. Surely, better than Gary Gilmore's had been when he was paroled.

So, when Abbott's hearing came up, my father wrote a letter endorsing Jack and his talent. He wasn't the only one who publicly vouched for Abbott, but perhaps he was the most famous. Jason Epstein and Errol McDonald of Random House, and Robert Silvers, editor of the *New York Review of Books,* also supported Abbott, and were instrumental in getting his memoir published. Later, we learned Abbott had actually been released thanks to information he'd given the prison authorities about other inmates. But at the time it happened, none of those who'd endorsed him, including my father, knew this. And Abbott, for obvious reasons, said nothing about it.

One morning during breakfast Norris told me she was furious with Dad for taking Jack under his wing. She had confronted him, saying, "Didn't you learn *anything* from Gary Gilmore?"

But my father paid no heed. He kept writing letters to Jack and didn't consider what might happen when he was released. Who would take care of him? Who would teach him how to live outside of prison?

Jack was released on June 5, 1981 and flew to New York. My father picked him up at the airport and took him to Brooklyn for a family dinner with Norris and my brothers John and Matthew. During the next few weeks Dad tried to keep him busy, enlisting various members of our family to help out. This sketchy plan proved disastrous. My father, never good at taking care of anyone if it took attention away from his writing, quickly went his own way and left Norris to do all the work. After a month, she got tired of being Jack's babysitter.

As they did every summer, Dad and Norris went to Provincetown in July with my younger siblings. Jack came up for a weekend. He'd never seen the ocean before and hadn't had an ice cream cone for thirty years. When Danielle took him out to see a film, he kept going to the men's room, and always returned rubbing his nose.

That Jack Abbott had few talents for life on the outside soon became obvious to everyone. But he knew how to handle a knife. One day he explained to Norris, over lunch, how to make a killing thrust with precision.

In August the family gathered in Maine. About a week before I arrived with Marco and Valentina, Dad had gotten the news that Jack Abbott had killed someone and was on the run from the police.

In the early morning hours of July 18th, Jack had gone with two women to a cafe on the Lower East Side called the Binibon. There he got into an argument with 22-year-old Richard Adan, a Cuban-born actor and dancer, who was also a waiter and night manager at the cafe. Jack wanted to use a restroom reserved for Binibon employees, but Adan refused, because the restroom could only be reached by walking through the cafe's kitchen. He led Jack outside to an alley, instead. Within a minute or two Abbott stabbed Adan in a single thrust to the heart. The young man was seen on the sidewalk staggering and clutching at his chest before he died.

By then Jack had urged the women to quickly leave the cafe with him. He fled New York, leaving the halfway house on East Third Street where he'd been living, and disappeared. NYPD Detective Bill Majeski worked the case; two months later, through informants, he discovered Abbott's whereabouts. Majeski sent the information to Louisiana police, who arrested Abbott at an oil pipeline yard where he was working as a roustabout.

Jack had lasted just six weeks on the outside.

The bare bones of the disaster were so familiar it was spooky. A man, unhinged and paranoid, gets drunk, gets into an argument, and stabs a guy, killing him. Dad had to see the connection with his assault on Adele. How could he not?

That afternoon in Maine when Norris told me about it, it felt like a karmic reenactment of that terrible time twenty years earlier. And I wasn't the only one who felt that way. My sisters Danielle and Betsy, Adele's daughters, had the same reaction.

A few days later Dad and I went for an afternoon walk and had a chance to talk privately. He told me he felt sick with guilt and remorse; plagued by Richard Adan's senseless death. He was angry with himself for not having taken care of Jack. He knew men who'd spent their lives in prison were wired to attack at the slightest provocation, real or imagined.

"But looking after Abbott turned out to mean I had to take time away from my work. I guess I was too naïve. I believed someone with Jack's talent should be helped. And I thought once his book was published, he would have a fair chance of making it outside. It was worth a try, I figured."

As he said this I remembered how, in my teens, he had never tired of repeating, "If you start something, you must finish it well, or it won't be worth your effort." Obviously, he had been unwilling to follow his own advice.

My father surely knew Jack was so tightly wired he could explode at any minute, but he had dismissed the possibility.

He said, "I should have known that the strain would be too much on Jack's psyche. I should have recognized the signs." I tried to empathize with Dad, but at the same time couldn't help but wonder how he could've blinded himself so thoroughly to the possibility of a violent outcome. He knew from his own experience what fame could do to a man's head. His intimate journey into the mind of a man who had spent his life in prison, Gary Gilmore, should have been a forewarning. He had written a one-thousand-page novel about Gilmore, whose life story was so similar to Jack's it was uncanny.

I'm sure he did see this. But my father was a gambler, and when the stakes were highest, that was when he placed his bet.

Added to all of the above factors, Dad had always had an urge to mold those who were close to him. With his children he demanded we be elegant and beautiful, or brilliant and socially savvy, or skilled athletes. All of which were qualities he'd wanted for himself and to some extent had acquired, though not without enormous effort. He'd sent to the basement the nice Jewish and very shy, skinny boy he'd been in Brooklyn, only letting him reappear in rare moments. His fake Irish brogue, the love of boxing, his enjoyment of playing tough characters, all were ways of getting out of his skin and becoming someone else.

We'd all assumed Norman's transformation had been due to the enormous success of *The Naked and the Dead,* when he had suddenly, in his twenties, become a celebrity. But I've come to believe that his change began much sooner, in the early 1940s, in the Army. He had been the "worst soldier" of his platoon, challenged to the limit of his strength. The army "Was the worst experience of my life and the one that changed me the most" he had often said. He had learned that to survive one had to be tough, take punches, and return them. Being loved and pampered did not prepare one for life, he decided. That had been the first real game-changer for my father.

In 1954 he wrote *Lipton's,* his marijuana journal, in which he elaborated on his theory of the saint and the psychopath, the high and base instincts waging a daily battle within us.

On page 234 of *Advertisements for Myself,* he wrote, referring to his experiments with marijuana, "…I was finally open to my anger. I turned within my psyche I can almost believe, for I felt something shift to murder in me…All I felt was that I was an outlaw, a psychic outlaw and I liked it, I liked it a good night better than trying to be a gentleman, and with a set of emotions accelerating one on the other, I mined down deep into the murderous message of marijuana, the smoke of the assassins, and for the first time in my life I knew what it was to make your kicks."

It is hardly surprising, then, that he would be attracted to Jack Abbott. Here was an intelligent and violent man who, in spite of all odds, and through writing, was on the road to transforming himself. He *was* a psychopath and a saint, a true character from the Mailer universe. Dad convinced himself that Abbott had a chance, with his help, to transform psychopath into artist. In so doing my father chose to dismiss all that he knew about prison life, about fame, about violence, and about madness. He clearly believed he could mold Jack Abbott's destiny, the way he had molded his own. But it turned out he was not willing to spend the time and effort this would have entailed. He loved to play Pygmalion, but the end of this tragic story was closer to the one in Garcia Marquez's *Chronicle of a Death Foretold.*

That summer, in spite of his dark mood, my father sometimes left his lair. On the only sunny day we had that month, we went on a hike to Acadia National Park, on one of the less dangerous trails. Dad marched at the head of his family, always the sergeant. Danielle and Maggie and the boys were his troopers. They walked right behind him, not afraid of the difficult turns and high drops. Being the oldest, I wasn't about to be left behind, so I too marched at their pace. Betsy and Kate, on the other hand, were annoyed at being forced up the hill, and always had an aversion to anything risky. They lagged behind, complaining bitterly, announcing every now and then, "Ok. I've had enough! I'm going back." But they didn't dare provoke Dad's wrath, so they kept going. Marco and Norris also went up that steep terrain, but at a slower pace, helping a three-year-old John maneuver the uneven stretches on the trail. Valentina was back at the house with Myrtle, now John's nanny. Dad led and cajoled us all. He rushed and scolded us, insisting we keep going until we made it to the top.

Another day he decided it was time Grandma Fanny took a walk, too. She was spending the month at The Griswold House with us and usually sat in a comfortable chair in the kitchen chatting with any family member who happened in. By that time, her energy had ebbed. She was happy to sit and reflect on her life. But Dad got it into his head that his mother needed to be snapped out of what he considered a lethargic mood. He convinced her to take a walk down the path to the mailbox.

Grandma could never say no to her son. She didn't want to go but mustered enough energy to attempt the walk. Betsy, Aunt Barbara and I walked beside her at a snail pace. Fanny moved slowly, one foot ahead, then another, out of breath and wobbling slightly. She didn't want help, though, and wouldn't hear of anyone taking her arm. She was determined to do it on her own. But after less than a quarter of a mile she asked to go back.

Aunt Barbara, Grandma and Valentina 5 months old. Maine, 1981.

Thinking about this later, I had to agree Dad was right. I felt, at first, he'd been too tough on her. But getting out of her chair and walking that half mile brought some of the old spunk back. Fanny was proud of herself for doing it.

Danielle was twenty-four at this time, in between jobs and boyfriends, so Marco and I invited her to come to Chile for a year. We mapped it all out for her. She'd have to learn to drive. We'd help her get a job teaching art at the International School in Santiago. And, of course she would live with us. We talked up the great weather, the majestic Andes, the healthy food. I wanted so much to have one of my sisters living close by, even for a while.

She was almost convinced, but when we laid out the plan to Dad he said, "Oh, no. I lost one daughter when you went to Mexico. I'm not about to lose another!"

In the end, Danielle didn't visit us after all. Not because of what Dad had said, but because that Fall she met Michael Moschen, who would later become her husband.

Marco, Valentina, and I left Maine after a three week stay and went back to Chile. I would have liked to remain with my family for the rest of the summer, but Marco had to get back to work. I could've stayed longer, but it would've meant losing my permanent residency: the Chilean green card. Once again, I felt unhappily wrenched from my surroundings. Only this time, I could feel my heart ache.

CHAPTER 29

Are you Norman Mailer?

ALEJANDRO WAS TWO YEARS OLD WHEN MY FATHER CAME TO Chile for the first time, in late 1986. Earlier in the year, on September 7, *El Frente Patriotico Manuel Rodriguez* (The Patriotic Front, a paramilitary organization and breakaway wing of the Communist Party of Chile) had tried to assassinate Pinochet. Immediately the government imposed a 12 AM curfew. Houses were raided, people taken prisoner, tortured and killed. Tension and fear tightened the air around us once again.

Dad came incognito on this visit. He didn't want it known that Norman Mailer was in Chile. He had no desire to meet with local authors, nor did he want any press or big social events. "If I am interviewed, I'll surely be asked what I think of Pinochet, fascism, and this government. I wouldn't want it to mean trouble for you and Marco. I came to be with you."

He added, "But I will have to work a few hours every day."

Having suspected as much, I'd already set up a desk next to the window of his room, so he could write without interruption. Once he settled in, his routine was the same as in New York. He woke early, we had breakfast, then off he went to his desk. I enjoyed walking in the garden, peering into the window where he was seated, bent over his yellow legal pads, writing and talking to himself. Such a familiar sight: my father, muttering sentences. The writer at work.

Back when he was planning this trip, I'd suggested he come alone. That is, without Norris. "We can have some quality together time without spouses."

Once Dad arrived in Chile, though, Marco and I organized a short daytrip to the seaside with him. When he saw my husband get into the driver's seat, Dad could barely disguise his surprise. I hadn't explained our no-spouses agreement to Marco, so he naturally felt included.

Clearly my father was thinking, *What the hell? I thought we were supposed to have quality time alone.* But he didn't say anything, probably not wanting to put Marco in an uncomfortable position.

~

What *had* motivated me to suggest he come by himself? Was I unwittingly merging Norris with Suzanne? Perhaps, but I was not aware of the possibility at the time. To be honest, as much as I'd come to love Norris, I didn't relish the idea of walking the streets of Santiago as her invisible companion. Or feeling like the ugly duckling once more, when Marco's family met her. I also felt embarrassed for this pettiness. For not "rising above it" as Dad would've said. But I couldn't help it.

In terms of my father, the motivation was more complicated. When I suggested he come alone, I had thought it would be a good opportunity to spend time together with no competition, no interruptions. But when we were planning the trip to the seaside, it never occurred to me to leave Marco behind. Somehow, I didn't realize the contradiction between my words and my behavior, until I saw the confusion and surprise on Dad's face.

Perhaps I wanted him to feel as shocked and surprised as I had been when, more than a decade ago, he had arrived in Denver with Suzanne. I might've wanted him to feel like the third wheel for a change. Or maybe despite what I had said, I didn't really want to be alone with him, and needed Marco as a buffer. It had never been easy to be around my father for long periods of time, and traveling in a car all day meant close quarters. And, who would drive? Certainly not Norman. He was a terrible driver. After Boulder, I didn't want to get behind the wheel with him next to me again. Marco as driver solved that dilemma.

The three of us went to Valparaiso, also called *Pancho* for its likeness to San Francisco. We headed to Viña del Mar, and then on to Zapallar, the Chilean equivalent of East Hampton, which was spectacularly beautiful. Dad was impressed by the forests that grew all the way down to the ocean; the well-tended gardens of the European-style homes that decorated the winding streets. He observed, "The rich certainly know how to choose the most beautiful places. But *Zapallar?* Zucchinni Land. Hmm, not such a great choice of a name."

Dad asked to have his picture taken in front of the "Mexican Reefer"
in Valparaiso. He got a kick out of the ship's name, 1986.

We took Dad to see a political play that was popular then, *Lo Que Está en el El Aire. What is in the Air.* A few months before, the leading actor's son had been kidnapped by the Chilean secret police. He was found dead the next day, lying on a dirt road with his throat slit. Even though Dad couldn't understand the Spanish dialogue, he was quick to pick up on the anguish that seeped into the main character's performance.

Afterward, he said, "I'm surprised the play was allowed on stage."

We explained the reason: it was a small venue, so the viewers would naturally be restricted to the size of the theater. Letting it run was a luxury the government could afford. An easy way for Pinochet to claim to the world he was actually a benign and tolerant leader.

Before Dad left, I threw a party for him, inviting my friends and the Colodro clan. That morning the two of us went for a hike in the nearby mountains. The walk uphill was strenuous, and Dad had to make an effort to keep up. I was used to hiking on weekends with my dogs. We were almost home when Dad tripped and fell, banging his forehead on the pavement and scraping one knee. Not severe injuries, but he was furious with himself for being so clumsy, and a little embarrassed later on when he had to explain to the party guests the ugly bruise on his forehead.

Of course, after a couple of drinks, he charmed everyone.

One day he expressed a desire to see where I worked. When we arrived, there was no one in the office; it was probably a Friday afternoon or a Saturday morning. As I opened the front door, he said, "Sue, don't tell me anything about your colleagues. Let me look around and see what I can figure out about them."

He recognized my suite immediately, because it had a couple of Danielle Mailer prints hanging on the wall. Then he walked into another empty office and said, "This woman is sure of herself, she's also an artist and has a no-nonsense quality."

He walked into a third. "The woman in this office is a private person. She keeps to herself and is probably just a touch severe."

"How do you know all that?" I asked.

"Well, I'm a novelist, after all. I should know something about people and the places they inhabit."

He was right about both of my colleagues. I was impressed.

~

He came to Chile again in September 1988, on his way to Uruguay. I was about to give birth to Antonia, my third child. He was writing *Harlot's Ghost* and wanted to include a section on Montevideo, so he'd decided to come and see it for himself. In Santiago, he specifically asked to go to the Hotel Carrera. Apparently, it had been a CIA enclave in the months before the 1973 coup.

We went up to the hotel bar, on the top floor. As we walked in, I noticed four United States Marines sitting nearby. They kept staring at us. Finally, one young marine approached our table, and addressed my father. "Sir, we have a bet going here."

"Oh, yeah? What kind of bet?"

"That you're Norman Mailer."

One hand on the table, Dad turned is torso to look up at the marine and asked, in the exaggerated Irish brogue he enjoyed putting on, "And which one of yas says I'm Norman Mailer?"

"I do."

"Well, yah can tell your buddies yah just won the bet."

"Really? They won't believe me. Can I please see your ID?"

Dad laughed and took out his driver's license.

I still find it hard to believe that four young marines stationed in Chile, probably guards at the American Embassy, would not only know about Norman Mailer, but also recognize him in person.

That was a short, sweet three-day visit. A week after my father left, I went into the hospital to give birth to Antonia.

~

Often people ask me what it was like to live under a military regime for almost ten years. But what no one ever seems to wonder about is what it felt like to live so long among people who knew nothing about me or my family.

Chile is a long narrow country surrounded by mountains. As isolated as an island, Chileans are, in effect, like islanders. Everyone knows someone who knows of someone who knows you. It is a place where your parents, your school, which branch of what family you belong to, are all cables that anchor you there in time and space, and help people figure out your position in the social ladder. This was especially so in the 1980s.

But I, the newcomer, was excluded from this web of relationships. I had no threads of my own. All anyone knew about me was that I was a gringa and that I was married to Marco. Most people could place his last name. They knew he was a leftist who'd worked for the Allende government. That he had left the country and come back in 1980, and that he had been married before and had three kids from that previous relationship. Marco also had Chilean classmates and childhood friends, political allies and enemies. Every time we went out together, he bumped into someone who knew him. Whereas I had no roots in Chile, at least to begin with.

I had always wanted to be known for myself, not as my famous father's daughter. Yet, when my wish finally came true, I didn't like it.

Once, while still in my twenties, I had asked Dad, "Do you ever wonder if people are attracted to you because of yourself, or because you're Norman Mailer?"

"But I *am* Norman Mailer," he said.

After my first few years of anonymity in Chile, I finally began to feel comfortable not only with the fact that *I am* Norman Mailer's daughter, but that I am also proud of it.

CHAPTER 30

The Big House

THAT DAD DID NOT TURN OUT TO BE A GRANDFATHERLY GRANDFAther came as no great shock. Though once in a while he did surprise me by going out of his way to do something nice for my children. When Valentina turned thirteen, Marco and I took her to New York. Outside the gate at Kennedy Airport my father was waiting with a big grin, ready to take us to our hotel. Later in the week he invited us to The Actor's Studio to see an unforgettable performance by Al Pacino in *Looking for Richard*.

But mostly the brief periods of time he had free after work were not spent on his grandchildren. He said, "It was hard enough to be a father, don't expect much from me as a grandfather."

It didn't bother me because all I expected from him now was to be welcomed in his Provincetown house, where together with my children and Marco, I enjoyed seeing the whole Mailer family for two weeks each July.

In February of 1985 Alejandro was born. That was the year of the big earthquake in Santiago, and the year my grandmother Fanny died. We came to Provincetown as usual, for the last half of July. My father had rented a condo for my grandmother and her nurse, but as soon as we arrived the nurse took a vacation, and Grandma moved into the Big House with Dad and Norris, while we settled into the condo. This was to be Fanny's last summer with us, although I can hardly say she was entirely with us. She had shrunk by then to a diminutive four feet six inches and had no short-term memory left. She would sit by the window looking out at the bay, and about every two minutes ask anyone in sight, "What time is it?"

"I think it's her way of finding out if she's still alive," Dad told us.

One day my brother Michael convinced our younger siblings Stephen, Maggie, and Matt to put a set of headphones connected to a tape recorder on Grandma's head. They recorded and timed her repetitive question. Then they taped someone announcing the hour of the day, every two minutes, changing the responding voice each time.

"What time is it?" Grandma would ask, headphones now in place.

"It's 12, Grandma."

Two minutes later, "What time is it?" was followed by "12 and 2 minutes, Grandma." And so on.

Fanny was appeased for a while. Until, in a moment of lucidity, she realized what was going on. She was terribly upset. So was our father, though he couldn't resist smiling as he gave Michael a thorough chewing-out.

Up to the end Grandma still recognized her son and daughter. She also knew who I was and guessed that the little girl and the baby were my children. She managed to link Marco to me, too, and knew we lived in a far-off place.

She'd ask me about Mexico, and then correct herself. "Dear, where is it that you live?"

Each morning my father would walk through the living room where Grandma was sitting and greet her.

"Good morning, dear, what time is it?" she would say.

He'd tell her, then make a quick exit to the dining room.

Aunt Barbara, who was staying a few doors down, came by at least twice a day to check on her mother. Many times, still not quite accepting that Grandma was unable to carry on a real conversation, Barbara tried to get one going with her.

Talking about death one day, my father told us he'd learned from Grandma's slow deterioration, and had decided, "It's better to go a little before than a little after."

Norris usually had the patience to sit for long stretches and listen to Fanny's stories, and I made a point of sitting by her side for a while every day. Just a little attention made Fanny happy, and usually helped her out of the mental haze. Her stories generally started with, "When you were a little girl." Then we'd reminisce about the past.

She also recounted tales about her father and mother, and family life in Long Branch, New Jersey, where she grew up. Then, stories of the old days concluded, she'd withdraw into her silence again.

She died on my birthday, August 28. By then we were back in Chile, so Aunt Barbara called with the news. When I asked about the funeral she said "Dear, I don't think it's necessary to come all the way back to New York. You won't make it on time; we're having the service and the burial tomorrow."

"But I want to come," I insisted.

"After the burial your Dad will be going off on a lecture tour, and all the kids have things to do."

I hesitated and reacted too late. The truth is, when she told me Grandma had passed, I couldn't feel a thing. I understood her words but felt cut off from what they meant. One faint inner voice said, *You have to go to New York and be there with the family,* but instead I listened to the other voices in my head. The ones that pulled me back to work. And to caring for my kids. All the too-obvious excuses to avoid actually feeling the experience of losing my grandmother. I stayed in Santiago.

The following year we went to New Jersey for the unveiling of Fanny's tombstone. Standing at her grave, which was next to Grandpa Barney's, I could feel the latch that had been locked for a year finally opening. I felt sorrow and sadness, and also relief to be able to mourn for her loss. Our bond had deep roots. From my first years of life up until my mid-twenties, Grandma Fanny had been my rock.

For decades we spent part of our summers with Dad and Norris in the Big House on 627 Commercial Street in Provincetown. Purchased in the early 1980s, it stood at the east end of Provincetown and was the only brick-construction home in the area. Its imposing view of the bay greeted us as soon as we walked in the front door. A large back porch and deck had steps that went right down to the water. Morning light streamed through the ceiling-to-floor windows of the spacious living room. Paintings by Norris, Danielle, and Maggie hung on the walls. The dining room also faced the bay. A bow window with a wide shelf the size of a love seat was always stacked with mail, manuscripts, books, seashells, and a large lamp. To the left was the kitchen. Right next to it was a small TV room with its own bathroom, where my father liked to rest and watch football in his last years.

A long, narrow bar with high stools also had a view of the bay. A ledge on the window there was just barely wide enough for us to sit on. If you were lucky, you got a stool and a bay view. Otherwise we stood or sat gingerly balancing our bottoms on that skinny ledge.

Norris and I usually drank Kir Royale, hers with ice. Dad preferred rum, orange juice, and seltzer in three equal parts, with lime or lemon on the rim. This drink he baptized the "Presbyterian." The bar was the bellybutton of the house, the gathering place where we sat and watched as the evening light changed, the blue sky turning to shades of violet, pink and purple reflected on the water, or on shallow tidal pools at low tide. Then sailboats rested patiently on their sides, waiting for the tide to rise and float them once more.

Up a grand stairway, on the second floor, were five bedrooms. On the third floor, originally meant as an attic for storage, was Dad's writing office, facing west, while Norris' studio there faced east. My father's space was definitely inhabited by him. It had its own atmosphere, different from the rest of the house. The room was kept dark since he was now sensitive to bright light. It held the musty, dry smell of papers and books, mixed with his own slightly salty, sweaty odor that blended with the sea-salt scent of the bay. A bare mattress lay on the floor for naps. His desk, covered with yellow legal pads and sharpened pencils, sat before a large window with a dark curtain, to protect his eyes from sunlight. From this window Dad enjoyed watching the bird formations that flew past.

The big house stretched along with each arrival. It didn't matter how many of us appeared, there was always room for one more: an extra mattress was put in a bedroom, or the studio couch in the TV room was opened, or someone slept up in Norris's studio.

A Rare Moment. Grandpa Norman Teaching Antonia and Isabella Chess. 1996.

Whenever I arrived with my family, Danielle always made a point of showing up, even if only for a few days. After her daughter Isabella was born she'd spend a week or two in Provincetown, then visit us in Santiago during our Southern Hemisphere summers in February. Betsy and her husband Frank usually stopped by for a couple of days. Kate and her husband-to-be, Guy, would arrive for a weekend. Michael and Stephen often showed up with girlfriends.

Maggie, John, and Matt were there the whole summer. They spent hours playing a game created by Matt that was loosely based on

Dungeons and Dragons. Matt was fourteen and John seven. They settled in a corner of the living room discussing their next moves, oblivious to the rest of the household. Sometimes Maggie joined in, but most of the time it was Matt as Dungeon Master, with John and his friend Dave.

We could've rented a separate place for our little family, but I needed to be in my father's home. I think he enjoyed having us there as well. I've always thought he originally bought that large house with the idea of welcoming all his children together. So, it was a given we would stay with him. Norris graciously put up with the annual summer invasion. It couldn't have been easy to have such a full house, even though we helped as much as we could with groceries and cooking, and chipped in for the cleaning ladies who came every other day. Still her privacy was invaded, her routine disturbed.

We also had a lot of fun together. Danielle, Norris, and I, and our girls Valentina, Antonia, and Isabella, always went shopping downtown. Every year, Danielle, Norris, and I took a trip to a jewelry store in Wellfleet, to buy each other a present. This was our ritual, a small tradition. In the evening Norris usually prepared supper. Then, sitting in the bar, she and I would sip our Kir Royales. Dad would ask Marco, "Lime or lemon?" for his vodka tonic, while we all marveled at the sunset. After that, in a frenzy, we'd set the table, then later wash dishes and clean up. Sometimes as many as thirteen stayed in the house at one time. It wasn't unusual to have twenty for dinner, including Aunt Barbara and her husband Al, who had a condo right across the street.

The seating at the dinner table was another ritual. Dad's place was always at the head of it, looking out at the bay. Every evening he would choose who to sit next to him on either side; usually the last to arrive during the week. It was an honor; we all wanted to be chosen. Sitting next to him was a treat because, aside from John and Matthew, none of us had grown up with Dad as a live in-father. He'd been a weekend dad, and even then we didn't get to see much of him between his work and a hyperactive social life. Choosing dinner partners was his way of saying *I'm happy you're here. Welcome!*

Mailer Girls: Betsy, Valentina holding my hand, Danielle, Norris and Maggie in the garden of the Big House. Kate is missing. Provincetown. 1987.

Still, whether you were chosen or not, conversations with my father were always intense, and often tricky. In the right mood he was charming and asked the type of questions that made you feel he was genuinely interested. He could also choose to tease, prodding his finger into old wounds. These comments usually had to do with our looks, how we expressed our ideas and, of course, our mothers. Danielle one day left the dining room in a fury because he made a disparaging comment about the way she dressed, ending the speech with his famous, "You have no idea of style, you dress just like your mother."

Sometimes he'd ask me or Betsy a question, then after we answered he'd chide us with, "Oh come on, you can come up with something better than that!" Or he'd say something to me like, "I see you got your looks back. I was worried there for a while."

Kate and Stephen sometimes raised their voices over Dad's; they were somehow not afraid of disagreeing with him especially if it was an issue that was sensitive to them. I was not so bold. If he hurt me, poking at a sore spot, I'd go into retreat mode and answer with a sarcastic "yessir" attitude. I wanted him to feel the full brunt of my indifference, but I'm not sure he ever really noticed. We all had different ways of dealing with his stinging comments. Sometimes, realizing he'd gone too far, he would apologize. But most of the time he'd just say, "Aw, come on. I know you can take a punch. Let's see what you've got."

I don't remember Dad deliberately getting under our brothers' skin with comments about their looks or how they dressed. Those judgmental morsels were reserved for his daughters. He did have one-liners for his sons, though: "You're not as dumb as you look." Or "The first time you hit me, and I notice you're in trouble." But usually, when it came to the male siblings, he was prone to criticize what they did and how they did it. And then to come up with a personal solution, always better than theirs, of course.

Cooking for an army of twenty was daunting, and though Norris was usually relaxed about organizing dinner, she finally got tired of being in charge of this task. So one summer Dad came up with the idea of kitchen duty. Every night two people would do everything, from shopping to cooking to cleaning. This assignment was to be on a rotating basis, and there were enough of us so no one would have duty more than once or twice during our visit.

When it was Dad's turn, he chose my son Alejandro, who was then ten years old, to be his helper. Instead of cooking something simple, Norman decided on an elaborate chicken dish, which he made even more complicated as they went along.

Dad was already notorious in the kitchen. He wasn't a good cook, although he was convinced, as he was with many other pursuits, that he had a unique flair for cuisine. He did have definite ideas about food. He thought one had to respect the integrity of each ingredient and handle it correctly. He once explained to me how important it was to cook a lobster in furiously-boiling water, because if it didn't die immediately the dread and pain would liberate toxins we would then ingest. At the time I'd rolled my eyes, thinking, *There he goes again with his weird ideas.* But hey, they don't seem so weird anymore.

Dad always improved as he went along, adding new spices to the mix as he lectured on each ingredient. He also had three chopping boards. With a magic marker he wrote ONLY ONIONS on one, ONLY FRUIT AND VEGETABLES on another, and ONLY MEATS on the third.

When we were kids, we too had helped him cook one of his favorite dishes. First, he took out a couple of cans of corned beef hash. "You're about to witness a transformation. Chop up the nuts and almonds and take out two pears and a handful of grapes from the fridge." He had us cut the pears in slices and the grapes in half. Then he opened the cans of hash. We'd all gag when we saw the slimy pink and white gook come out of them. Unperturbed, he put the corned beef hash in a frying pan and let it brown. Then he'd added the other ingredients, and finally served a small portion on each of our plates.

"Kids, you are about to taste '*Ash de la Poire,*'"he proudly announced, in a put-on French accent.

As I recall, it wasn't that bad. But what did we know about cooking? We were under his spell, just tickled to have his attention.

Dad had chosen Alejandro as his helper with another purpose in mind, as well. He thought the best way to get to know more about his oldest grandson would be to work with him.

On the appointed day they went to the A&P in the early afternoon. Then, after Dad took a short nap, they worked nonstop for hours, chopping onions, shallots, carrots, and celery. Alejandro helped Dad bone the chicken and cut it into good-sized pieces. He washed the potatoes and put them in the oven. Then he set the table and helped serve the meal. By the time the food was on our plates, Dad was so tired he couldn't eat. He sat down with us until he was satisfied we all approved of the dish, then excused himself, leaving Alejandro to deal with cleaning up. Knowing, of course, everyone else would help him out.

Dad later told me he thought he'd bonded with Alejandro that afternoon. "You know Sue, he's not so bad." His typical way of saying he was actually a good kid. "He's very smart. You and Marco need to guide him. I think our cooking together was good for him. He's used to things being easy, and this was hard work, believe me. He needs more of this. It will make him tougher and better equipped to go out in the world."

Always afraid of too much coddling, he had wanted his children, and now his grandchildren, to be tough.

The full day spent preparing the meal with Alejandro was unusual, because Dad still rarely took a day off from literary labors. His routine was as regular as the tides, with few exceptions, even for kids or grandchildren. His choice, of course, but I couldn't help recalling something he had written once about being a galley slave to his imagination. Yet he was available for appetizers, pre-dinner drinks, long, boisterous family meals, after dinner drinks, and later on, poker. Texas Hold'em, which he grew passionate about in his late seventies.

There had been few established rituals in my own life. I had been bounced back and forth in childhood, living in many different homes until adulthood, but the Big House became my family landmark. It held a kaleidoscope of images and memories for my siblings and our spouses, and later on for our children. Every time we met in Provincetown, the joys outweighed by far the dark clouds. This eventually helped us grow into a resilient family, with traditions and strong bonds.

Mailer Boys: Matt, Stephen, Norman, Michael and John.
In the garden of the Big House. Provincetown, 1987.

CHAPTER 31

Is This Really Happening?

I N EARLY FALL OF 1991, I RECEIVED A LETTER FROM NORRIS. SHE'D found credit card bills that led her to suspect my father was having an affair. When she confronted him, he at first denied everything, but soon, with a mountain of evidence against him, he confessed to one affair. Then after a while he admitted to having not just the single involvement, but three long-standing ones, plus a myriad of one-night stands.

In her note Norris said, *I still haven't decided what I'm going to do. But I wanted to let you know what's going on . . . I love him despite his infidelities, and I also love you all.* She ended the note with *. . .there's always a silver lining in every dark cloud. I've lost 20 pounds and look like myself again.*

The news landed like a bomb. For over fifteen years we'd had stability in the family. The two of them were a team—they seemed to get along well, in spite of all the bumps. Norris had navigated living with my brothers Michael and Stephen during their teens, not an easy age for any boy, and especially not easy for Norman's and Beverly's sons. She had deftly handled Dad's irritability and cranky moods. I couldn't imagine our family without her, or our father with yet another woman. I was outraged. How could he be so irresponsible, so selfish? Was he really incapable of thinking of anyone beside himself? Could he not, for once, put his family's needs first?

I knew he couldn't. My father was in love with the excitement of seduction. As much as he loved Norris, he probably chafed under the domesticity of their daily routine. It killed the passion that fueled his life. So, on second thought, it wasn't surprising that he'd cheated, then left the evidence for her to find. That, of course, would have made it all even more exciting.

When Aunt Barbara asked why he'd done it, he said, "Life was getting too safe."

I might've not been so surprised, but I was still furious.

Norris and I met a few months later. She told me she'd left Dad for a few weeks and had her own affair. "But even though he was young and handsome, I missed Norman and our life in New York, and I also missed the family terribly." She came back ready to give it another try. But only after Dad promised to never do it again. He swore he'd never again cheat or lie again.

It felt as if there was a missing piece to the story Norris told me. I'm sure she loved my father, and that she also loved the family, as she said. But I wondered if she didn't also love being Norman Mailer's wife, and perhaps didn't want to become yet another Mailer ex-wife. I remembered she had said, "I missed Norman and our life in New York."

What also came back to me was how, whenever anyone asked if she was Norman's sixth wife, she'd always answer, "No, I'm his last wife."

I was delighted she was back. I could not imagine getting used to another stepmother; I could not even imagine my father with another woman, though I had no doubt there soon would have been one. But more important, I also happened to care about this wife.

One day, Norris asked me point blank, "Sue, when Norman went to Chile five years ago, did he bring along one of his lovers? Is that why he didn't want me to go?"

I was embarrassed, certainly not proud of what I'd done. I would've loved to sweep it away but I had to tell her the truth about my desire to see only Dad on that visit, and not her. I'm pretty sure she believed me, but I don't think she got over the fact that I had deliberately left her out. In the end, she never did make it to Chile.

~

Conversely, Dad and I never touched on the topic of his infidelities directly. Whenever he mentioned them to me, it was with a typical euphemism, "When all of this happened." He seemed embarrassed by the whole thing. I don't know if it was because he had been unfaithful, or because he had been caught and chastised. Probably the latter.

I wanted to ask him what had happened; the reasons behind this destructive compulsion. But his guarded avoidance foreclosed the possibility. We had an open relationship by then, and talked about many personal things, but this time he set boundaries.

Norris, on the other hand, had no such qualms. She went into all the nasty details with me. And for a while I lent an ear, but I wasn't comfortable being her confidante. After all, the bad guy in the story was my father. So I wanted her to back off. I got a "too much information" kind of feeling, and realized Norris also had a problem with boundaries. She just didn't get it. We loved each other, and we were close, but I was also her husband's daughter.

In retrospect, I'm glad my father kept his personal life to himself and spared me the specifics of his many amours. Candid to a fault about so many things, this time he drew a circle of silence around his secret life with other women, at least with his children.

Even though Dad and Norris didn't separate, there was a shift in their relationship. She was still angry and showed it. Yes, she'd come back, but she was not about to let him off the hook so easily. They bickered at the drop of a hat, over everything and nothing. Often at dinner now they would begin arguments. In the past she might have joked about things Norman did or said that angered her, or just ignored them. But now, more and more, she was like a dog with a bone.

One night, Dad was talking about what constitutes good writing, and he opined that plot was highly overrated.

Norris countered, "That's nonsense, Norman. Of course plot is important."

"And, of course *you* would think that. You love plot, you can't live without plot; all those best sellers you read only have plot," he shot back.

"And what do you suggest instead?"

"Mood, rhythm, character."

She set down her fork. "That's why *your* books go on and on and are so boring; that's why no one can finish them. They need more plot."

I admired Norris' spunk. Not many people had ever stood up to Norman and had the last word.

Sometimes the fights got nastier, though. We'd watch in silence until someone suggested a drink or a poker game or simply left the table.

But at other times the atmosphere was lovely. One night, we had just finished our dessert, and Dad said to Norris, "Hey, Honey, why don't you sing for us?"

"Oh no," she said demurely. "I just ate, I don't think I can sing right now."

"Yes, please do," we all replied in chorus.

"Okay, but just a bit," she conceded at last.

She sang "Amazing Grace," beginning softly and slowly building up. By the time she finished the hymn her voice was vibrating through the entire dining room. Listening to Norris, I felt I was in a Baptist church and able to catch a glimpse of her religious upbringing; a period of her life she rarely spoke about.

Dad's most recent affairs were seldom mentioned, yet they never left the family alone for long. There was always some mention of them, both old and new, on Page 6 of the *New York Post,* or in other gossip rags. Resurrecting those old scandals.

～

Nine years after Norris found out about the affairs, she was diagnosed with cancer. On an evening shortly after we had heard the terrible news, Dad was feeling guilty. Facing the damage he'd caused he brought up his infidelities. He believed – no, he *knew* – he was partly responsible for Norris's illness.

He said, "I don't think she's ever forgiven me."

I was silent. What could I say? He was probably right.

Norris had gone in for a routine operation and come out with a serious diagnosis. The surgeon had found a rare type of sarcoma in her peritoneum. The prognosis was bleak. Chemotherapy and radiation were a brutal combination that kept her ill for days at a time.

Although she gradually lost all her hair, Norris still managed to look elegant using wigs and scarves. She was also busy finishing her first novel, *Windchill Summer.* That kept her in good spirits, which in turn helped her heal. By the summer of 2000, she handed Danielle and me the final draft to read. I was happy to sincerely tell her, "It's a page turner and I think it'll be a success." She had been true to herself: the story had a good plot.

My father had health issues as well all through this period. He was having trouble with his teeth and his hearing was getting worse. The arthritis in his joints became so painful he finally caved in and went through a hip replacement, just a few weeks before Norris was diagnosed with cancer. Afterward he had to walk with two canes.

Whenever I asked if it hurt, he'd say, "I'm always in pain, but it's all right. I figure I'm paying my karmic dues."

In spite of these difficult times, both Dad and Norris kept an incredibly busy schedule. In 2001 they did stage readings of *Zelda, Scott and Ernest,* assembled from the letters of those three writers by Terry Quinn and George Plimpton. It had started off as a benefit reading for a school in Vermont, then blossomed into a year of travel as they staged it in venues from Paris to London and many cities in between. Norman played Ernest Hemingway, George was Scott, and Norris portrayed Zelda. These readings were probably what they enjoyed most during that period of their lives. When they were in New York they went out constantly, but in Provincetown they spent their time writing.

～

In 2002 Norris' father, James Davis, died. The following January, her cancer came back. Due in part no doubt to the strain of going to Arkansas every month and watching her beloved father, whom she had adored, fading away. Added to that was the emotional weight of taking charge of her mother, Gaynell, with whom she had never gotten along. It all became too heavy a load for Norris: This time the cancer was even worse.

I happened to be in New York at the time, since it was close to my father's eightieth birthday and Norris's fifty-fourth. Dad was scheduled to speak at the Barnes & Noble in Union Square. Just before his talk he got a call from Norris, telling him the doctor had again found cancerous tumors in her abdomen and was very pessimistic. Visibly upset, with all the color drained from his face, Dad got up in front of the audience and spoke for more than a half hour. He took a few questions, then called it a night. All nine children were there. Earlier, we'd heard the news not all was well with Norris and had arrived en masse to lend our support to Dad.

After his talk we gathered in the back of the bookstore's large speaking room. Convening between the shelves, we settled on a course of action for the next few days. We'd all go to Boston for her operation. It would be a difficult procedure, and her surgeon feared she might not live through it.

The next day Aunt Barbara and I took the train to Boston, arriving just in time to see Norris before visiting hours came to an end. Her surgery was scheduled for 6 AM the following day. We all got up before dawn and made a pilgrimage to her room to wish her luck, surprising a smile out of her. With the help of his two canes Dad practically ran through the hospital corridors to get to her room in time. He held her hand and said, "I love you. You are beautiful."

They spoke privately for a few minutes, until the nurses came in and she was taken away.

Norris came out of surgery at mid-morning. She'd survived the operation, but her recovery was going to be slow, the treatment even more aggressive than the last time, the surgeon announced. But she was alive, and that was all that mattered at that moment. We felt she'd probably won a few more good years, at least.

That day we all spent in Boston supporting Dad and Norris was unforgettable. There was laughter, lots of it, mixed with tears and anxiety.

The scene that stands out in my mind happened while most of us were sitting in the lobby of the hotel we had booked, waiting for Norris to come out of surgery. Our ears were numb and red from the freezing weather; our hands sorely chapped. Guy, Kate's husband, took out a large tube of Aveeno moisturizing lotion from his backpack and applied some to his hands.

My brother Stephen, in TV-commercial voiceover tones, said to Guy, "Would you like to try some of mine? It's ah-*mazin*."

"Some of your *what*?" Guy said brusquely.

Stephen changed his voice again. "This! You Bermudian prick." And he showed him a small tube of Neutrogena Norwegian Formula Fragrance-Free hand cream. "It's the best. And I should know, I wash my hands a hundred times a day."

By this time, Guy was smiling. We all were. He said, in his perfect British accent, "Why, then, should I trust such an obsessive compulsive? Be off with you at once."

"Try it, you *schmuckus*!" Stephen roared.

"I never stray from the power of my glorious, cultivated, colloidal moisturizing lotion." Guy sprang to his feet and confronted Stephen in a fencing pose, Aveeno in one hand. In a deep voice he cried, "*En guarde!*"

Stephen jumped up with his tiny, outmatched Neutrogena tube, and they fenced for a few seconds, then collapsed onto a sofa, laughing uncontrollably.

We were all roaring by then, tears running down our cheeks. Definitely in a manic mood, we joked, we giggled. We burst into laughter over anything, then got teary eyed and sentimental. We drank lots of coffee and ate gooey muffins and donuts.

The day after the surgery, exhausted from stress and lack of sleep, we split up into three cars and went back to New York. Yet, still unable to separate, we followed each other on the highway for a while, caravan style. Late in the evening, Michael dropped me off at my place. John drove our father back to Provincetown. He would return to Boston to pick up his mother in a few days.

A week later cousin Peter and I drove to Provincetown to help take care of Norris and Dad. Aunt Barbara was already there but would be going back to New York in a few days. Peter was to stay for a week, while I would leave with my aunt.

The atmosphere in the house that day was grim. Norris was clearly miserable, in pain and considerable distress, and could barely get out of bed. The house was dark, except for the dining room and the kitchen. Norris had a thing about light in the house. There was a lamp in every corner, nook and cranny, high and low, all of which she lit every evening and turned off before she went to bed. Now the house was gloomy and dim. Her illness hung in the air of the unlit rooms.

Peter and I had arrived that evening to a broiled chicken Aunt Barbara had prepared. Norris made an effort and came down to sit with us. But soon Dad began picking on her. He was annoyed because he hadn't slept well the night before.

He complained, "You move around in bed too much."

"But Norman, I'm in pain. I'm trying to find a good position."

"Well, it's damned annoying."

"Maybe you should sleep someplace else," she shot back, looking hurt.

"I believe I will. That way I won't have to hear you moaning. Oh, how you moan and groan, how you moan and groan."

We stared, unable to believe what we were hearing.

Aunt Barbara snapped, "Stop, Norman. Enough!"

I left the table and went to the kitchen. Norris got up, crying, and Peter helped her up the stairs to her bedroom. Dad sat alone in the dining room for a long time while Peter, Aunt Barbara, and I washed the dishes in silence.

At last he got up and slowly came into the kitchen. "I'm sorry," he said. "I was out of line."

"Yes, you were," we replied, almost in unison.

"And you must apologize to Norris," Barbara said, with unusual vehemence.

He looked forlorn.

Furious as I was, I could sense his fear. He looked lost. This wasn't supposed to happen. Norris wasn't supposed to get sick, or be on the verge of dying. *He* was the old man who needed care.

Dad went upstairs to Norris and didn't come down again.

After that night he slept in one bedroom on the east side of the house, while Norris stayed in the master bedroom. I believe his outburst produced an irreparable tear in their relationship. Even though later Norris told me they still cuddled and held each other, they never shared a bedroom again.

And, just as Dad had said to me, I don't think she ever forgave him.

CHAPTER 32

Being There

"SO, HOW ABOUT TAKING A YEAR OFF AND GOING TO NEW YORK?" Marco asked one Saturday morning, while we were having a cappuccino at our favorite café. It was 2003, and the beginning of spring in Chile.

"You mean, like, when? Next year?"

"Yes. Like next year."

A playful remark, one he'd made before. While we drank our coffee, we talked of all the things we could do in the City. Still I assumed it was a whimsical what-if, soon to be forgotten. He'd floated the idea many times over the years; a promise Marco had made to me when we first moved to Chile. But soon we were busy with jobs and kids, and so the notion was always shelved.

Now we began thinking seriously about it.

The timing wasn't great; my practice was very busy. But if I were to always take this into consideration, there would never be a good time. Marco was also busy. He had just turned sixty-four, and after ten years of high-profile positions in the government he felt he needed time to think about what he kept calling "the last quarter of my life."

We have the freedom to do this. So why not? I kept saying to myself. I also thought about my aging parents. Both Norman and Bea were eighty-one. I didn't know how many more years they would have. Our kids were twenty-three, nineteen, and sixteen. The two oldest were at university, but still living at home, Chilean style. Our youngest, Antonia, could come with us. She'd often talked about going to live someplace else, and New York seemed just the ticket. Now we had to find her a school.

The plan started taking shape. So, before Marco changed his mind, I got to work.

I wanted to take full advantage of my year in the City. I first organized the time, signing up for three study groups that began in September. This would be a unique opportunity to learn and interact with psychoanalysts I respected and whose books I'd read and taught at the Chilean Psychoanalytic Institute. I planned to spend time with the family too, of course. And also visit museums, go to the theatre, and eat fantastic food. Absorb the energy of the streets of New York.

Dad and Norris were living full time in Provincetown, so Marco thought we might be able to move into their Brooklyn Heights apartment. Then, instead of paying rent—something Dad would never have accepted anyway—we could contribute to its renovation. Over the previous years Matt and Maggie, as well as cousin Peter, had lived in the place off and on, so it certainly needed a facelift.

Norris immediately accepted our offer. She was still quite ill at the time but the idea of refurbishing the apartment was a boost to her energy. She quickly got in touch with an architect and a contractor, and in the months before our arrival had them remodel. The ropes and hammocks were removed. They modified the stairs that went to the second landing and put a handrail along the ledge that led to my old bedroom. The windows were sealed with silicone and she gave some old furniture away. She redecorated the main bedroom and put in a new bathroom. Instead of white, as the walls had long been painted, Norris decided on a dark green.

After the renovation was finished, Dad went to New York to see the result. When he walked in, he told me he'd been speechless. Not only were the ropes and hammock gone, but Vertical City, his vertiginous futuristic city made from 10,000 Lego blocks of five colors, had disappeared. This construction had been a central piece of the apartment since 1967, taking up an area of about six square feet in the living room. Dad had designed it and had it assembled by Beverly's half-brother Charlie Brown and a Provincetown friend, Eldred Mowry. He considered the Lego construction to be his unique contribution to city design, and put it on the cover of his 1966 book *Cannibals and Christians*. Yet after 25 years the city had lost its luster, and many pieces were missing.

Norris wasn't attached to it. "It was impossible to dust," she often said. Without asking Dad, she had it taken apart, and gave each of his children a chunk. Holy relics, of a sort. One piece was donated to the newly established Norman Mailer Society to be auctioned off. I wasn't interested in owning a block, so I settled for a photo of the complete city, and asked Dad to sign it for me.

My father was relieved Norris had bounced back with such zest, but it took the wind out of him to see the place where he'd lived since 1962, with four wives, and off and on with all of his children, become gentrified. It might've looked better, but it had lost much of the old quirky charm.

Initially I felt reticent about living there. I thought the place would be full of ghosts from the past. But after Antonia got into a school five blocks away, I decided it was the best possible choice.

Leaving Santiago turned out to be harder than I'd expected. Saying goodbye to patients and closing my office brought back memories of loss that I felt in my aching neck and shoulders, and in a disgruntled gut. But I was also very excited about the move and was in the midst of a constant flurry of activity.

I worried about my two oldest children. Because of my own childhood experiences, I had always tried to protect them from emotional hardship, especially the feeling of an empty home. Now the image of "the big empty house" was a large shadow looming over me. I knew they were no longer kids, and that my fight was with the ghosts in my own nursery, not theirs. Janet, our trusted cook and housekeeper, would stay on and be a principle of continuity. Our two golden retrievers, Dante and Laica, would keep them company. Valentina and Alejandro could visit us in New York during their vacation breaks.

Antonia, Valentina and Alejandro, before our move to New York, 2004.

We asked Valentina, our oldest, if she'd be willing to take charge of the house in our absence. She agreed and did a splendid job the year and a half we were away.

We took the place at the beginning of July, reaching Brooklyn Heights fourteen hours later. We then lugged six large, very heavy suitcases up four flights of stairs. Only to discover we couldn't get in. There was a new lock on the door and I didn't have the key! It must have been 90 degrees at the top of that airless staircase. I felt queasy and had no idea what to do. We didn't have a cell phone, and it was high summer, so most of the family was away, and of course Dad and Norris were in Provincetown.

In a flash Judith McNally, my father's secretary, came to mind. She lived a few blocks away, so I went to the nearest pay phone. Fortunately, she was home and had the new key. Twenty minutes later we walked into a steaming hot, newly-painted apartment. Its shiny floor was squeaky clean, but the place had no air conditioning!

The phone rang the moment we walked in. Norris, wanting to know what we thought of the changes. Dad sounded tired, but he too got on the line and welcomed us; no longer the paterfamilias at the door welcoming his offspring home. His tone was wistful. We'd taken charge of the old apartment which had always been his terrain. It was modified and gentrified, and we had contributed to this change. Always sensitive to even slight shifts of power, surely he couldn't help but feel a touch of melancholy. Norris was happy, though, probably already making plans for their move to New York after we left, while Dad was inclined to remain for the rest of his life in Provincetown. But it hadn't come to that yet, during the summer of 2004.

Very soon after we drove to Provincetown for two weeks, renting a house a few doors away from the Big House. The whole extended family arrived: my siblings, my children, Alejandro and Valentina, and Marco's daughter Daniela with her newborn baby girl Tali and husband Daniel. They lived in Cambridge; he was getting a PhD at Harvard while she worked on a PsyD at a psychoanalytic institute. We did all the traditional activities: hikes with the kids, swimming in Long Nook, walking across the flats and the dunes, shopping. And the Whale Watch cruise, Marco's usual outing with the children.

Dad stuck to his longtime routine, but there was something different about him now. He stayed at the breakfast table longer, reading the newspapers and playing solitaire. He was more amenable to chatting before going up to his studio to work. In his early eighties, he had grown gentler.

That summer he was busy with *Hitler's Mother*, an early working title for his last novel, *The Castle in the Forest*. His studio was filled with books on the Holocaust, Germany, WW II, and Hitler, as well as references on bees and apiculture. He had been studying the German language and was considering taking a trip there. He also had severe angina and popped nitro pills and aspirin like candy. He still needed canes to walk, and he was always in pain. His neck was stiff; his joints creaked. Yet he was resolved to finish this book. He felt "the great novel" had always eluded him, and this time he hoped to deliver.

Norris was also writing a novel, the sequel to her first. They worked in their studios on opposite ends of the third-floor attic. If someone wanted to get a message to Norman, they often emailed Norris, who then walked a dozen steps and laid a note silently on his desk. Both were ill, but the severity of my father's heart condition hadn't yet been realized.

During our stay in Provincetown Dad and I had several conversations. He knew he was sick and getting old, but it wasn't so bad, he said. "If my knees hurt or I get chest pains, I figure it's karmic compensation, a way to pay back for the mistakes I've made." He felt age had its perks. For instance, "I can concentrate on my work without a nagging feeling I'm missing the action. Even though my body is not in great shape, my instincts are still sharp."

Though he was still prone to fits of irritability, he wasn't as angry as in his youth. This was a relief for everyone. He also couldn't drink the way he had in the past, so he was free of the punishing hangovers he had so aptly described in *Tough Guys Don't Dance*. His favorite drinks now were a whisky sour with "all the garbage," as he put it, cherries and various fruit slices, or the proverbial Presbyterian: a jigger of white rum with equal parts of water and orange juice, and a big slice of lemon.

For me, the most important change in my octogenarian father was the emergence of a brisk sweetness I had only seen before on rare occasions. Perhaps this persona dated all the way back to that nice young Jewish boy from Brooklyn. He was clearly vulnerable now. Sometimes in the morning I'd walk over to the big house and see him laboring to prepare his breakfast. I'd offer to help and, following his precise instructions, cut two oranges, then scramble two eggs which usually didn't come out exactly the way he liked. I'd set a mug of black coffee on the table, no sugar, with toast and butter on the side. I enjoyed taking care of him. He'd grumble, "Don't hover over me."

But it was obvious he needed, and secretly enjoyed, the attention.

After breakfast we'd both settle down to read the newspaper, or he'd play his favorite game of solitaire to "comb his mind."

Now that I too was free of anger, I could be a doting daughter, ready to enjoy whatever he had to offer. Just being with Dad in the morning—we didn't speak much—and looking out at the bay with its unique light was enough. After breakfast he'd slowly make his way up to the third floor to work, and I would go back to my family.

Every time I visited Dad, we followed our ritual of going out, just the two of us, for a meal. He did the same with my siblings, either lunch or dinner. But that summer, Norris warned me "Under no circumstances is Norman to drive." Half blind and with poor reflexes, he was a danger to himself and to others, but he didn't want to accept that.

Forewarned, I arrived at his house for our date. "Hey, Dad. You ready?"

"Yes. I thought we could go to Pepe's and take the car. There's a parking lot there."

Oh shit, I thought and immediately said, "Ok, I'll drive."

"I see Norris talked to you. She's got it into her head that I can't drive anymore, and she's full of shit."

"Dad, really, I can drive. It's no problem. You don't have to prove anything." I realized, too late, that was exactly the wrong thing to say.

"I won't hear of it. Don't be ridiculous, I'll drive."

He was determined. He took his canes and with difficulty got into the car. "Hop in," he ordered. But getting his seat adjusted took some time. He had to hike up the driver's seat, get his legs close to the pedals and his body close enough to the steering wheel. Then he adjusted the side mirrors to his eye level; not that he ever used them. All of this fiddling irritated him so much, he refused to put on his seat belt. So, he hobbled up out of the car and stood there, waiting for me to buckle it over the empty seat before he got in again.

I figured, *What the hell, I'll just go along with this. It can't be that dangerous driving down Commercial Street.*

We started on our way, and Dad was doing pretty well. But soon, we came to a complete stop. A commercial van, trying to make a difficult turn into a very narrow street, was blocking our way. We waited a minute, then a few more.

Dad shifted in his seat. He stuck his head out the window to look. "What's going on? Why isn't that van moving?"

"I'm sure it'll get going in a few minutes." I said, trying to calm him down.

He honked the horn; first a few short beeps. No response. Another honk. Finally, a long and very angry one.

The van still didn't move. But a big, tough-looking woman with a buzz haircut, in shorts and a T shirt with cut off- sleeves, got out of the van and walked slowly over to our car. Her expression was grim, her mouth tight, the whole effect menacing.

Leaning on the door, she poked her head into the open window on Dad's side. "Hey, hey! Gotta problem?"

"You're damn straight I gotta problem," Dad growled. "Why the fuck you blocking the street? People gotta move here."

"Oh, yeah? Well, that's too fucking bad."

"What!" Dad shouted. "What did you say? Fuck you!"

"Fuck *me*?" she spat out. "Fuck you, buster!"

She stood there a few seconds glaring at him. Then walked away, got back in the van and, taking her time, turned off into the side street.

"Phew!" Dad exclaimed. "I was worried for a moment there. I thought I was going to have to hobble out on my two canes and have it out with her, and she would've beaten the shit out of me."

We both burst out laughing and drove on to Pepe's with no further incidents.

We had a great time at lunch, but when we got back into the car to go home, Dad again insisted on driving. While trying to get out of the parking space, as usual he didn't look into the rearview or side mirrors, nor did he turn around to gauge his distance from a car parked nearby. He was too stiff to turn his head. So, of course he got too close to the other car and lightly scratched its paint. He was so embarrassed he handed me the keys and said, "Here, take them. Better you drive."

Dinners were not quite the same in his last years. My father was hard of hearing and no longer the center of the conversation. He still decided who sat next to him but, as the evening progressed, the strain of listening and barely hearing was tiring. I could see him drifting off into his thoughts, only perking up when dinner was over and Texas Hold'em could begin. I wasn't good at poker, so I usually went into the living room with Norris or some other uninterested straggler.

But Dad regularly insisted that poker was the game for me. "It'll help you read the subtle, unspoken expressions of the other players. And that'll be helpful when you're with your patients." He was probably right, but I don't like card games.

Norris wasn't well that summer either. The tumors had returned, and she was scheduled for another operation in August. She checked into Mass General early that month. Due to the radium treatments she'd taken in previous years, the soft tissue of her abdomen had been severely damaged. Her surgeon was obliged to take out a considerable amount of small intestine. He performed an ileostomy, a rerouting of the small bowel that required a colostomy bag be attached to a port in her lower abdomen. She would only have it for a few months, while her intestines healed. But she was embarrassed by the leakage and the smells that came from the bag. With her usual facility, Norris became proficient at changing it. A few months later, she would be creating beautiful bag-bags out of old purses, and joking about her condition. But immediately after the operation she was in a sour mood and had no use for humor.

Norris specifically asked that no one visit. "I have no energy. I can't entertain anyone," she told Norman.

But Dad asked me to go anyway, so I called and insisted on seeing her. I spent two days at the hospital in what turned out to be a special time between us, with no makeup and no lies. I knew she realized she might die, and I didn't deny the fact, nor did I make light of it. My being honest, and just being there, I think gave Norris a break from her lovely, elegant, always-appropriate self. For me it was a relief to not have to make nice, or to remember to tell her she looked beautiful. Nor to lie and say that everything would be okay. We both knew she was at a crossroads.

My father was grateful I'd gone to the hospital. Staying in Boston would have been impossible for him. He and Norris got on each other's nerves, and he was inept at the kind of gentle interaction she needed just then. He resented her illness, and at the same time felt awful for being so selfish—the same old split in his sensibility. Seeing her suffer was unbearable, but at the same time he was angry she wasn't her usual self. At the root of these conflicted feelings was the knowledge that his wife was ill with cancer, a disease he'd written about in the sixties and had mentioned many times in interviews, as well as in family conversations. He had long believed cancer was brought on by unexpressed dread and anger, and by exposure to plastic.

He again reproached himself for all his infidelities, all the emotional pain he had inflicted on Norris. Several times in the years before he died, he told Marco and me, "I'm sure she's never forgiven me and it's probably one of the reasons she got cancer." But once said aloud, it was too hard to face, and he would again blame Norris for getting sick, for not letting out her anger. For "being so damn southern with all the bullshit sweet talk and good manners. Never able to stop being the well-behaved, sweet Southern Baptist belle."

My father wasn't to blame for everything. Cancer, as he had intuited in the 1960s, has been linked to depression and trauma as well as stress. And the last couple of years had been particularly difficult for Norris. Her father had died the year before. After his death she had packed her mother's clothes and taken her to Provincetown to live in the Big House. A bad choice, because Gaynell had no desire to leave Arkansas, and she and her daughter had never gotten along. But a sense of duty dictated Norris must take care of her mother. And since she felt she couldn't leave Gaynell alone in Arkansas, after much pleading Norris had convinced her to come to Provincetown. Gaynell was severely depressed, though, and there was nothing her daughter could do to make her happy.

When I saw her that summer in Provincetown, I told Norris her mother needed to see a psychiatrist and start taking antidepressants. Her mood lifted, but it was still an untenable situation. She was an albatross around Norris's neck. Try as she might to make her mother happy, Gaynell was never satisfied. So, after a few months in the Big House, and thanks to a forceful push from my father, Norris finally realized everyone would be better off with Gaynell in an assisted living facility nearby. Although my father and Norris and even Gaynell were happier with the arrangement, all the stress took its toll on Norris and the cancer came back.

I was happy to be around during that summer. I had missed so many important events in the family. To be there for both of them for a change gave me deep satisfaction. I was in the center of the storm and it didn't feel bad. For once I wasn't being informed of events long distance. Now, I was the news bearer.

In September Antonia started school in New York. At sixteen, and without her close friends and siblings around, she was trying very hard to adjust. I knew exactly how that felt and tried to help as much as she'd let me. She did manage to enjoy New York and some of her courses, and even made a couple of friends.

It was easier for me; I was in known territory. Everything from the apartment, to the neighborhood grocery stores, to the subway we took to get to the city, was familiar. But Marco and I lacked our usual routine and felt at loose ends. We had longed for a life without schedules and appointments, but at first so much free time was unsettling.

Family Gathering in Brooklyn Heights. 2005. In back:
Danielle, Antonia, Marco, Kate, Betsy and her husband Frank Nastasi
Sitting: Stephen with son Teddy, Isabella Moschen with Natasha Lancaster
(Kate's daughter), Cal (Stephen's oldest), Guy Lancaster (Kate's husband) and
Christina Marie Nastasi, (Betsy's daughter.) I took the photo.

Dad came to New York in early September, but he stayed with friends. He said the apartment's stairs were getting to be too much for him, but we understood he didn't want to impose on us. We insisted he stay with us the next time he was in the City. He came into town a few more times, and his visits became a painful treat. Even with the canes, walking a block was an ordeal. He had to stop every few minutes to catch his breath. Every step demanded an enormous amount of effort and will. Once we got home to Brooklyn Heights, he somehow managed to climb up the four flights. Then he'd walk in and collapse onto the nearest chair.

During these visits I would cater to his needs. He didn't complain about my hovering any more. In the morning I'd fix his breakfast and he'd crack a joke about my being such a caretaker. "Didn't know you had it in you, kid, but you're doing pretty good. Not bad at all."

Taking care of him was gratifying. He'd finally become the father I had always yearned for. Now he was gentle and appreciative. Occasionally irritable, but it didn't scare me anymore. I enjoyed just watching him read the *Times*. Sometimes he'd ask me to open his mail or to sit next to him while he taught me a new game of solitaire. He was still writing *The Castle in the Forest,* so he'd hand me new pages to read. Then we'd discuss them. He listened closely to my comments, but of course in the end paid no attention to them. "You can comment all you like, but I'll do what I want," seemed to be his motto. He didn't listen to his editor either, so I didn't take it personally.

I felt an old wound beginning to heal.

The next year, on the last day of April, Matt and his girlfriend Salina got married on San Padre Island, Texas. Dad and Norris were both in poor health. But nothing short of death would have stopped Norris from seeing her oldest son take his wedding vows, and Dad, also keen to be present, hobbled onto the plane on his canes.

But later that year Dad's breathing problems got worse.

Our youngest brother John was his companion on many of his speaking engagements, which were still considerable. One day, John called me at the Brooklyn apartment and asked if I could meet him in Provincetown. He was exhausted after a week on the road with Dad. He told me the night before had been hairy.

"This time I thought it was the end. We got home and sat in the dining room to rest a bit before dinner. Pops wasn't feeling well all day; he hardly ate at dinner and said he had an awful pain in his chest. He started popping nitro pills and aspirin like crazy. He was sweating and very pale and I began to panic. I insisted on taking him to the ER, but eventually the pain subsided, and he went to bed. I wasn't sure I'd see him alive in the morning. But I thought, *so be it*, he'll go the way he wants to go."

I took a plane to Provincetown. When I walked into the house, I hugged my twenty-five-year-old brother. He had a heavy load, taking care of two ailing parents.

My father finally went to a heart specialist and agreed to have open-heart surgery that summer. But before the surgery, he had to have his remaining teeth extracted, to reduce the risk of infection.

Suddenly he looked ten years older. I could see defeat in his eyes, the shame of being a toothless old man. He told a friend, "You lose your manhood when you lose your uppers." My father had hated plastic for as long as I could remember. Having false teeth was his idea of torture, and he took them out at the oddest moments. Trying to be funny, he would come down for breakfast and give us a toothless grin. Sometimes he had the false teeth right next to him in a glass of water and would pop them in when someone visited. It became an ordeal for him simply to chew his food.

One evening, in the summer in Provincetown, a couple of my siblings, Aunt Barbara, Norris, Marco, and I were having dinner when suddenly we heard strange hacking noises coming from Dad. He'd swallowed a piece of meat, but it had stuck, and he was trying to cough it up. He tried a few more times but couldn't get it out. We could tell he was choking, and desperate, but we sat in our seats paralyzed, unable to move. Marco sprang up from his chair and gave Norman the Heimlich maneuver three times. Dad finally spat out the chunk.

After thanking Marco, Dad turned to Norris very angry and upset. "Goddammit! Why do you cook meat for dinner when you know I can't chew it."

The heart surgery was set for September. All his children and the older grandchildren went to Mass General to see him beforehand. After surgery I walked into his hospital room and saw a tiny old man in a funny-looking bed that snuggled him closely and held him in an upright position, like a baby with acid reflux. His voice sounded otherworldly, with the hollow, metallic quality produced by a person speaking through an electro-larynx device. The doctors said it was an aftereffect of the intubation during anesthesia.

But he was full of energy and gusto. "I've had some interesting insights about this experience, kiddo. I can't forget them because I'll want to write about them later. Can you imagine, Sue? Doctors take your heart out and connect you to a machine that gets your blood pumping through your body while they get to work on your arteries.

Right now, I'm sure my heart is in shock, not to speak of the cells. I mean, to have your blood flowing through a machine that probably has plastic parts must do some job on your cells. Some of them die during this whole process and those that don't have the taste of dread in them. No wonder people get depressed after this operation. Me? I'm feeling great."

But of course, he was high on pain killers.

A month later Marco and I went to the rehab center in Orleans to see him. We would be going back to Chile in a few weeks, so it was a sad visit for the three of us. I'd never before thought much about my father dying, but now his death was becoming a real possibility. What affected me most was to see how depressed he was. The operation had taken its toll and weighed on his spirits, though physically Dad was slowly recovering. He diligently did the breathing exercises, walked on his canes, and was doing his best to get back to Provincetown. At the same time, he was growing more impatient with the delay, and itching to get home.

As we were leaving he said to me, "Sue, I'm so happy you spent this year in the States. It was a treat having you both here. Don't take too long to come back."

Marco and I walked out, got into the car, and cried.

CHAPTER 33

It's Better to Go a Little
Before Than a Little After

Dad in Brooklyn Heights, May 2007.

IN LATE AUGUST OF 2007 MY FATHER WENT TO BOSTON, FOR A
checkup at Mass General. He must've been feeling awful to leave
Provincetown and his own doctor. But once he entered the hospital the

old vim came back for a short period. When Marco and I arrived, he was bickering with Norris. He looked at us, then turned back to her. "Now that Sue and Marco are here, why don't you go shopping."

She shrugged it off with a joke. "I can never say no to shopping, so I shall leave you with him."

The doctors had to run a series of tests and wanted him to stay for at least a week. He protested that he had to get back, because my sister Maggie was getting married in a week. In the end, I'm not sure how many tests were done, but I know he left without a clear diagnosis, looking ashen, without energy and very frail.

Maggie's wedding took place in Provincetown at the Big House, on September 8, a cool, windy day. Her big blue eyes sparkled with excitement, and her long dark hair cascaded in curls down to the middle of her back. She wore a long cream-colored dress. When she descended the stairs, the combination of pale dress, dark hair, and bouquet were perfect. She looked radiant and was especially happy Dad had been able to make it to the ceremony.

But our father could barely walk. He sat quietly on a chair on the beach right outside his house, the wind blowing during low tide, while the ceremony unfolded before us.

Michael, Stephen and John are the toastmasters of our family. Later, on the deck overlooking the bay, they regaled Maggie with warm and funny childhood memories. Then we all went inside for cocktails, dinner, and dancing. Dad sat next to Aunt Barbara in the living room nursing a drink. He tried his best to talk to all the guests who stood in line to greet him, but instead of his usual low bass his voice was a whisper; he could not get enough air. He made an effort to stay for dinner but by that time felt too weak; he kissed the bride and was helped upstairs by John.

After Maggie's wedding, Norris went to New York for a scheduled event. Marco and I decided to stay for another week in Provincetown. So did Aunt Barbara, as well as Mike Lennon, Norman's biographer, and his wife Donna Pedro. We all got together every evening for a game of Texas Hold'em, the one activity Dad still totally enjoyed. Bill

Majeski, a friend and the retired New York City police detective who had tracked down Jack Abbott back in the Eighties, also came to visit for a couple days. I took a photo of the three "tough guys": Dad, Bill, and Marco, each wearing an NYPD cap.

Norris and Norman had hired Dwayne Raymond two years earlier to work as a personal assistant. He came for a few hours each day, sorting out my father's papers or his mail, or cooking when Norris was busy with another task. My father now spent a lot of time in his bedroom or in the little TV room off the kitchen, mostly sleeping. He had no energy. Dragging in each breath of air was like running a marathon. He'd lost forty pounds over the last year.

It finally came time to leave, and we wanted to get an early-morning start. The night before, Dad said to me, "If I'm not down by the time you finish breakfast, come upstairs to say goodbye."

That morning, I went up the stairs to his bedroom, knocked on the door, and walked in.

He was sitting at his desk with the light on and the shades down.

"Dad, we're leaving in a few minutes. I just wanted to say goodbye."

"Yes, yes, come in. I was waiting for you. Sit down." He gazed at me with tired eyes, and said, "Susie, I'm happy you and Marco stayed these few days. I appreciate it and want you to know I enjoyed being with both of you. But there is something else I wanted to tell you." He paused, struggling to take in a breath.

I leaned closer. He hadn't called me Susie in a long time.

He finally got sufficient air to speak again. "This family, our family, is a fine tapestry. I want you to make sure it doesn't unravel."

I felt honored and panicked at the same time. I was the oldest child, true. I knew that in some way it was my responsibility to keep the family together. But I had no idea at that moment how to do it. I lived in Chile. How could I keep all my siblings together? At the same time, I knew he wasn't talking about geography, but about spirit. It wasn't necessary for me to be in New York. I could maintain the family tapestry with emails, by phone calls, and during summer visits. And I wasn't alone. Aunt Barbara, all my siblings, and Norris would help with the task I had just inherited.

But I said none of this. Instead I murmured, "Oh Daddy, I'm so sad." And began to cry.

"Don't cry, honey, I'm fine, really, I'm okay with this."

We embraced then, and he had tears in his eyes. I was sobbing.

"Okay Sue. Go now," he said. "You don't want to keep Marco waiting. I said goodbye to him last night. I love that guy, tell him I love him. Okay?"

We drove away from Provincetown a few minutes later waving goodbye to Aunt Barbara. Later on, Mike and Donna would be arriving, and also Dwayne, to cook and help with paperwork. I felt slightly better knowing Dad wouldn't be alone.

Norris decided she could no longer live in Provincetown fulltime. In March she moved back to Brooklyn Heights. She'd been talking about doing this for a while. Out at the end of the Cape, it was windy, cold, and nearly deserted for several months of the year, in winter. She'd felt she was fading there; withering away. She missed the family members who lived in and around New York City, and now that her son Matthew and his wife Salina had Mattie and that Jackson was on the way, Norris wanted to be closer to them.

Although Dad understood and supported her choice, he refused to follow her back to the City. He often said he wanted to die in Provincetown listening to the water lap against the deck. He was determined to stay on. Provincetown was now his home. But during those months, from March until June, it was obvious he was lonely. Provincetown still had a winter chill even in spring, and few friends lived in town at that time of year. He called Norris several times a day on his cell phone, which never left the pocket of his fleece vest.

Fortunately, Mike and Donna had made "P-Town" their permanent residence while Mike was writing the lengthy authorized biography. A real blessing; they went to see Norman practically every night, and either stayed for dinner or arrived later for a night of poker. Sometimes they stopped by for a drink or took him to doctors' appointments. Aside from social visits, Mike was busy writing and researching the biography, as well as with a book he and Dad had been writing together. It was a running conversation on my father's ideas about God, which was published later that year under the title, *On God: An Uncommon Conversation.*

Dwayne was not only an assistant; he was a writer himself, and a very good cook. He proved to be a loyal friend for both my father and Norris during Dad's last year. Before Norris left for New York, the three of them had agreed Dwayne would not only spend a few hours each day sorting and answering mail, and helping with Norman's papers; he would also cook for him, arriving in the morning to fix breakfast, work on Dad's projects, then give him his lunch and leave dinner ready, if necessary. He also bought the groceries, and spoke regularly to Norris, or emailed her several times a day to report on the state of affairs at the Big House.

Still, in spite of friends dropping by and the close attention and care he had, the bottom line was that Dad was living alone for the first time in his life. During that period, to my great surprise, he called me in Chile a few times just to say hello. "When are you coming to New York?" he would ask.

During one such call in May, he even went so far as to suggest I hop on a plane right then and come see him. I couldn't remember the last time he'd asked me to drop what I was doing just for him. Once I married Marco, he had treated me as an adult, making a point of not interfering with my relationship with my husband or the details of our life in any way. So his impulsive request touched me. I canceled all appointments for ten days and hopped on a plane.

As luck would have it, Dad was in New York, so I didn't have to drive all the way to Provincetown after all. We spent a good deal of time together at the Brooklyn Heights apartment. We read and chatted, he slept, I made him a meal.

One afternoon I felt the urge to ask him about the stabbing episode.

For quite a while I'd wanted to know more. And many times, he'd told me we would talk about it when I was old enough to understand. I was certainly old enough by then, and also felt we might not get another chance. I was thinking about this when, without any prompting from me, he began talking of Adele and that night in November 1960.

"We were both out of our minds with drinking and drugs. At each other's throats. It was a bad time. Very bad."

This wasn't anything I didn't already know; what was new for me was his tone. I could tell he was still grieving about the incident.

He said, "Sue, I'm sorry for all the harm this caused the family. I know the damage was profound and irreparable. All my kids have had to carry this burden." His tone was full of concern and sadness. I'm sure he must've often thought of the stabbing and felt tremendous guilt over what he had done. But unlike on other occasions, this time there was no avoidance of responsibility and no anger in his voice. It was the first and only time I can remember him saying, "I'm very sorry I hurt you and everyone else in the family." A rare and precious moment of intimate communication. It felt as if he had read my thoughts. And since Dad didn't have much time left, it was truly *carpe diem*.

During the last week of September, I was back in Chile having lunch at my son's new home when I got an urge to call my father. In fact, such a strange and strong urgency it couldn't wait until Marco and I got home.

Dad answered the phone. "Oh, Sue, I'm so happy to hear from you, I was just about to call you. I've made an important decision I want you to know about. I've decided to have an operation."

"What kind of an operation, Dad?"

"It turns out I haven't been breathing well because I have a collapsed lung filled with fluid, and the other lung is only functioning at 75 percent. And I finally found a doctor I trust, at Mount Sinai. She's smart and seems to know what she's talking about. She says during the operation they will cut out the damaged lung tissue, and then be able to inflate it. I'll be able to breathe well again, and might have a few good years left. I figured, what the hell, I can't live this way anymore. If I go, so be it."

I was worried the surgery would be too much for him but didn't say anything to try to change his mind. He'd already made it up. And of course, he was right; he couldn't keep on living like this. He couldn't accept fading slowly. He preferred to go out with a fight.

The first week of October Marco and I flew to Spain for a conference. The weather in Madrid couldn't have been better. As we sat on a park bench on a sunny afternoon, sunlight filtering through the trees, I again had a sudden urge to call my father. Two years before I had worried about him during his quadruple bypass, but now I had a strong feeling he could die at any moment.

Right there in the park on Marco's cell phone, I finally reached Aunt Barbara. She told me Dad had been operated on the day before and was doing well. Relieved, I hung up and enjoyed the rest of the trip. Only to come back home to Santiago and discover by then he was not at all in good shape.

I got on a plane to New York a few days later.

Dad's operation had gone very well at first. In three days he was taken out of the ICU. He had visitors, was reading books and newspapers, and already thinking of what he would do when he got home. Mike Lennon had arrived with newly-released copies of *On God*, which gave Dad a boost. He'd been in good spirits. But a couple of days later he suddenly had difficulty breathing. His epiglottis was closing due to the aftereffects of intubation during the operation; not an uncommon occurrence, according to his doctors. He needed to be on a respirator for a few days, and so was put under sedation.

When I walked into the ICU and saw him, I had to take a step back. My father was lying in bed, asleep with his mouth open, a tube going down into his lungs, and the respirator whooshing in and out. The oxygen had dried the tissues surrounding his mouth and throat, so his lips were terribly chapped, even cracked. He appeared helpless and tiny. It was painful to look at him.

Later that day the family had a meeting with the doctors, who suggested a tracheotomy to alleviate his discomfort. They could connect the oxygen tube to Dad's larynx. That way he would be able to close his mouth and feel more comfortable. But taking that step also meant he wouldn't be able to speak.

None of us were thrilled with the solution but it was better than seeing him sedated with that horrible tube going down into his lungs. We figured it would be a brief treatment measure, and he'd soon be back to normal.

When he woke up after the tracheotomy, Dad seemed happy to see me. But he was also angry at the doctors, at the hospital, at all the tubes and the many medicines being pumped into his system. With the tracheotomy, and connected to a respirator, the only way he could communicate was in writing. But his cursive was an illegible scrawl, so few of us understood what he wanted. Norris was pretty good at deciphering his scribbles, but the rest of us could only guess, erring most of the time, which only added to his mounting irritation.

"Does something hurt?"

He'd shake his head. *No.*

"Do you want to read?"

Another terse shake of the head.

"Would you like me to read you the *Times?*" No, once more.

Finally, frustrated with angry sparks all but flying out of his eyes, he'd pull at his tubes and respirator. That message was quite clear: GET ME THE HELL OUT OF HERE!

All he wanted was to be back in Provincetown.

But once you're in a hospital, and in critical condition, you become a helpless prisoner of the system. The doctors tried to keep his spirits high so he wouldn't give up. They came up with a solution for each new obstacle. The lung doctor had thought Dad would be able to breathe well once he healed from the surgery. But she hadn't expected so many post-operative complications; and more were mounting daily. Each solution brought with it a new problem, which then suggested new procedures which carried their own troublesome results, and so on.

After the tracheotomy he got an infection in the groin which required an operation. He was put on strong intravenous antibiotics. A few days later, the gastroenterologist diagnosed a stomach lymphoma; a tumor which had been there for some time, apparently. By then my father was too weak to undergo another operation. It was evident he was dying.

Still the doctors insisted, "We can try another procedure. It will help him breathe. He'll be more comfortable, and he's strong."

Why didn't we just take him out then?

Norris was against it. She couldn't cope with the idea of him dying in Brooklyn Heights, and wouldn't hear of him being subjected to a long and painful ride home to Provincetown. She probably needed the protection of the hospital organization at that point. Her father's death surely still loomed in her mind, and she was weak from her own illness. Unlike my father, she had faith in the medical establishment.

Another important part of the equation was our hope that Dad might yet pull through these emergencies, just enough to get him out of there and back home where he wanted to be. We accepted all the medical procedures because we also felt helpless and didn't know what else to do.

But Dad knew he had to get out of there. He was desperate. He couldn't say so, but with his eyes he implored us. He tried writing it down. His gestures indicated the tubes: *Get these needles out, get me out of here.* But we were trapped in a labyrinth. Our father had been captured by the medical establishment he'd mistrusted for most of his life.

Finally, the family gathered in a meeting room the hospital had kindly provided for us. John said, "We could insist on his release and take him to Provincetown. He could get a last look at the sea and breathe some fresh air for a change."

But what if he died on the way? One of the young and sympathetic doctors sitting next to us said, "I know you'd like to take him home, and that he wants to go back to Provincetown. But he won't withstand the trip. He's even too weak now to be transferred to Brooklyn Heights."

And so our father stayed in Mount Sinai day after day, procedure after procedure. And I felt I needed to get back to Santiago. I knew he was dying, but figured I could still return to Chile for a few days.

I told him I had to leave; he nodded. His gaze asked when I would be back.

"Soon, I just have to take care of a few things." I had a class to teach, a conference presentation to give, patients to see. All the details of everyday life that at that moment seemed important enough to get me on a plane back to Santiago. In truth, I needed some air. It was all too painful to bear. And at the same time, I desperately wanted to stay.

The morning of my departure I met a friend at Le Pain Quotidien on 11th Street and Broadway. Suddenly, in the middle of our breakfast, I started to weep—my whole body was shaking. "I don't want to leave," I kept saying, "I want to stay."

She said forcefully, "So stay!" And handed me her phone. "Call the airline and cancel your trip."

I extended my time in New York, but only for another two days. When I walked back into the hospital room that day, Dad's eyes lit up, as if to say, *You're still here!*

I did return to Santiago, though I spoke every day to Norris or Aunt Barbara. Then a couple of days later, early on the morning of November 8, I got a phone call from Norris. "Sue, Dad is asking for you. I think you should come."

"Tonight?" I asked, still not fully comprehending this was the end. I felt paralyzed; I didn't know what to do. My mind raced with various worries. *I need to call my patients. I should let the Institute know I won't be teaching the next few seminars. Do I have time? Should I leave tonight? Tomorrow?*

I called Marco but couldn't reach him. I had to talk to someone about it, so I called a close friend.

"Susan, what is wrong with you? Of course you have to leave immediately. How will you feel if your father dies and you arrive the next day? Call the airline right now and get a seat, no matter what."

Which is exactly what we did.

～

Marco and I reached Aunt Barbara's house at 9 AM on November 9th. We dropped our bags and immediately headed to Mount Sinai. I called Antonia at Hampshire College, then bought a ticket for Valentina and Alejandro to fly in the next day.

Dad was still in the ICU. The doctors summoned the family for a meeting. All eleven of us filed into the conference room: Norris, all the siblings except for Stephen, who was acting in Arizona, Aunt Barbara, and Peter.

His primary doctor said "I'm afraid there's nothing else we can do. Your father is slipping away. We think he has only a few hours left."

Stephen was on speakerphone, crying. "I'll get the first plane out to New York," he said.

We were all in shock. In spite of the mounting evidence, we simply didn't believe our once-towering, indestructible father could die. Yet now it was happening. All the tubes would be taken out and he'd be transferred to another room in the hospital some time that afternoon, we were told.

Then Michael had a brilliant idea. He asked the doctors if Dad could have a drink. They said, "Whatever you think will make him feel better."

Michael went to the nearest liquor store and brought back a bottle of rum, some OJ, seltzer, and ice. When we entered the room with all those bottles, Dad's eyes lit up. He gestured with his hand, one-third rum, one-third water, one-third OJ. Just the way he liked it.

Peter apologized for the plastic cups, but Michael found a real glass for Dad's drink somewhere and put ice in it.

By then most of his tubes had been removed. The tracheotomy site was camouflaged with a gauze bandage. We stood in a circle around his bed, all of us, including our spouses, his sister Barbara, and Peter. Michael helped Dad sit up.

He took a couple of sips of the drink, and then he motioned for the straw to be taken out. The old fire was back for a few seconds. Norman Mailer was damned if he was going to have his last drink from a plastic straw! He sipped straight from the glass, coughed, and then smiled.

Lifting a thumb in approval, he then gestured for all of us to take a swallow from the same glass.

Kate asked, "Dad, are you ready?"

He lifted a hand and moved it in a "more or less" gesture. As if to say, *Is one ever totally ready for such a thing?*

Then Michael said, "Hey Dad, it'll be a great adventure."

I hope so, he mouthed.

I just wanted him to feel how much I loved him. I looked at him, searching for his eyes. Then smiled and squeezed his hand. He smiled back. He knew. Even though he was dying, he was still alive, all of him. And I was deeply grateful we could all be there to say goodbye to our father.

I remembered what he'd told me as I was leaving Provincetown in September. This big unruly band of brothers and sisters, this family, was a fine tapestry. It had never felt as strong as in that moment.

We left. He was wheeled to another room on a different floor. Next time we saw him, he would be free of tubes, the doctors had said.

We had a few hours until then, so we decided to grab a bite to eat. Always a hearty, hungry bunch, the fifteen of us headed to Sarabeth's in the East 90s. We sat together at a big round table. Once again in that goofy, excited, slightly frenzied mood that came over us when there was a storm brewing.

After dinner we went back to the hospital. Dad *was* looking better; sleeping calmly, connected to the vitals machine, but with no tubes. Only the oxygen beneath his nostrils and a morphine drip, which was shut off at that moment.

Stephen arrived shortly after, and said he'd sleep in the room with Dad that night.

Norris was quiet; she wasn't feeling well. John took her home, and soon the rest of us left. We would meet again at five AM to accompany our father to the departure point of his last voyage.

~

But in the end he beat us to it. Norman Mailer died at 4:38 AM on November 10th, 2007.

A few minutes before five, the phone rang. Immediately, Aunt Barbara came into the bedroom and told us in a low voice Dad had just passed.

We didn't speak, just quickly got dressed and left for the hospital. When we arrived at Mount Sinai, Michael and Stephen were already there, Betsy and Kate arrived soon after, as did Danielle and Maggie. John and Matt were with Norris and would come a little later.

Stephen told us that after we all left the night before, he had held Dad's hand for a while and fallen asleep next to him.

Some time later, suddenly the vitals machine went off, bells ringing, waking them both up.

Dad had opened his eyes and looked right at Stephen. Then he grinned at him— eyes shining—and died. Stephen held him for a while, then called the nurses.

We sat, we cried, and at last fell quiet. Marco took me aside. "Don't you think we should say Kaddish?"

We wandered the halls of Mount Sinai until we found the rabbi's quarters. He gave us a couple of prayer books and a few yarmulkes. Betsy and I washed our father's hands and dried them while the men read the Kaddish. I felt good when we all said, "Amen." We needed some kind of ritual, for Dad and for us. I thought Grandma would be pleased.

Norris arrived soon after with John and Matthew. She said a casket had to be chosen and asked, "Who wants to go to the funeral parlor?"

We all did. When we arrived, a slim man in a dark suit ushered us in with a doleful *I'm sorry for your loss* kind of look. Twenty people filed in, including Valentina and Alejandro, who'd just gotten off the plane.

"The caskets are upstairs. Are you *all* going up?" he asked, looking around at our large group in disbelief.

"Yes, of course," Stephen answered.

Upstairs a large, well lit room had four or five caskets on display. Norris was serious about the matter; she was in charge and the one listening to the undertaker.

But the rest of us got into a giddy, irreverent mood once again. We couldn't help cracking jokes about the different styles.

"Oh, I think *I* would prefer *this* one," Stephen said, imitating a flamboyant gay voice.

"Or perhaps plain pine would suit Norman best," countered Michael. "He'd go for the simple, rugged style."

The man in the dark suit led us to another large room. This held displays of the most lavish and expensive caskets, with prices all the way up to one hundred thousand dollars.

"Oops, I think we just stepped into the Mafia room." joked Stephen. "I'm sure Dad would like to lie in one of those. Should I try it out for him?" He lifted a leg as if he were actually going to climb inside.

We all giggled.

Fortunately, the man in the suit was talking to Norris and didn't seem to have noticed Stephen's gesture.

Of course, in the end Norris decided, choosing a sober, elegant wood casket with white satin lining. We found out then that nowadays all caskets were made of some kind of metal to prevent leakage. They were only wood lined for a more down-to-earth look. So, Dad wouldn't return to the earth, as he had wanted, but would decompose inside his coffin in the Provincetown cemetery. An unsettling image; one that every once-in-a-while still pops into my head.

We waited for Norris to fill out the paperwork, then we all left the funeral home, and went out to eat. Again.

~

My siblings and Norris always talked about visitations from the dead, but I'd never bought into that stuff. The first night after my father died, we were still at Aunt Barbara's. I went to bed and dreamt I was at a crossroads and couldn't decide which path to take: left or right? Dad was standing next to me. He said, "It doesn't matter which one you take. Go ahead and do it."

I woke at 4:38 AM with a jolt. Dad was close to me. Alive. Then I remembered he wasn't. That he'd died the night before at the exact same time.

An ache, an almost unbearable pain rose in my chest that made it hard to breathe. I couldn't remember ever feeling such overwhelming woe before. I cried uncontrollably, the pain throbbing in my chest. He was dead, and I still couldn't comprehend what that meant.

We had spent so much time apart. I had protected myself against his loss my whole childhood. Trying either to ignore his absence, or else attempting to get used to his presence. Cloaking myself in a veil of indifference— an emotional burka. But not recently, not in his last years, and not now. Now I ached for my father. I loved him and felt it. And even though I was in pain I was grateful to feel the enormity of the loss.

～

We rented a car and drove up to Provincetown with Valentina, Alejandro, and Antonia, arriving in the afternoon. Some of my siblings had left the City earlier and were already at the house; the others would be there soon. Norris was busy at the funeral parlor. The wake and burial would be the next day. Most of us stayed at the Watermark Inn.

That night we had our first supper at the big house without Dad.

All the lights were on. The house felt warm and inviting. We walked into the dining room and for a few moments looked at his chair, wondering who would sit in it now. I don't remember if anyone did.

After the meal, we went up the stairs to his bedroom. When we opened the closet, his characteristic slightly acidic, peppery scent came rushing out. His desktop was oddly neat and clean. On it was a yellow legal pad, some small notebooks, and of course, his favorite yellow No. 2 pencils. Betsy and Danielle could feel his presence. I wasn't sure, but I definitely wanted to feel it. Then we went up to the attic, to his studio. His empty chair faced the desk before the big window that overlooked the bay. It felt as if some invisible presence was sitting there.

If he was anywhere, it was here.

～

The next day at the funeral parlor, I was surprised to see it was an open-casket viewing. In the Jewish tradition, once the departed has been washed and put into a shroud, the casket is closed. There is no viewing of the dead.

I wasn't sure if I wanted to see him. But I walked up anyhow, feeling anxious, and stared down at a face that looked like a bad imitation of my father. He was dressed in his usual dark flannel shirt and the fleece vest that had become his uniform.

My son passed me on his way up to the casket. He showed me the orgonite amulet he had made for his grandfather and given him last Christmas. It had stayed on Dad's night table since then. Alejandro had gone up and gotten it earlier in the morning.

He said, "I'm going to slip it into Grandpa's vest pocket."

The room was large, with indirect soft lighting. A nondescript sofa sat at the back, with a few armchairs covered in paisley fabric. I don't remember the color of the walls, but the room stuck in my mind as being dark. White, pink and lavender flowers in vases were set on tables, and a few wreaths stood by the casket. Because Dad was a veteran, a folded American flag was atop it. Poster-style photos of Norman and Norris stood nearby on easels. Next to these was a large picture of my father in his WWII Army uniform.

At that moment, a dream emerged from the night before. Dad had been standing in front of me, very young, as he was in this photo. Dressed in the same uniform, with the exact same posture and expression. Was last night's dream a visitation? I wondered, or perhaps hoped. As I stood by his coffin, those dream images still in my mind, I wondered where he was now. Certainly not in that dark parlor.

I walked around the room feeling removed from the scene even as I talked to many of the people who had come to pay their respects. They were mostly Provincetown residents. John was crying quietly, his head on Norris's shoulder. Later he went over to the coffin and put a card, the ace of spades, into the other pocket of Dad's fleece vest. Michael was acting in his official role as older brother, shaking visitors' hands. My sisters and I stood together, holding hands, by the coffin, not saying much, feeling the warmth of our affection. Matthew put a family photo taken in Maine on Dad's chest, and Norris stood by the casket for a long time. She later told me she'd slipped in a letter for him to read on his way to wherever he was going.

When it was time to leave, we got into our cars. Two motorcycle policemen escorted the funeral cortege through town, first passing by the Big House, then all the way down Commercial Street and up to the town cemetery. People stood on the sides of the road to say goodbye to Dad.

It was Norman Mailer's last trip through Provincetown.

After my father's death I thought of him every day, several times a day. I often cried alone, usually while driving. Did I miss him? Not exactly. I felt his loss in my body; my arms and legs felt heavy, my mind was muddled. I was always tired. When I taught, it was hard to find the right words. I constantly lost my train of thought and was easily distracted. While with patients, in my office, I often found myself slipping into reverie.

On the first anniversary of his death I actually got sick. I hurt for him. But I don't think the simple phrase "I miss him" expresses what I felt. That hollow aspect of absence; of longing to be with or talk to someone who has gone, was not part of my grief. We had lived together in spurts, our relationship intense but fractured in time and space. Many curtains had been draped between us, and many aspects of his life I had only been able to glimpse. I had spent too many of those years resenting the center of his life, writing. And this resentment had prevented me from understanding that, ultimately, no one could hold onto him.

Many times he had told me, "I cannot be the father you want me to be. My mind is captured by my ideas and by the need to write them."

So, I couldn't say only that I missed him. Instead, I hurt for us. For the unique circumstances of our life together, for what we hadn't lived together. For all I had missed.

~

In April, five months after his death, a large memorial ceremony was held for my father in New York. Two thousand five hundred people came to Carnegie Hall to celebrate the life of Norman Mailer.

At the start of it, my siblings and I, together with Aunt Barbara and Peter, and our second cousin Sam, walked onstage, where twelve chairs had been set out. Each of us, one at a time, from oldest to youngest, stood at the microphone to read a personal anecdote about Norman. For the first time in our lives we were center stage. Dad's photo was projected on a huge screen behind us, his aura always present. But this time he was in the background.

After that day something shifted in me. My eyes focused in other directions, and I began to think about the possibility of a fresh design for my life. I still loved my profession, but I needed more. Another ingredient. Gradually, I felt the urge to write; a new and, until then, unknown desire. I let my hand open, and said to myself, "Why not?"

I wrote about us, my father and me, and while I wrote he came back to me again. His voice was reassuring, championing my step into new places. I remembered the dream I'd had after he died, the dream in which I was standing, undecided, between two roads, not knowing which way to go. And he had said, "Go ahead and do it."

I finally understood his message. Writing, what my father had loved most, what had been his essence, could now also be a part of me.

Acknowledgements

A published book is a creation of many minds, many hands.

I'm grateful to Kaylie Jones for helping me nurse an idea to life. To Mike Lennon, Norman's biographer, for his wealth of knowledge, support and endless patience. To my agent Chris Tomasino for her sense of humor and for being there beyond the call of duty. And to Lenore Hart, my editor, for her wise advice and razor-sharp eye. To my friends Michele Golodetz and Clara Rosenblutt, readers of the early drafts. And to Laurie Lowenstein and Ross Klavan for their insights. To my friends at the Norman Mailer Society and the Provincetown Public Library, where I read parts of this book. And to Larry Schiller for his attention to the photos. Also, to Donna Pedro. With Love to Marco and my children Valentina, Alejandro and Antonia, my personal cheering squad. And to all my siblings, Aunt Barbara and Peter, for their stories and fact checking. Most of all for being essential players in my life.

With appreciation to Northampton House Press.

Photo Credits

From the Author's Private Photo Collection:
Smiling in Grandma's arms, 1951. Awkward in Mom's arms,1951.
Mom and me at 3 months,1949. Me and Dad at Grandma's, 1953.
The Two Sals, 1958. Salvador, Mom and me, 1958. Me with Pixie
haircut holding Danielle 9 months old, 1957. Dad took this photo a
few days after I arrived in New York. 1957. Chelo and me dressed for a
play. 1962. Me on Terrace of Brooklyn Height apartment, 1963. Ech-
everría, Norman, and me. 1973. The family at Aunt Barbara's, 1975.
Me and John eight months old, 1978. Me and Marco, 1980. Mailer
kids. 1981. A Rare moment. Grandpa Norman teaching Antonia and
Isabella Chess, 1996. Aunt Barbara, Grandma and Valentina, 1981.
Norman Mailer in Valparaíso, 1986. Mailer Girls, 1987. Mailer Boys,
1987. Antonia, Valentina and Alejandro, 2004. Family Gathering in
Brooklyn Heights, 2005. Dad in Brooklyn Heights, May 2007.

Courtesy of Barbara Mailer Wasserman.
Norman and Bea, 1948.
Adele, 1957.
Grandma on a horse in Vermont, 1971.

Jeanne and Kate, 1962. Courtesy of Kate Mailer
Jose Torres, 1965. Courtesy of J. Michael Lennon
Norman, Sue and Beverly during campaign, 1969. Reproduced with
permission of AP.
Carol and Maggie, 1975. Courtesy of Maggie Mailer. Photo by Beverly
Pabst.
Norris Glam photo, 1976. Courtesy of Matthew Mailer.
Robert Lindner. Udel Brothers. Rinehart and Co.

Northampton House Press

Northampton House publishes select fiction – historical,
romance, thrillers, fantasy – and lifestyle and literary nonfiction,
memoir, and poetry. Our logo represents the Greek muse Polyhymnia.
See our list at www.northampton-house.com, and follow us on
Facebook – "Northampton House Press" – for more great reading.